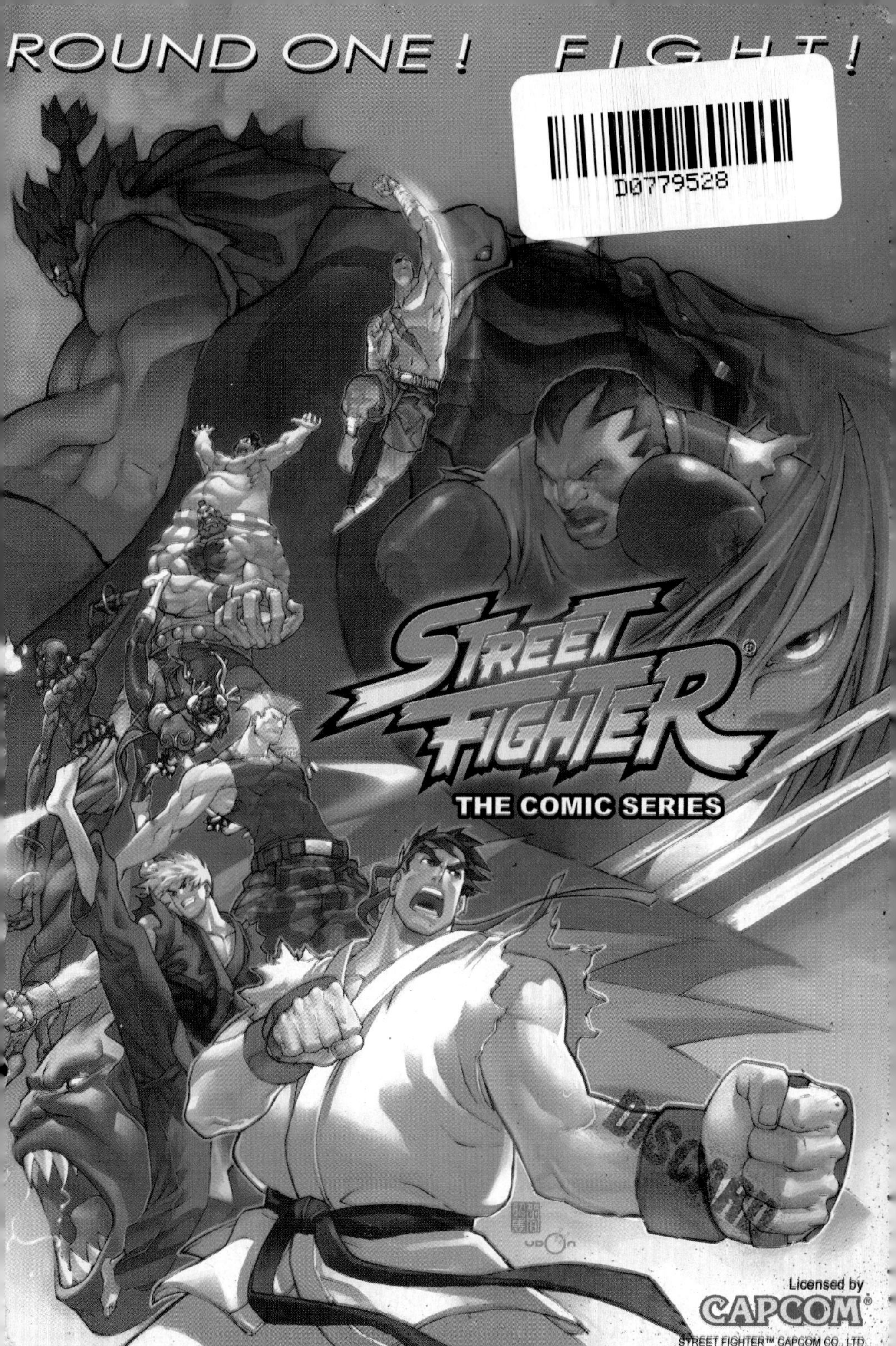
ROUND ONE! FIGHT!
STREET FIGHTER®
THE COMIC SERIES
DISCARD
UDON
Licensed by
CAPCOM®

Cover Art by: Arnold Tsang

Street Fighter®

Chapter 00: MASTER

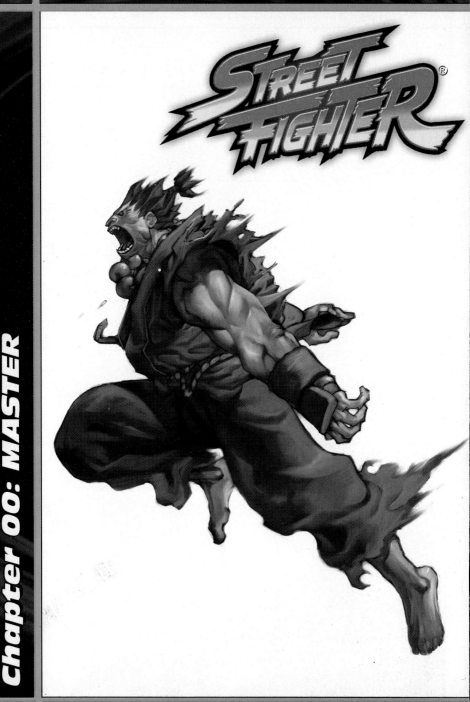

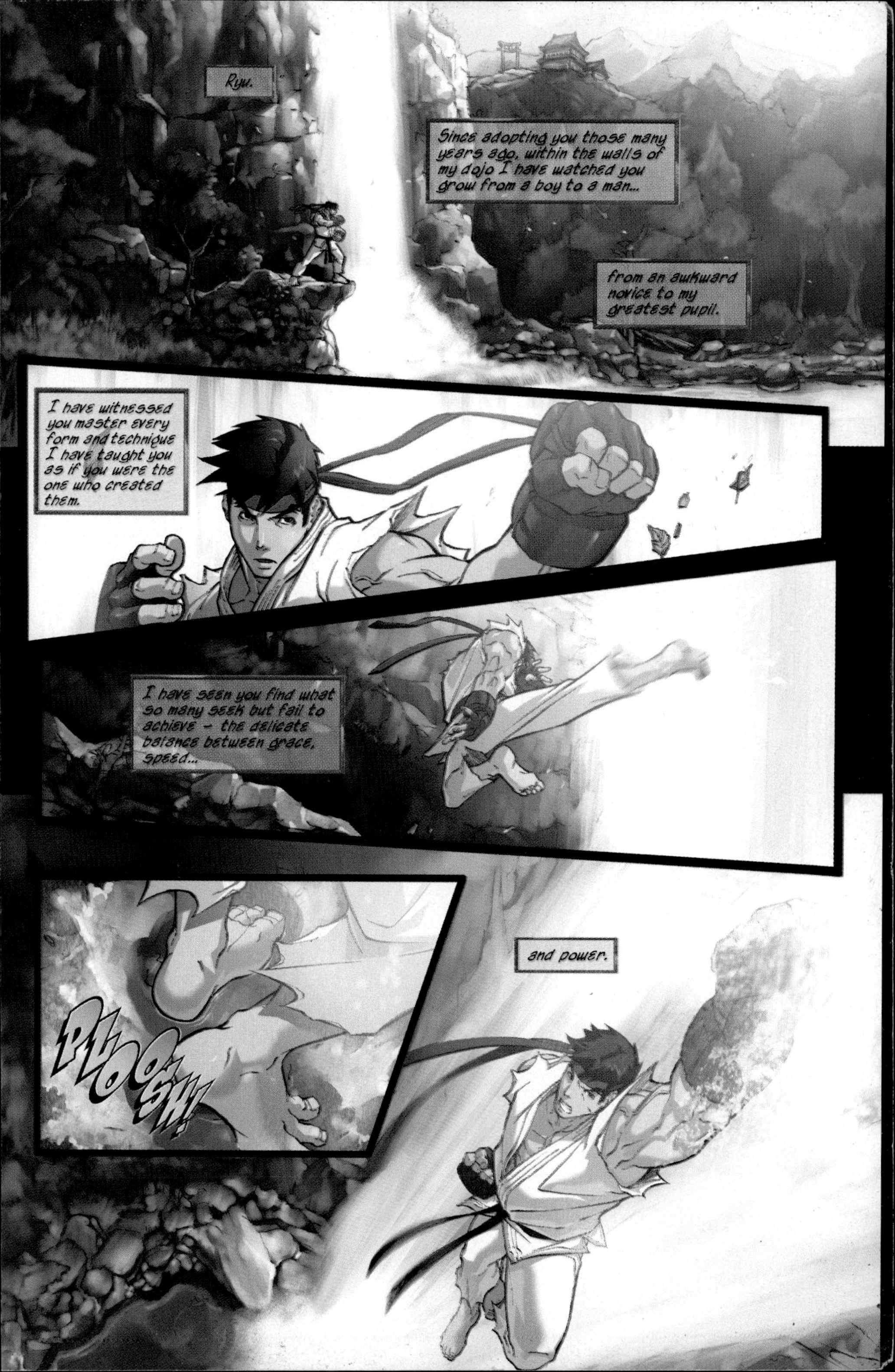
Ryu.
Since adopting you those many years ago, within the walls of my dojo I have watched you grow from a boy to a man...
from an awkward novice to my greatest pupil.
I have witnessed you master every form and technique I have taught you as if you were the one who created them.
I have seen you find what so many seek but fail to achieve - the delicate balance between grace, speed...
PLOOSH!
and power.

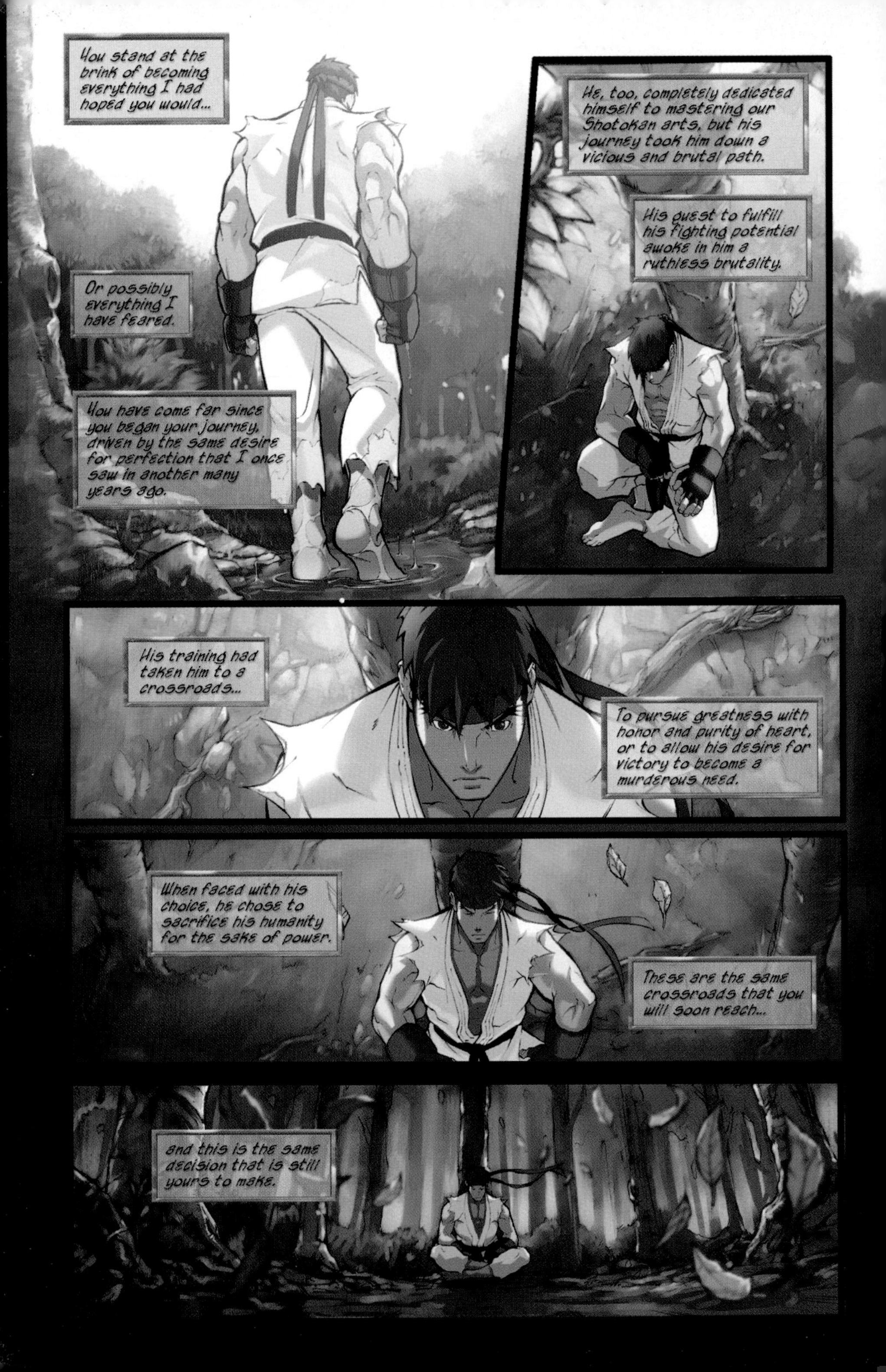
You stand at the brink of becoming everything I had hoped you would...
Or possibly everything I have feared.
You have come far since you began your journey, driven by the same desire for perfection that I once saw in another many years ago.
He, too, completely dedicated himself to mastering our Shotokan arts, but his journey took him down a vicious and brutal path.
His quest to fulfill his fighting potential awoke in him a ruthless brutality.
His training had taken him to a crossroads...
To pursue greatness with honor and purity of heart, or to allow his desire for victory to become a murderous need.
When faced with his choice, he chose to sacrifice his humanity for the sake of power.
These are the same crossroads that you will soon reach...
and this is the same decision that is still yours to make.

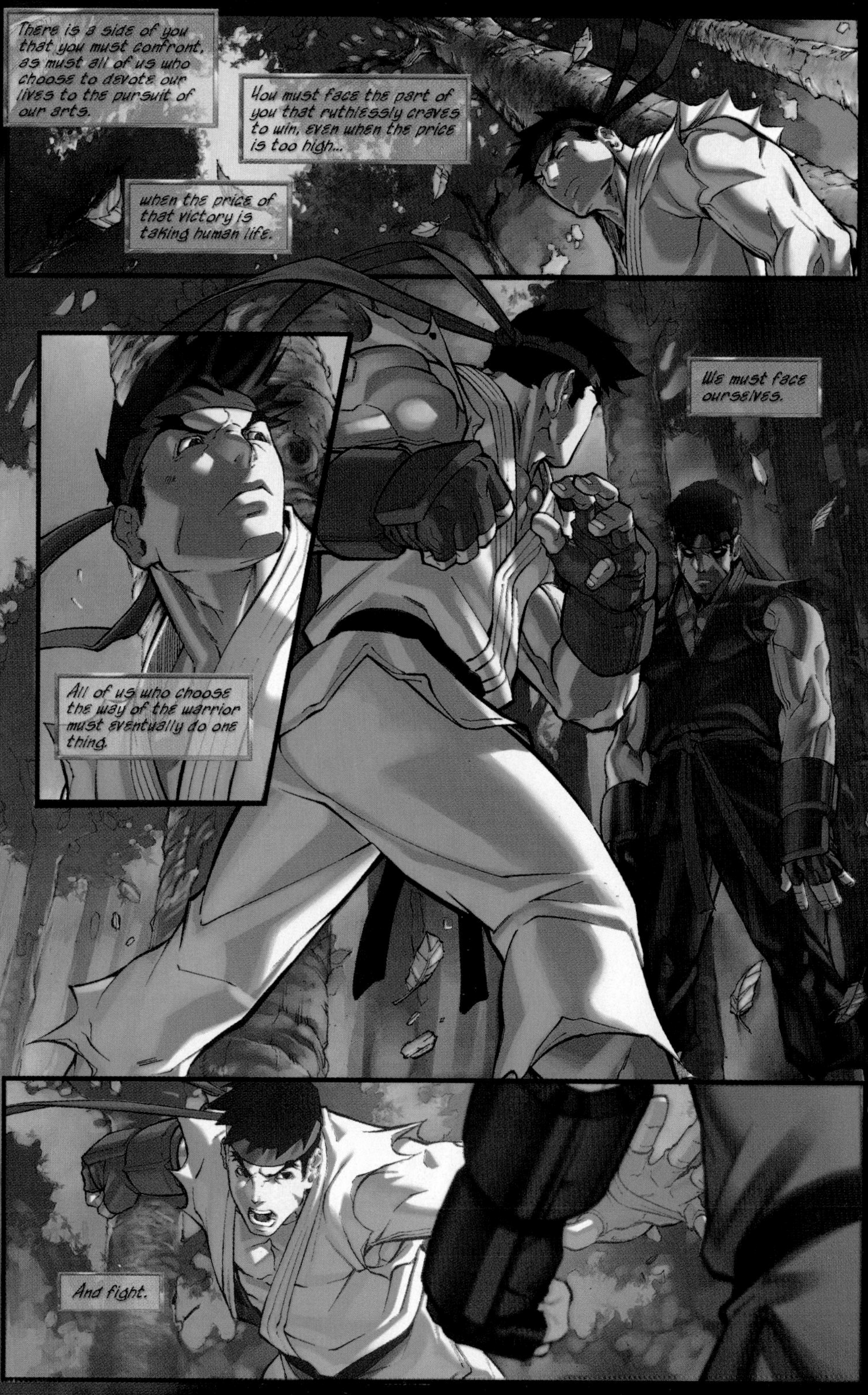
There is a side of you that you must confront, as must all of us who choose to devote our lives to the pursuit of our arts.
You must face the part of you that ruthlessly craves to win, even when the price is too high...
when the price of that victory is taking human life.
We must face ourselves.
All of us who choose the way of the warrior must eventually do one thing.
And fight.

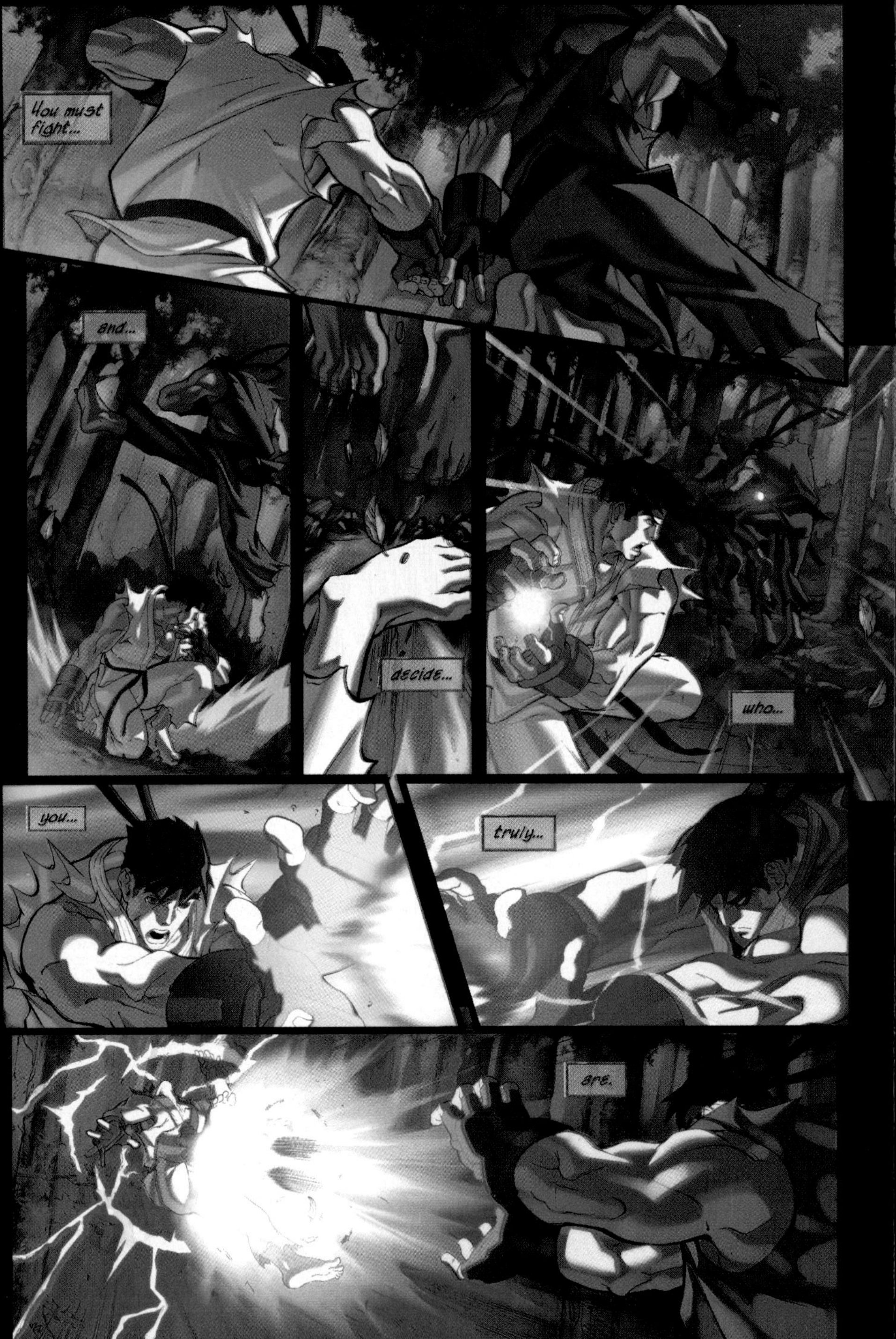
You must fight...
and...
decide...
who...
you...
truly...
are.

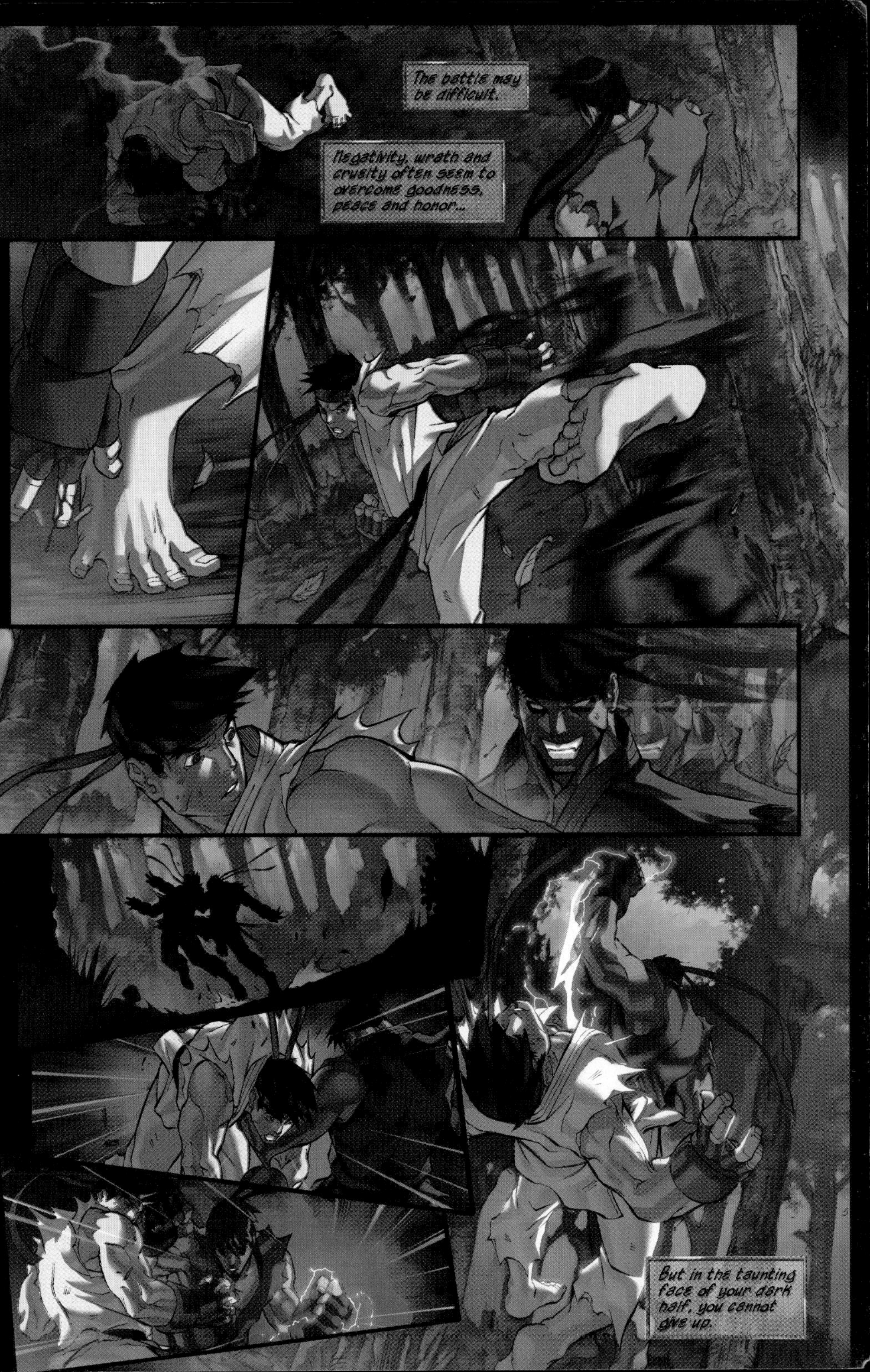
The battle may be difficult.
Negativity, wrath and cruelty often seem to overcome goodness, peace and honor...
But in the taunting face of your dark half, you cannot give up.

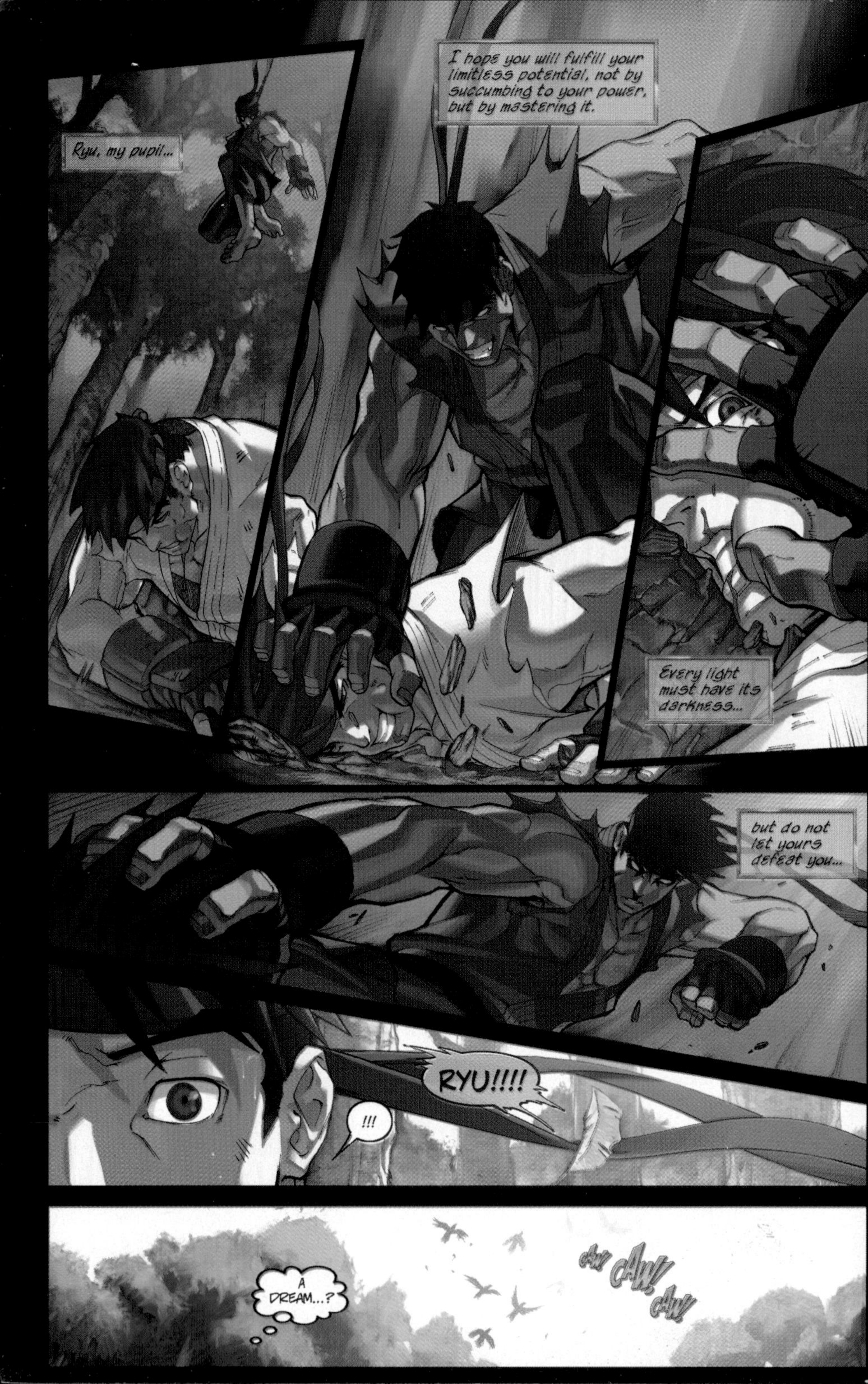

Ryu, my pupil...
I hope you will fulfill your limitless potential, not by succumbing to your power, but by mastering it.
Every light must have its darkness...
but do not let yours defeat you...
RYU!!!!
!!!
CAW! CAW! CAW!
A DREAM...?

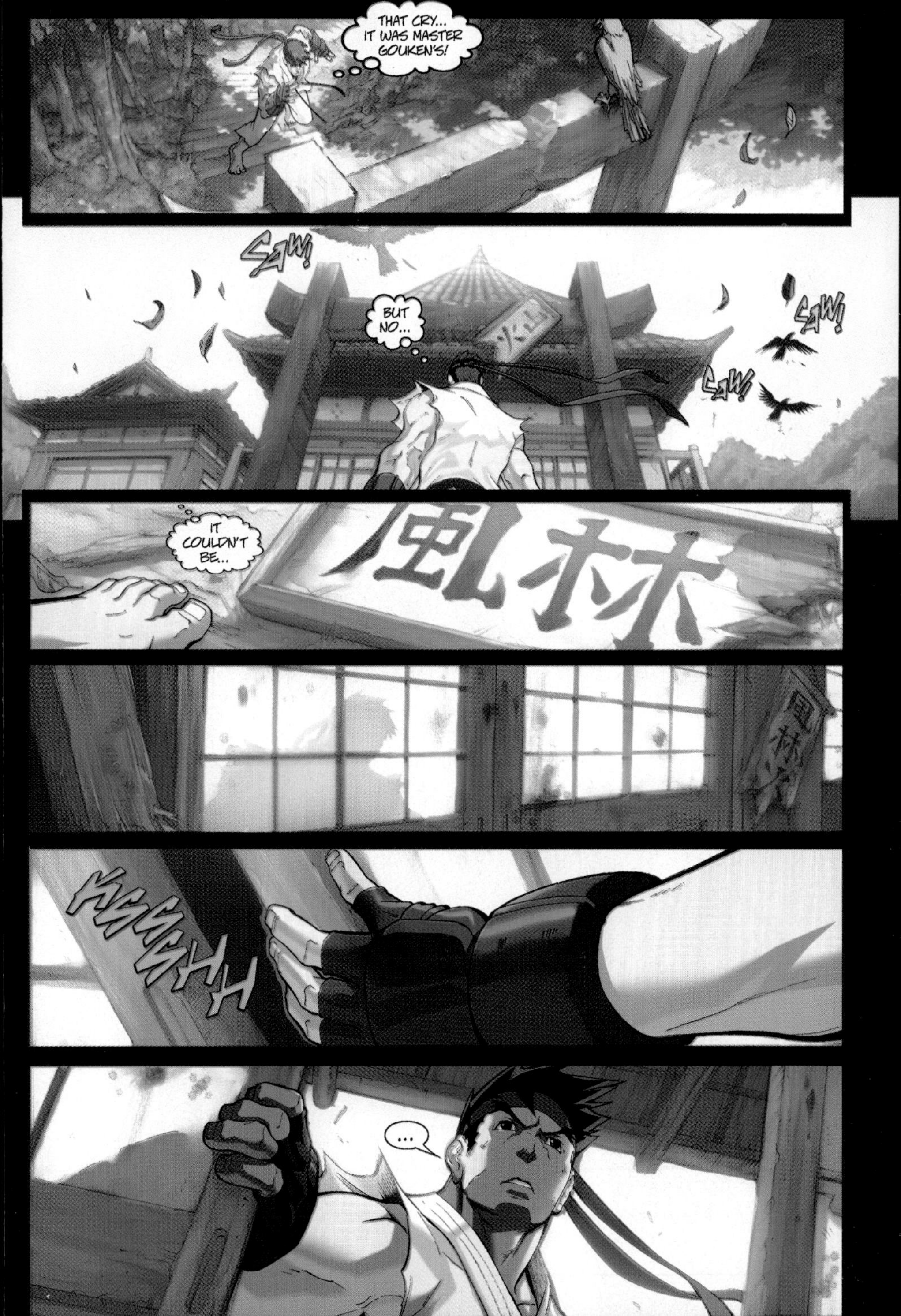

THAT CRY... IT WAS MASTER GOUKEN'S!
CAW!
BUT NO...
CAW!
CAW!
IT COULDN'T BE...
風林
KSSSHH
...

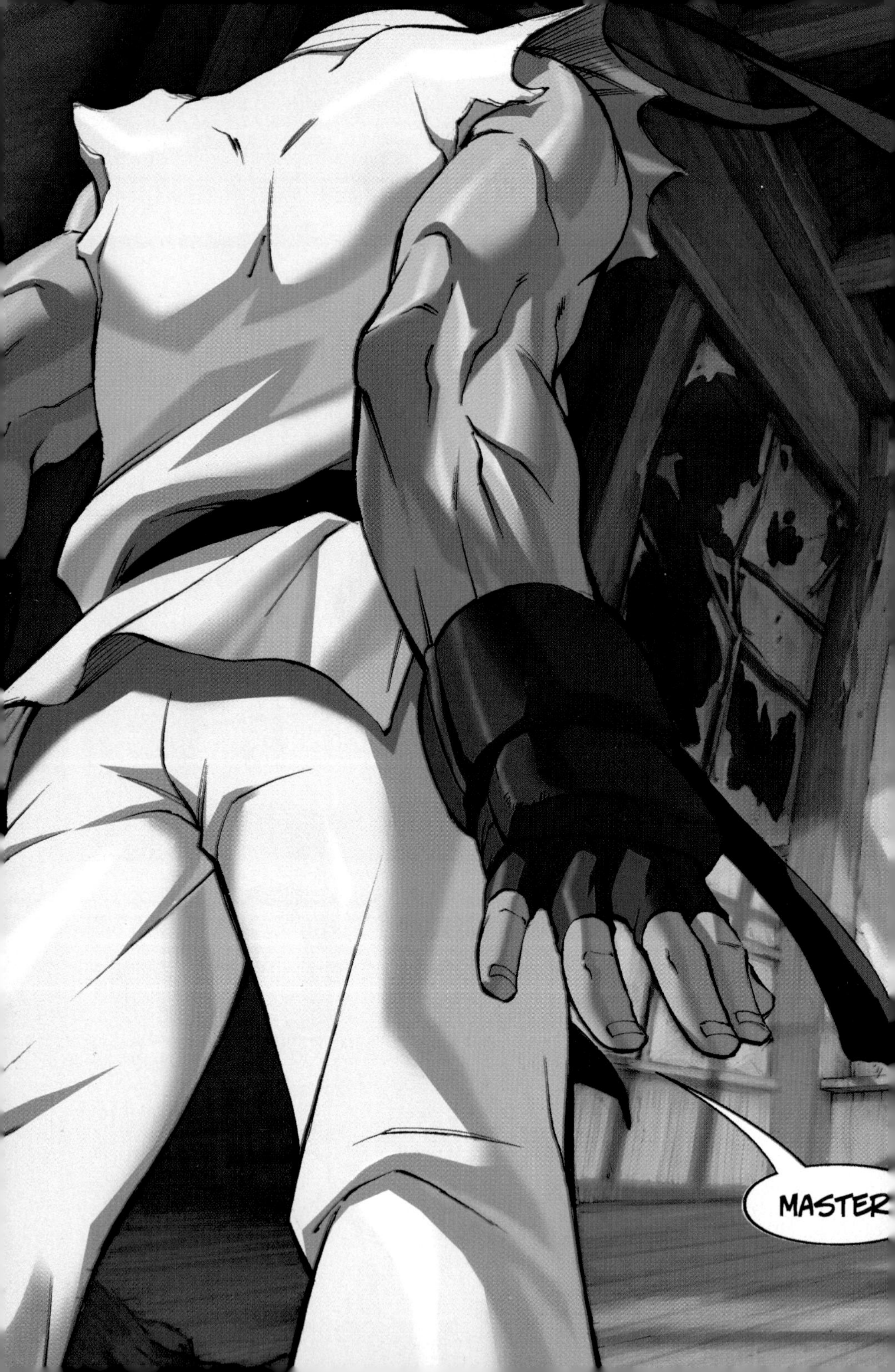
MASTER

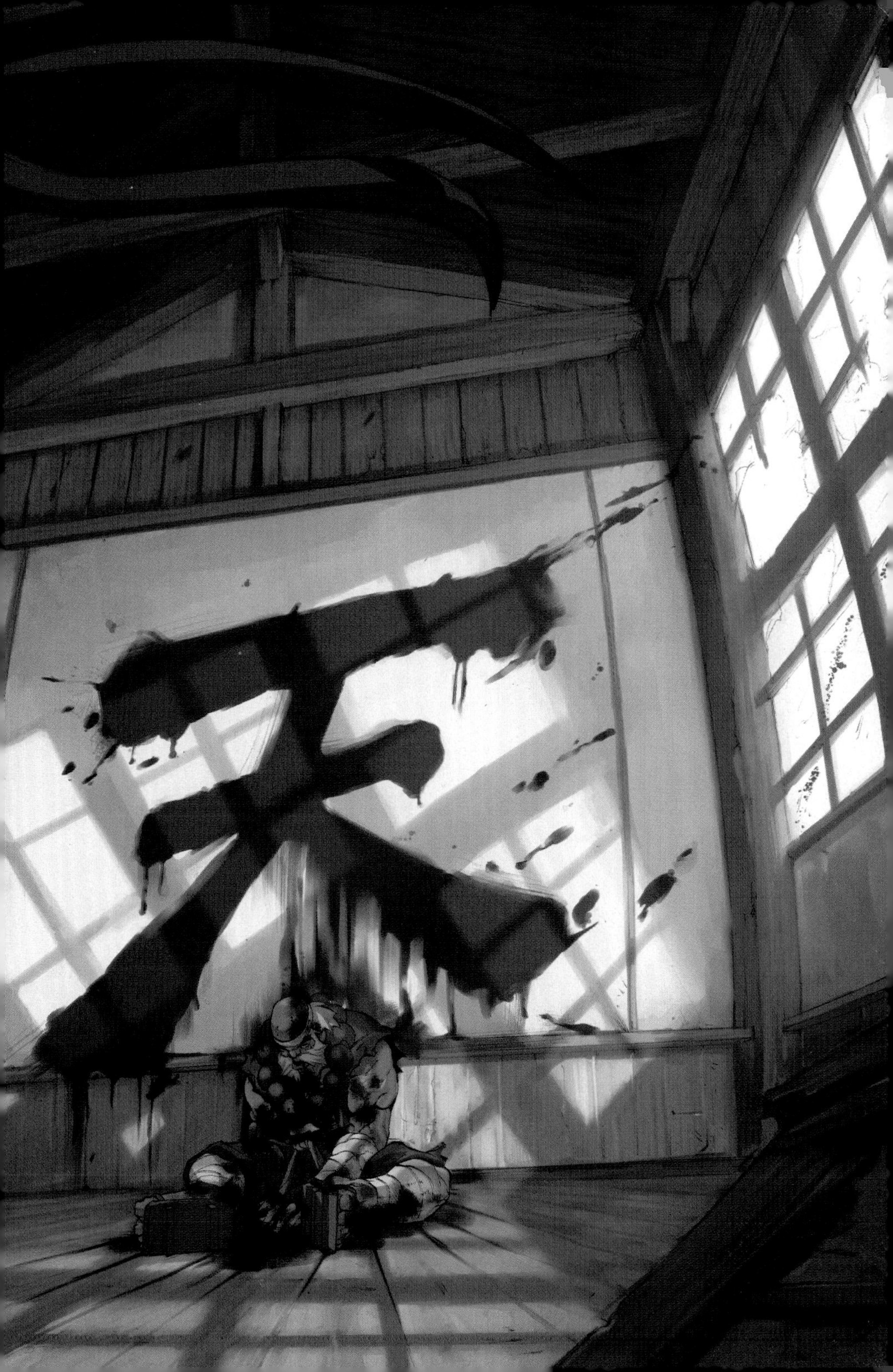
天

Cover Art by: Arnold Tsang

Chapter 01: OLD FRIENDS

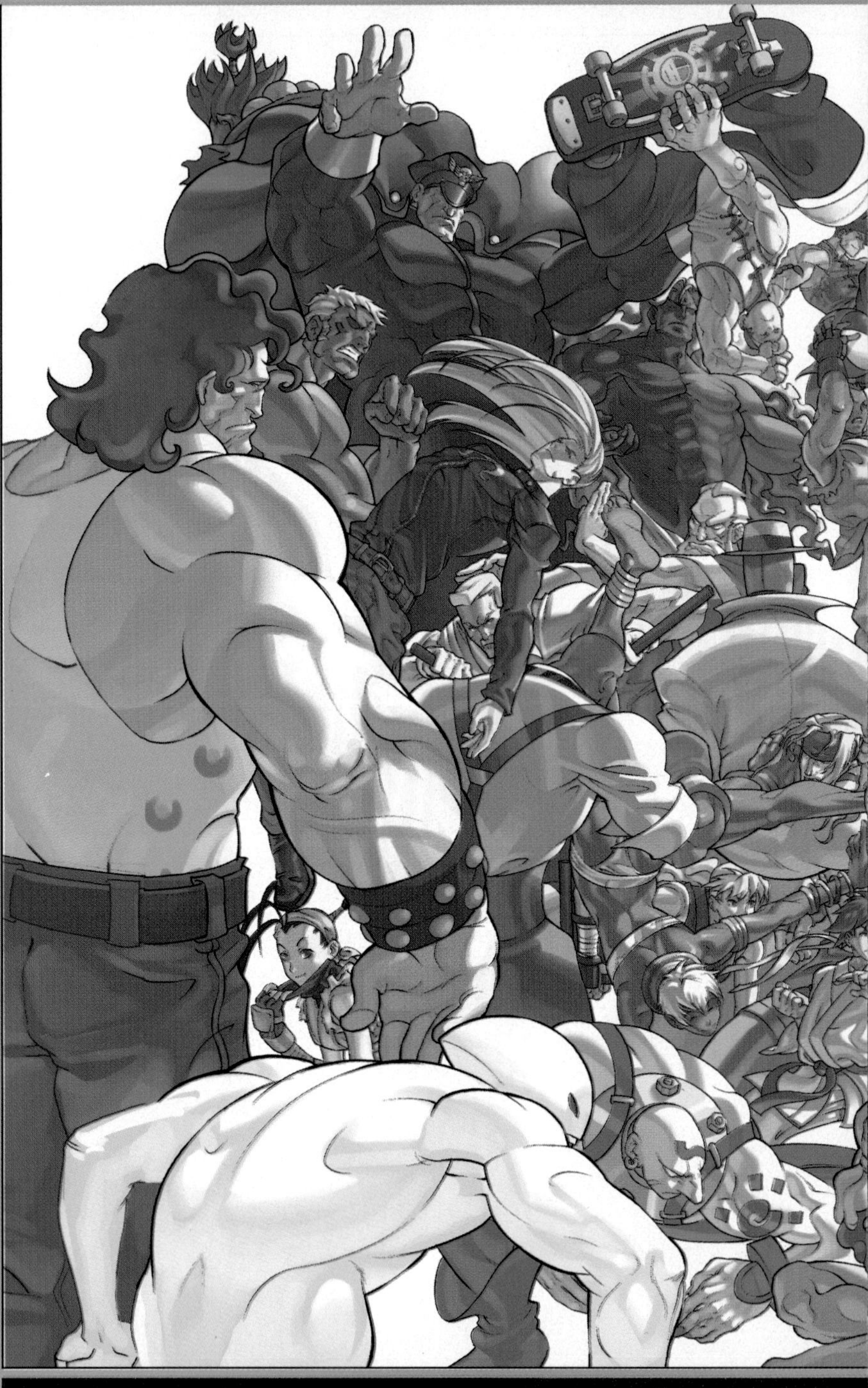

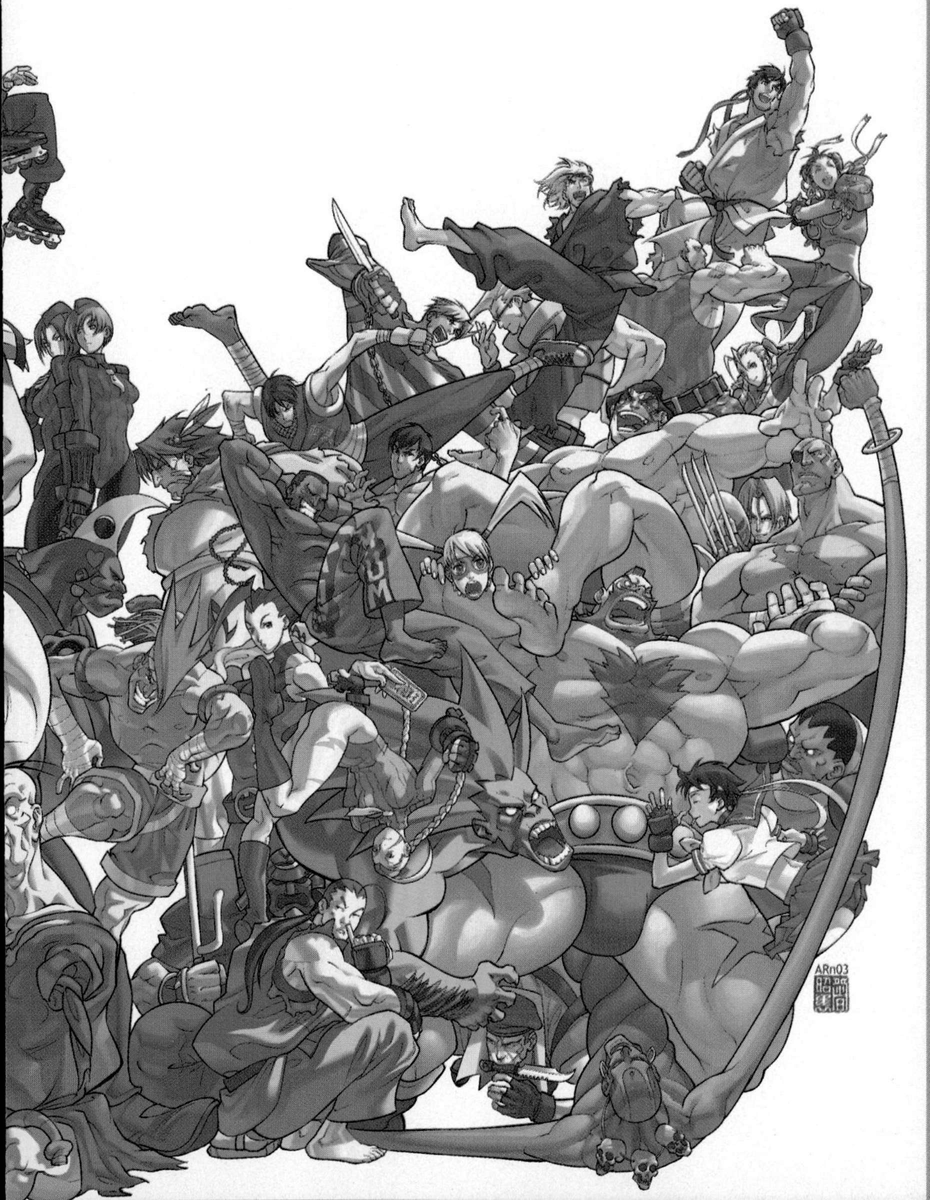
ARn03

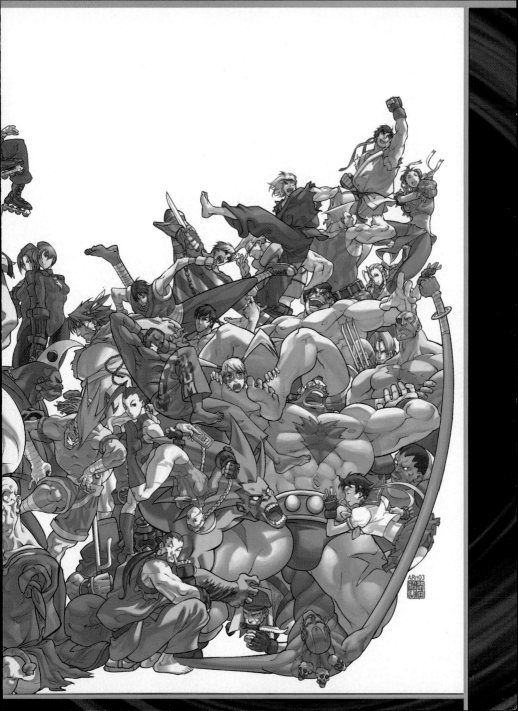

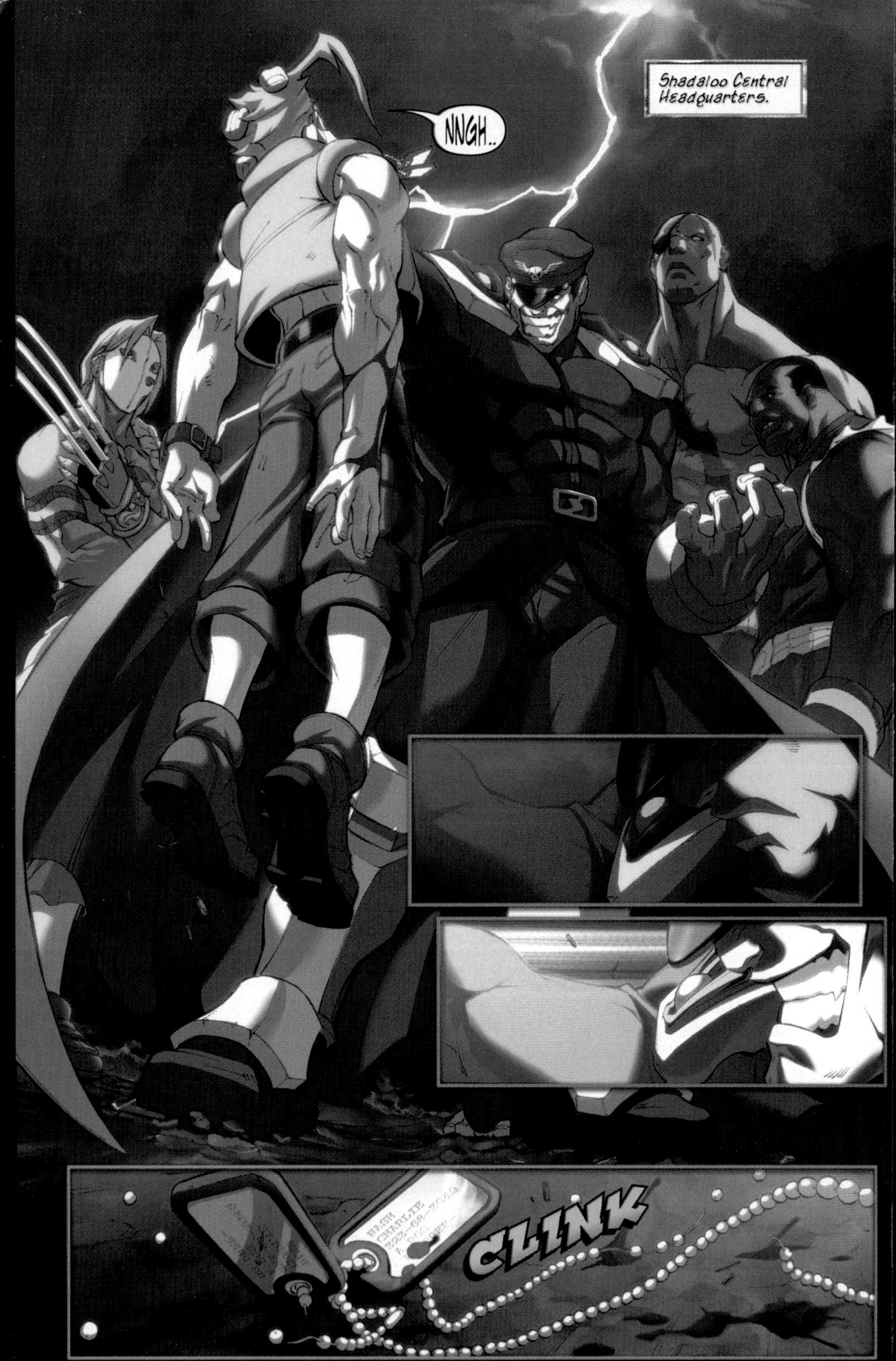
Shadaloo Central Headquarters.
NNGH..
NASH
CHARLIE
323-68-7049
CLINK

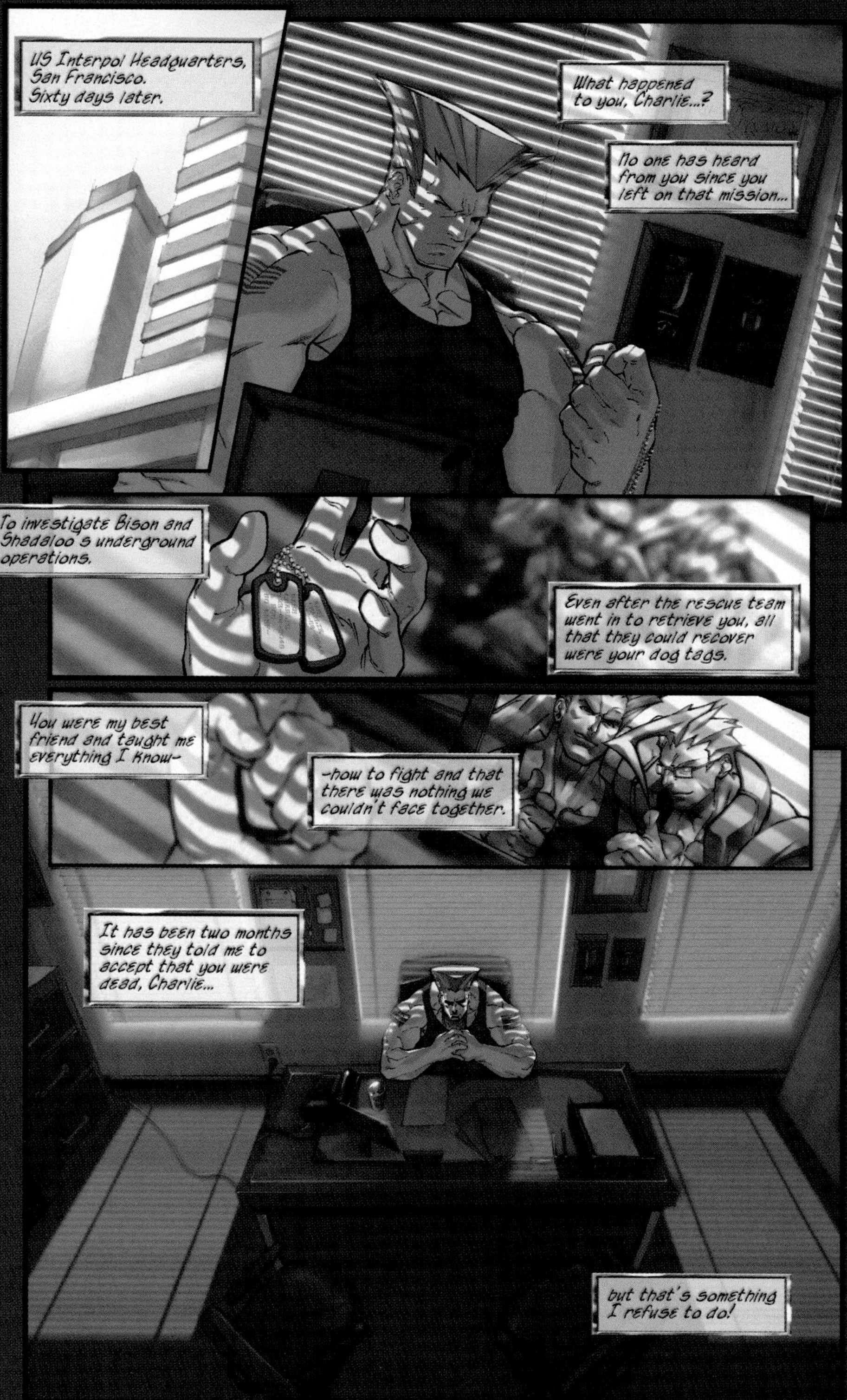
US Interpol Headquarters, San Francisco. Sixty days later.
What happened to you, Charlie...?
No one has heard from you since you left on that mission...
To investigate Bison and Shadaloo's underground operations.
Even after the rescue team went in to retrieve you, all that they could recover were your dog tags.
You were my best friend and taught me everything I know-
-how to fight and that there was nothing we couldn't face together.
It has been two months since they told me to accept that you were dead, Charlie...
but that's something I refuse to do!

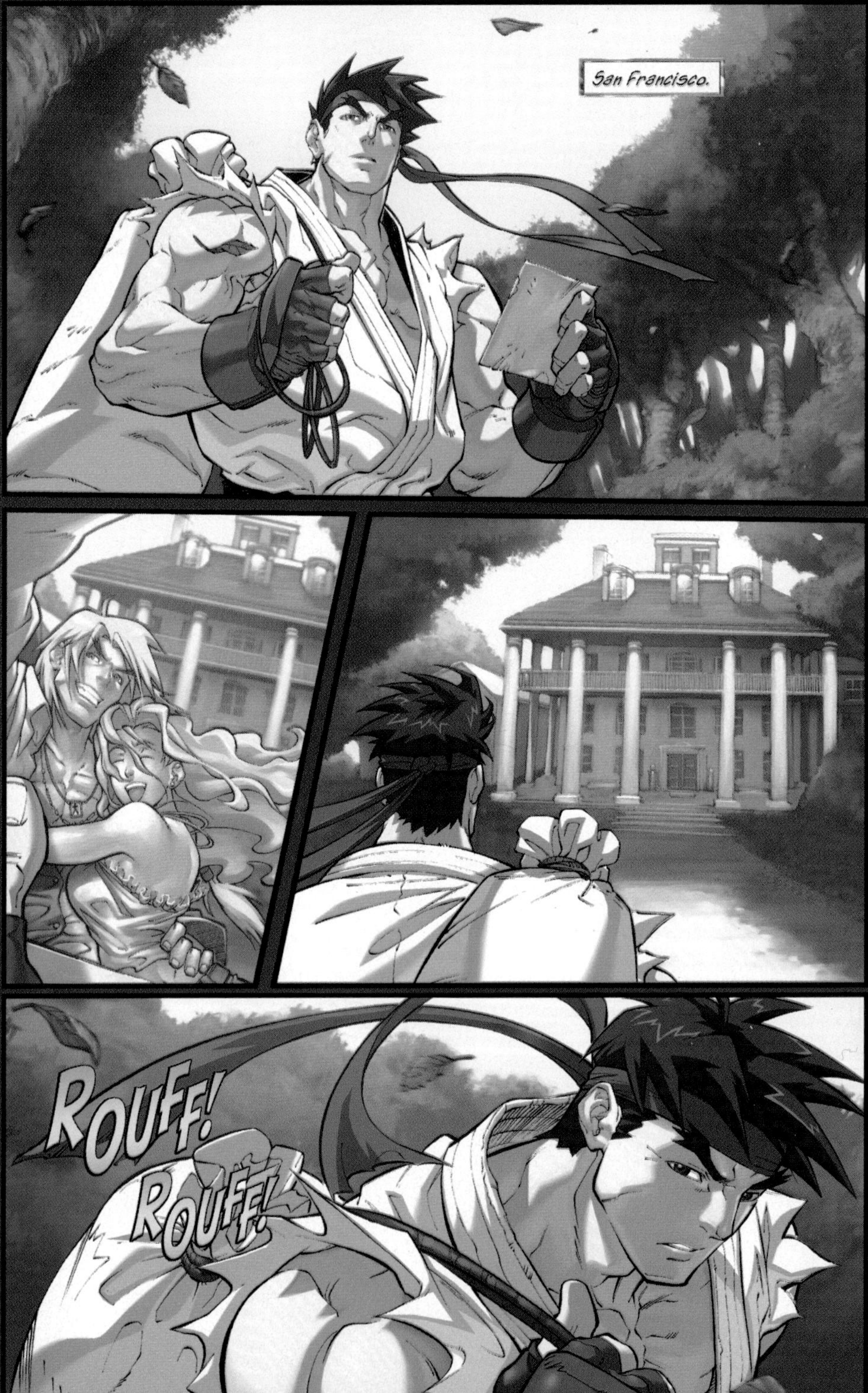

San Francisco.
ROUFF!
ROUFF!

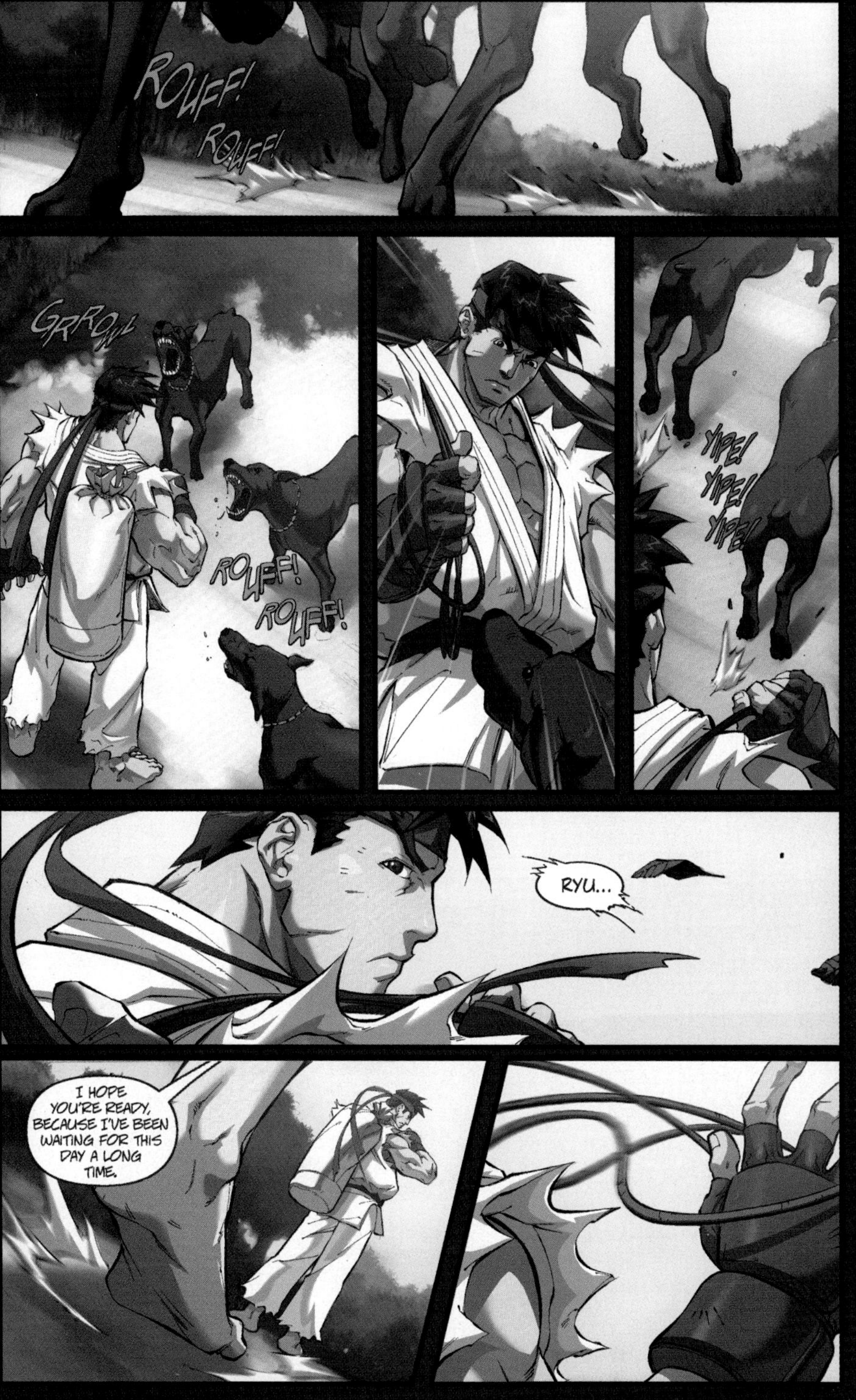
ROUFF!
ROUFF!
GRROWL
ROUFF!
ROUFF!
YIPE!
YIPE!
YIPE!
RYU...
I HOPE YOU'RE READY, BECAUSE I'VE BEEN WAITING FOR THIS DAY A LONG TIME.

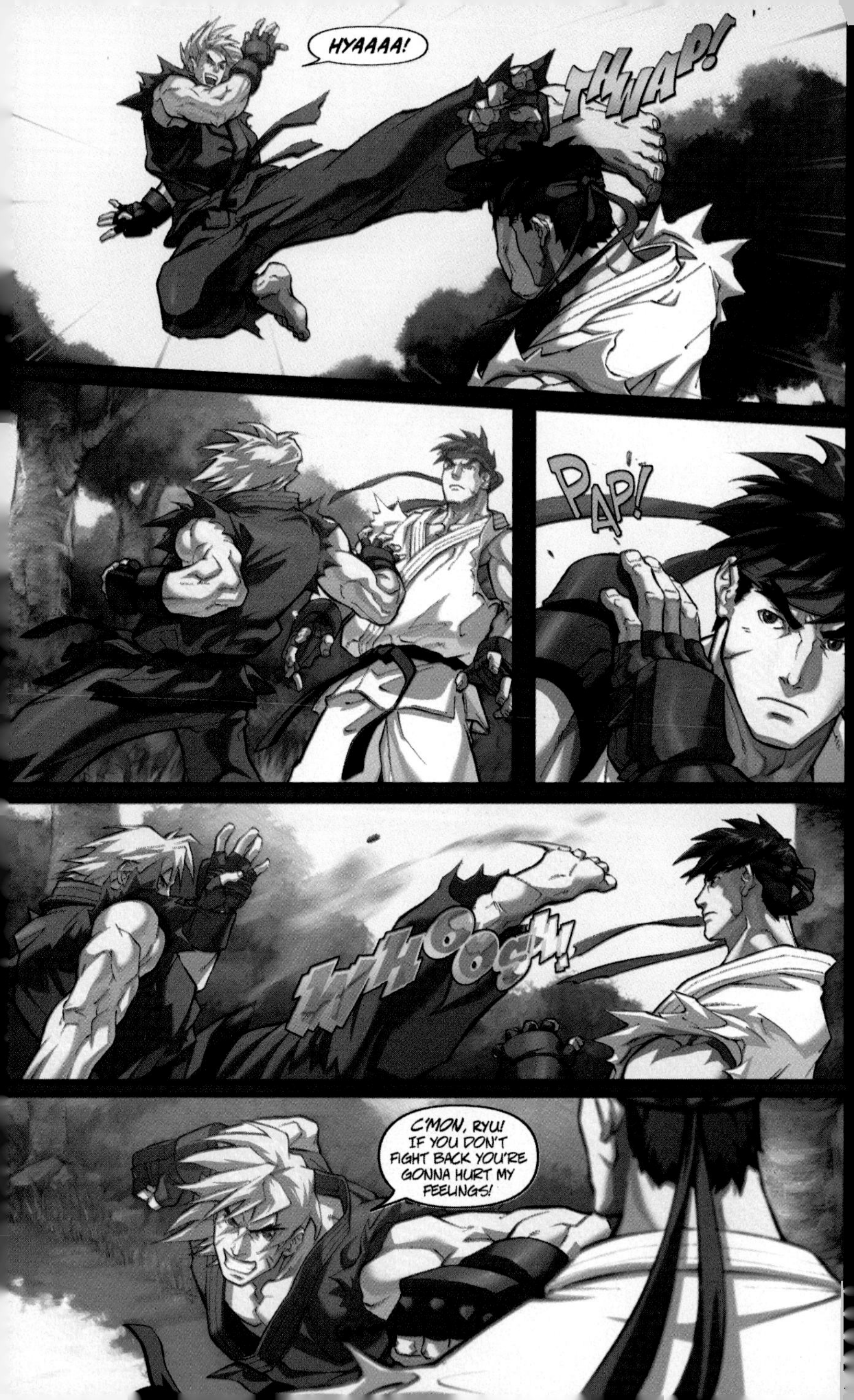
HYAAAA!
THWAP!
PAP!
C'MON, RYU! IF YOU DON'T FIGHT BACK YOU'RE GONNA HURT MY FEELINGS!

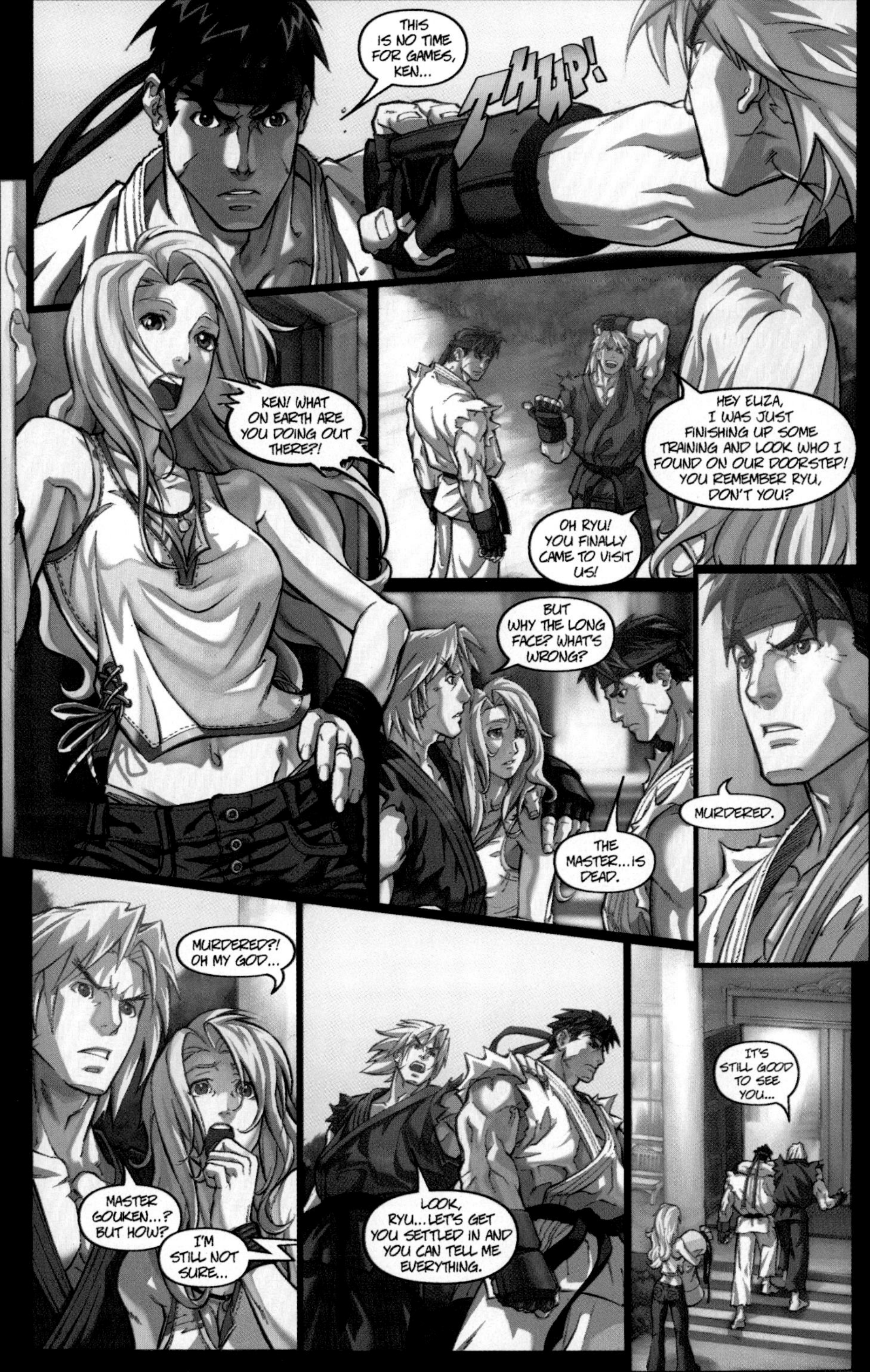

THIS IS NO TIME FOR GAMES, KEN...
THUP!
KEN! WHAT ON EARTH ARE YOU DOING OUT THERE?!
HEY ELIZA, I WAS JUST FINISHING UP SOME TRAINING AND LOOK WHO I FOUND ON OUR DOORSTEP! YOU REMEMBER RYU, DON'T YOU?
OH RYU! YOU FINALLY CAME TO VISIT US!
BUT WHY THE LONG FACE? WHAT'S WRONG?
THE MASTER...IS DEAD.
MURDERED.
MURDERED?! OH MY GOD...
MASTER GOUKEN...? BUT HOW?
I'M STILL NOT SURE...
LOOK, RYU...LET'S GET YOU SETTLED IN AND YOU CAN TELL ME EVERYTHING.
IT'S STILL GOOD TO SEE YOU...

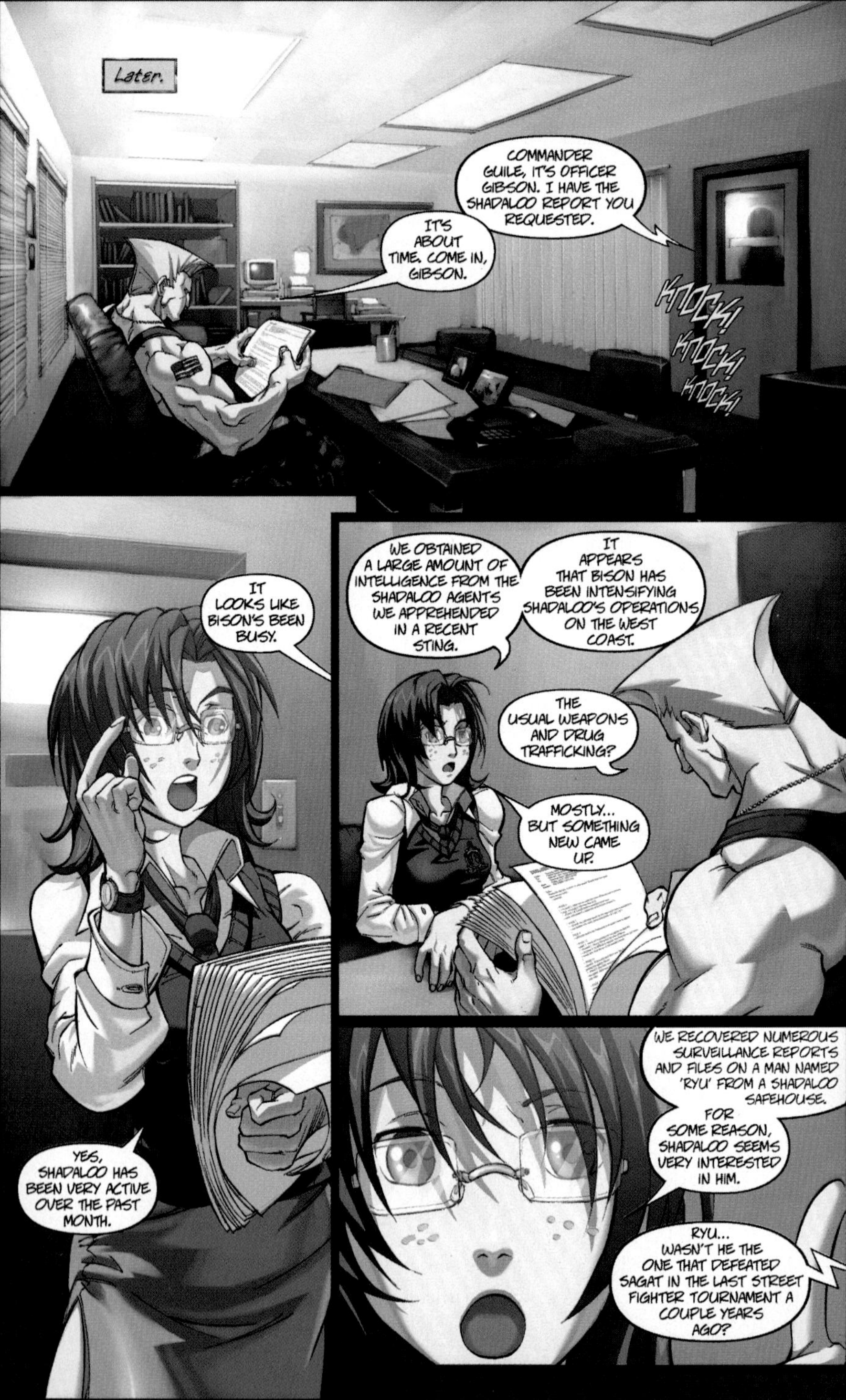
Later.
COMMANDER GUILE, IT'S OFFICER GIBSON. I HAVE THE SHADALOO REPORT YOU REQUESTED.
IT'S ABOUT TIME. COME IN, GIBSON.
KNOCK! KNOCK! KNOCK!
IT LOOKS LIKE BISON'S BEEN BUSY.
YES, SHADALOO HAS BEEN VERY ACTIVE OVER THE PAST MONTH.
WE OBTAINED A LARGE AMOUNT OF INTELLIGENCE FROM THE SHADALOO AGENTS WE APPREHENDED IN A RECENT STING.
IT APPEARS THAT BISON HAS BEEN INTENSIFYING SHADALOO'S OPERATIONS ON THE WEST COAST.
THE USUAL WEAPONS AND DRUG TRAFFICKING?
MOSTLY... BUT SOMETHING NEW CAME UP.
WE RECOVERED NUMEROUS SURVEILLANCE REPORTS AND FILES ON A MAN NAMED 'RYU' FROM A SHADALOO SAFEHOUSE.
FOR SOME REASON, SHADALOO SEEMS VERY INTERESTED IN HIM.
RYU... WASN'T HE THE ONE THAT DEFEATED SAGAT IN THE LAST STREET FIGHTER TOURNAMENT A COUPLE YEARS AGO?

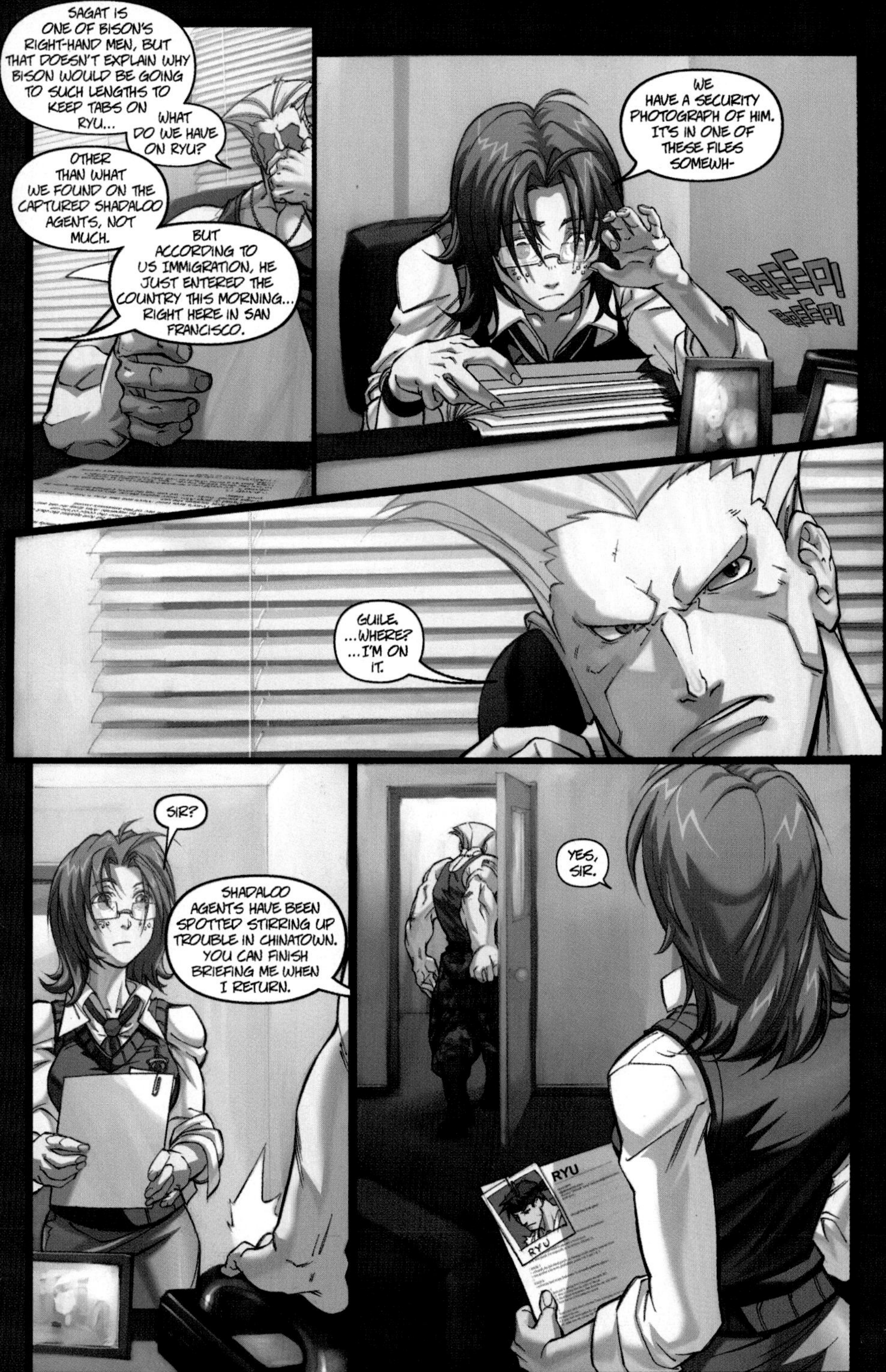
SAGAT IS ONE OF BISON'S RIGHT-HAND MEN, BUT THAT DOESN'T EXPLAIN WHY BISON WOULD BE GOING TO SUCH LENGTHS TO KEEP TABS ON RYU...
WHAT DO WE HAVE ON RYU?
OTHER THAN WHAT WE FOUND ON THE CAPTURED SHADALOO AGENTS, NOT MUCH.
BUT ACCORDING TO US IMMIGRATION, HE JUST ENTERED THE COUNTRY THIS MORNING... RIGHT HERE IN SAN FRANCISCO.
WE HAVE A SECURITY PHOTOGRAPH OF HIM. IT'S IN ONE OF THESE FILES SOMEWH-
BREEEP!
BREEEP!
GUILE. ...WHERE? ...I'M ON IT.
SIR?
SHADALOO AGENTS HAVE BEEN SPOTTED STIRRING UP TROUBLE IN CHINATOWN. YOU CAN FINISH BRIEFING ME WHEN I RETURN.
YES, SIR.
RYU
RYU

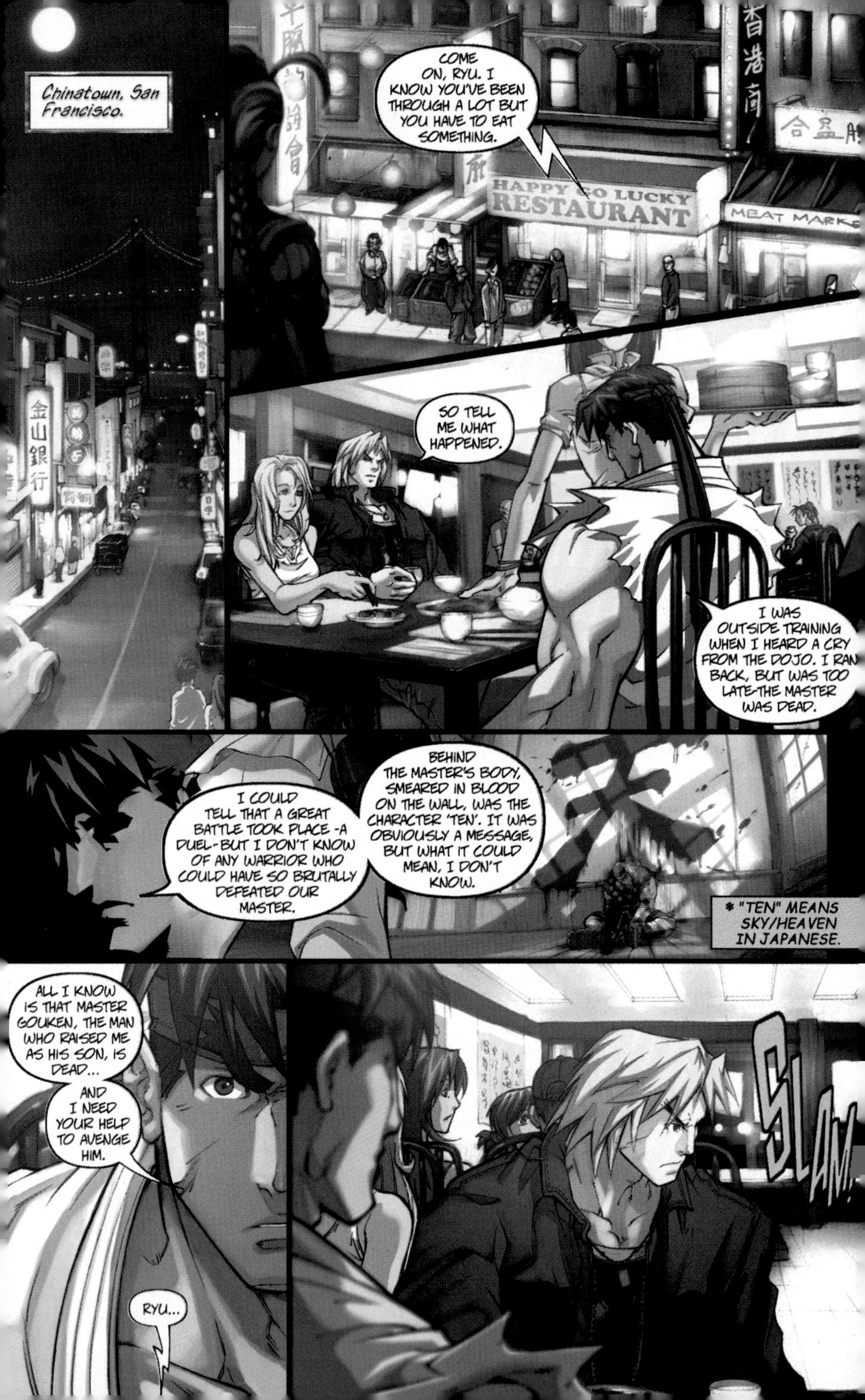
Chinatown, San Francisco.
COME ON, RYU. I KNOW YOU'VE BEEN THROUGH A LOT BUT YOU HAVE TO EAT SOMETHING.
HAPPY GO LUCKY RESTAURANT
MEAT MARKE
SO TELL ME WHAT HAPPENED.
I WAS OUTSIDE TRAINING WHEN I HEARD A CRY FROM THE DOJO. I RAN BACK, BUT WAS TOO LATE-THE MASTER WAS DEAD.
I COULD TELL THAT A GREAT BATTLE TOOK PLACE -A DUEL- BUT I DON'T KNOW OF ANY WARRIOR WHO COULD HAVE SO BRUTALLY DEFEATED OUR MASTER.
BEHIND THE MASTER'S BODY, SMEARED IN BLOOD ON THE WALL, WAS THE CHARACTER 'TEN'. IT WAS OBVIOUSLY A MESSAGE, BUT WHAT IT COULD MEAN, I DON'T KNOW.
* "TEN" MEANS SKY/HEAVEN IN JAPANESE.
ALL I KNOW IS THAT MASTER GOUKEN, THE MAN WHO RAISED ME AS HIS SON, IS DEAD...
AND I NEED YOUR HELP TO AVENGE HIM.
RYU...
SLAM!

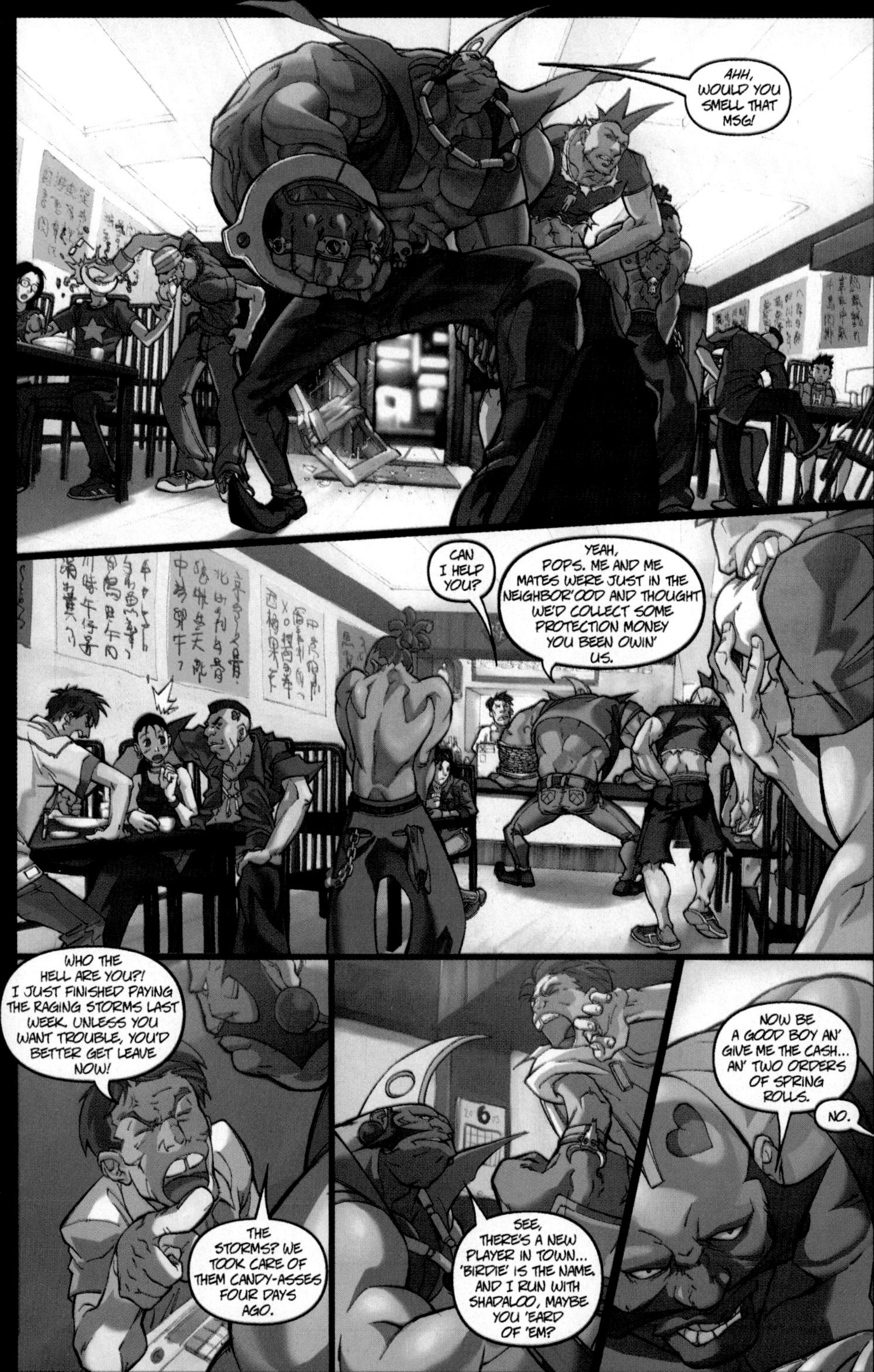
AHH, WOULD YOU SMELL THAT MSG!
CAN I HELP YOU?
YEAH, POPS. ME AND ME MATES WERE JUST IN THE NEIGHBOR'OOD AND THOUGHT WE'D COLLECT SOME PROTECTION MONEY YOU BEEN OWIN' US.
WHO THE HELL ARE YOU?! I JUST FINISHED PAYING THE RAGING STORMS LAST WEEK. UNLESS YOU WANT TROUBLE, YOU'D BETTER GET LEAVE NOW!
THE STORMS? WE TOOK CARE OF THEM CANDY-ASSES FOUR DAYS AGO.
SEE, THERE'S A NEW PLAYER IN TOWN... 'BIRDIE' IS THE NAME. AND I RUN WITH SHADALOO, MAYBE YOU 'EARD OF 'EM?
NOW BE A GOOD BOY AN' GIVE ME THE CASH... AN' TWO ORDERS OF SPRING ROLLS.
NO.

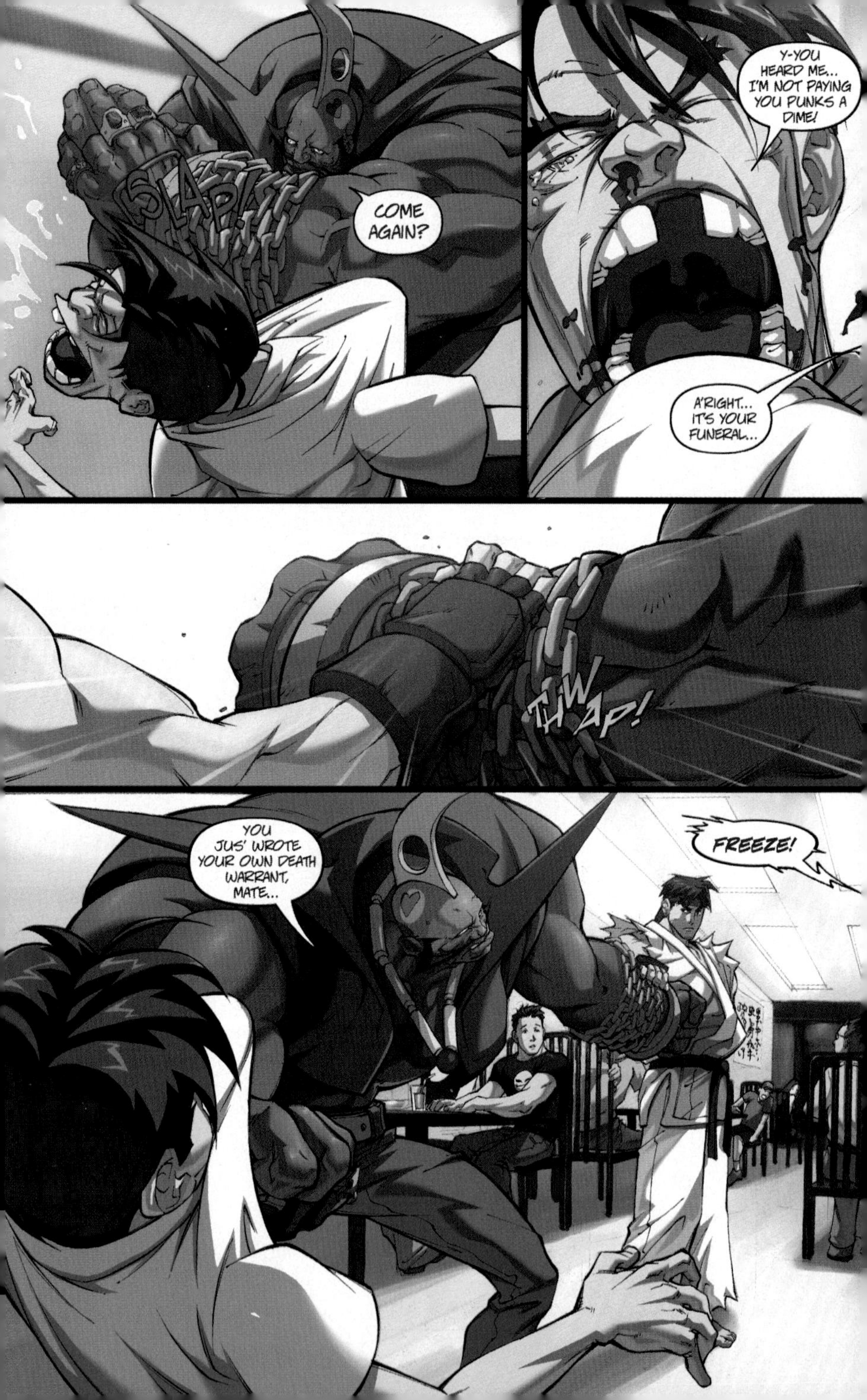
SLAP!
COME AGAIN?
Y-YOU HEARD ME... I'M NOT PAYING YOU PUNKS A DIME!
A'RIGHT... IT'S YOUR FUNERAL...
THWAP!
YOU JUS' WROTE YOUR OWN DEATH WARRANT, MATE...
FREEZE!

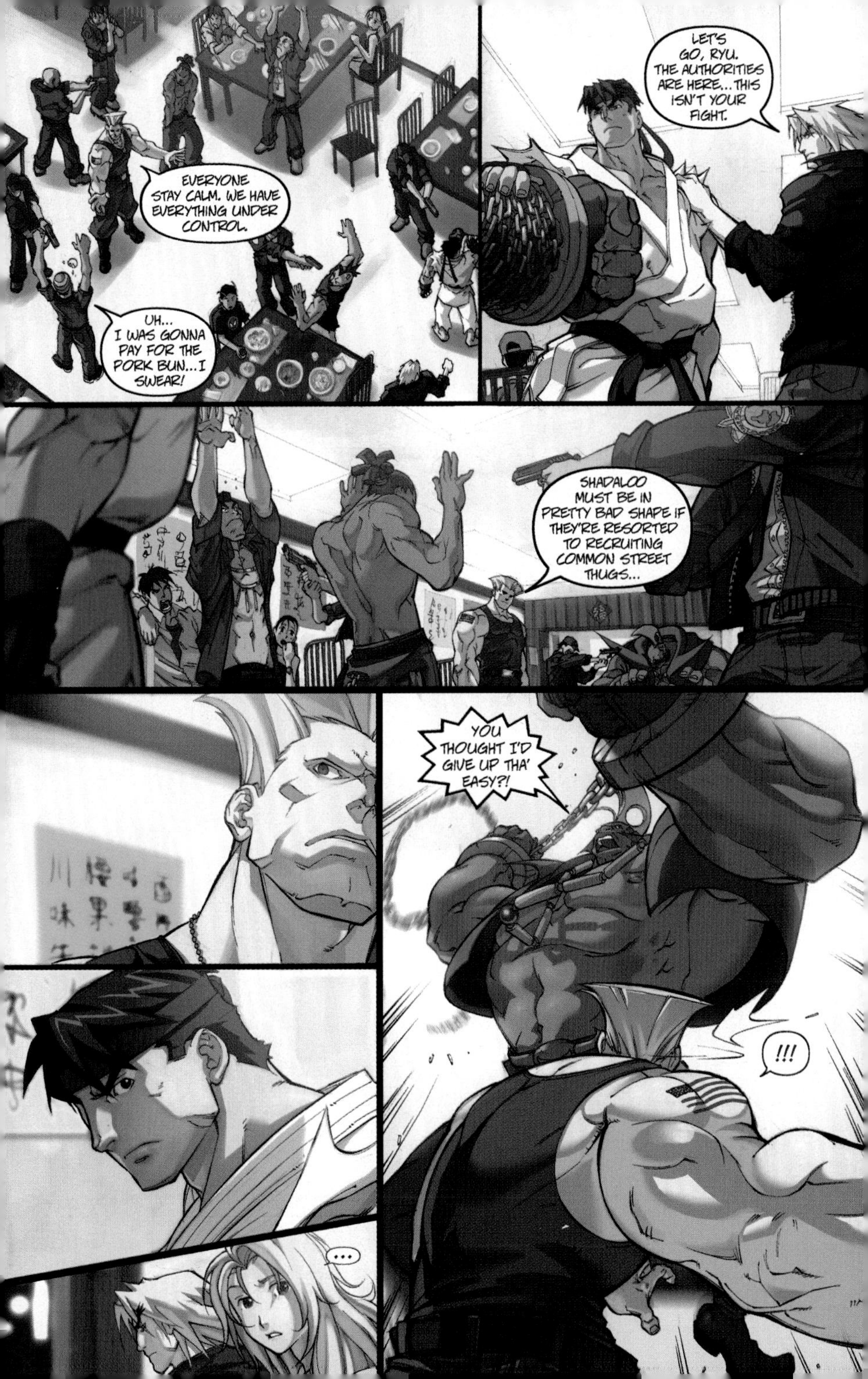
EVERYONE STAY CALM. WE HAVE EVERYTHING UNDER CONTROL.
UH... I WAS GONNA PAY FOR THE PORK BUN... I SWEAR!
LET'S GO, RYU. THE AUTHORITIES ARE HERE... THIS ISN'T YOUR FIGHT.
SHADALOO MUST BE IN PRETTY BAD SHAPE IF THEY'RE RESORTED TO RECRUITING COMMON STREET THUGS...
YOU THOUGHT I'D GIVE UP THA' EASY?!
!!!
...

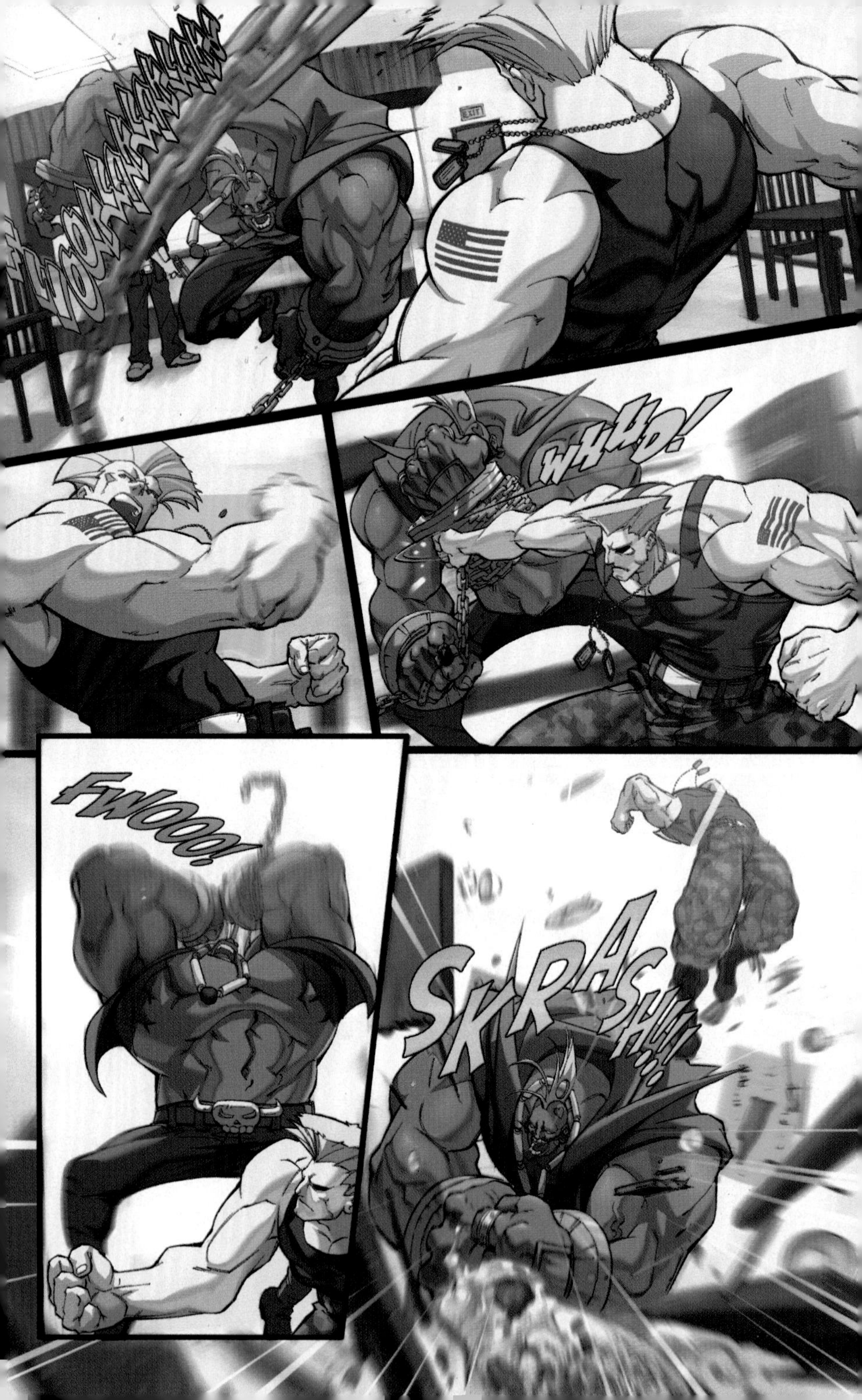

WHUD!
FWOOO!
SKRASH!!

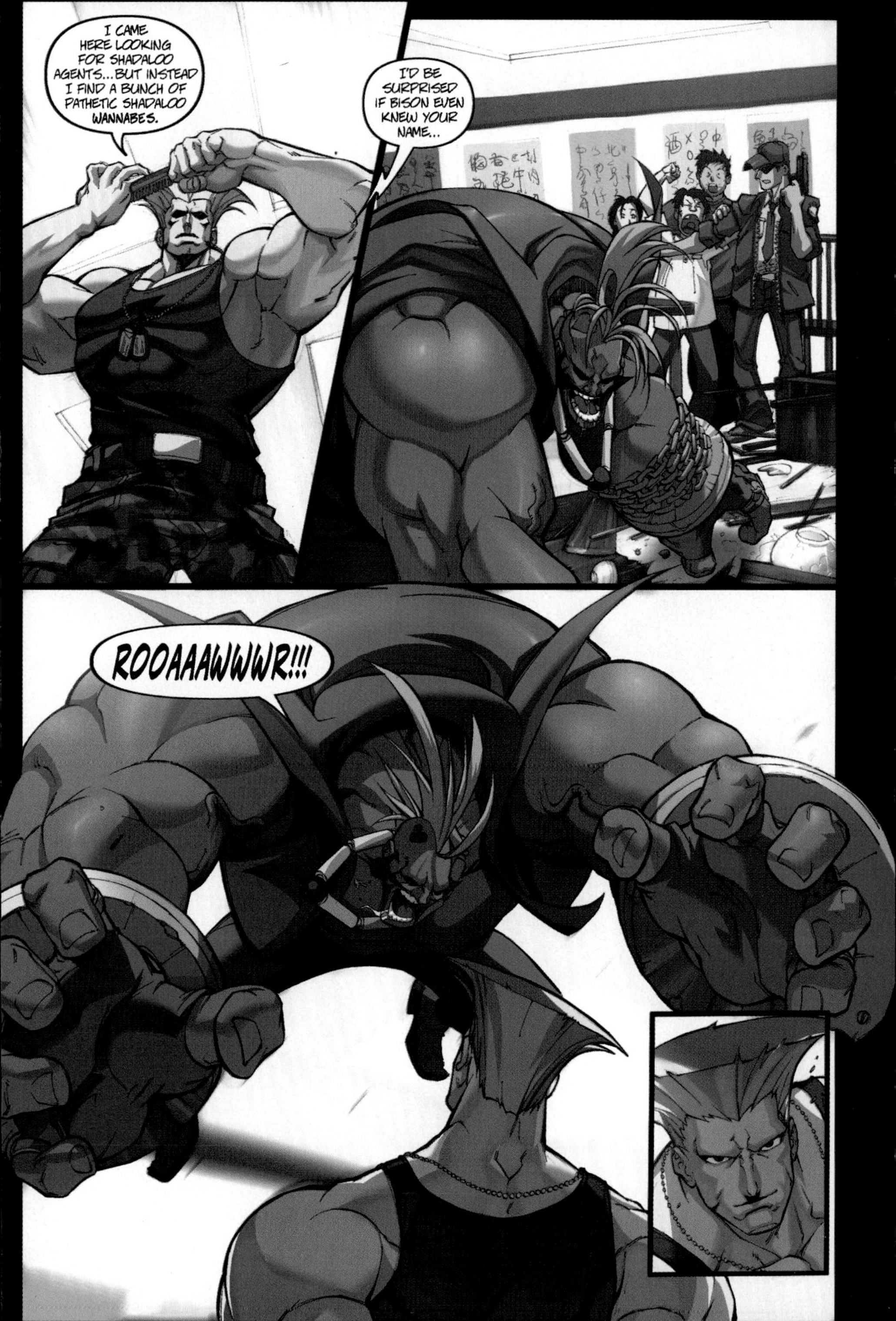
I CAME HERE LOOKING FOR SHADALOO AGENTS...BUT INSTEAD I FIND A BUNCH OF PATHETIC SHADALOO WANNABES.
I'D BE SURPRISED IF BISON EVEN KNEW YOUR NAME...
ROOAAAWWWR!!!

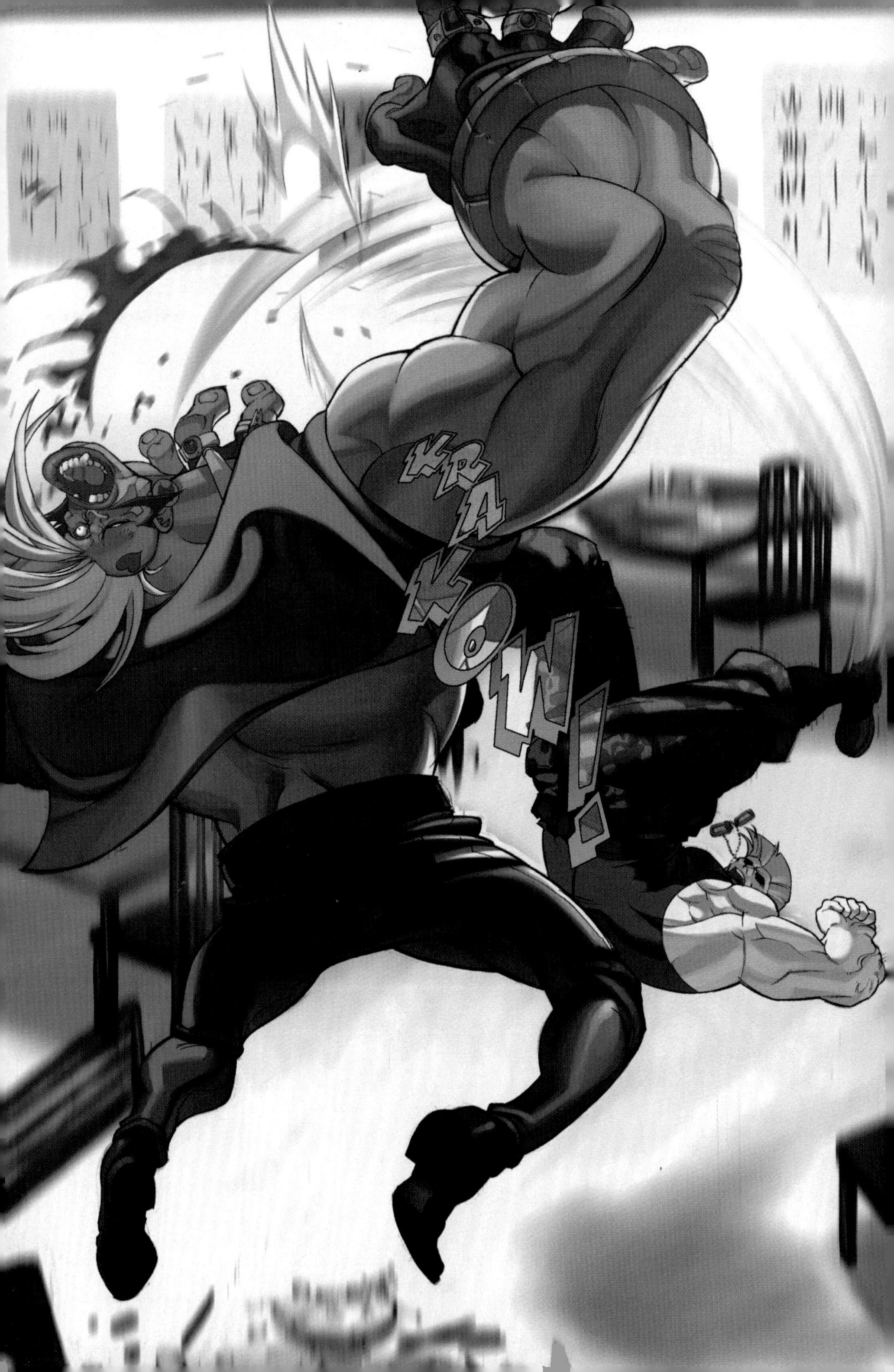
KRAKOW!

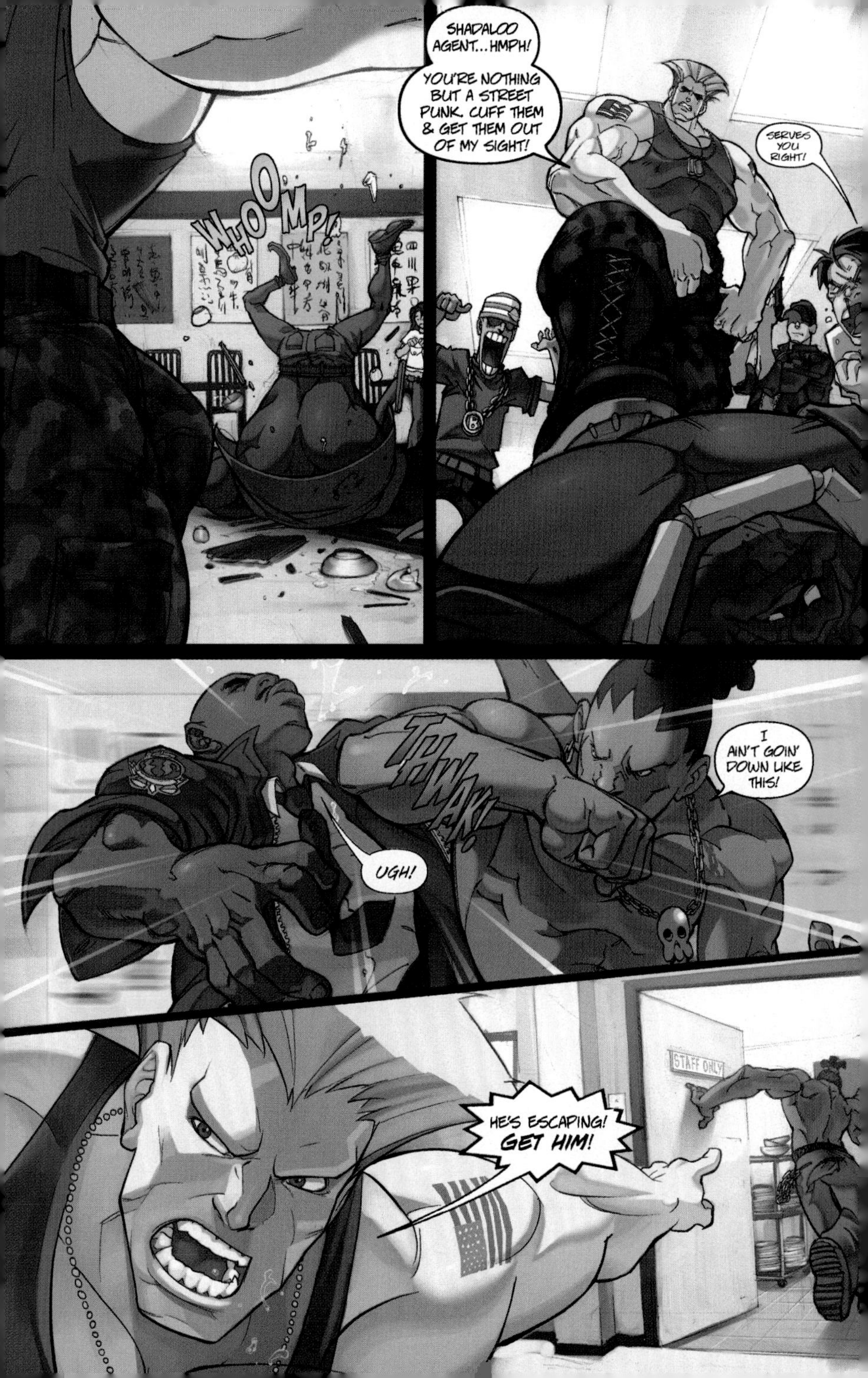
WHOOMP!
SHADALOO AGENT... HMPH!
YOU'RE NOTHING BUT A STREET PUNK. CUFF THEM & GET THEM OUT OF MY SIGHT!
SERVES YOU RIGHT!
THWAK!
I AIN'T GOIN' DOWN LIKE THIS!
UGH!
STAFF ONLY
HE'S ESCAPING! GET HIM!

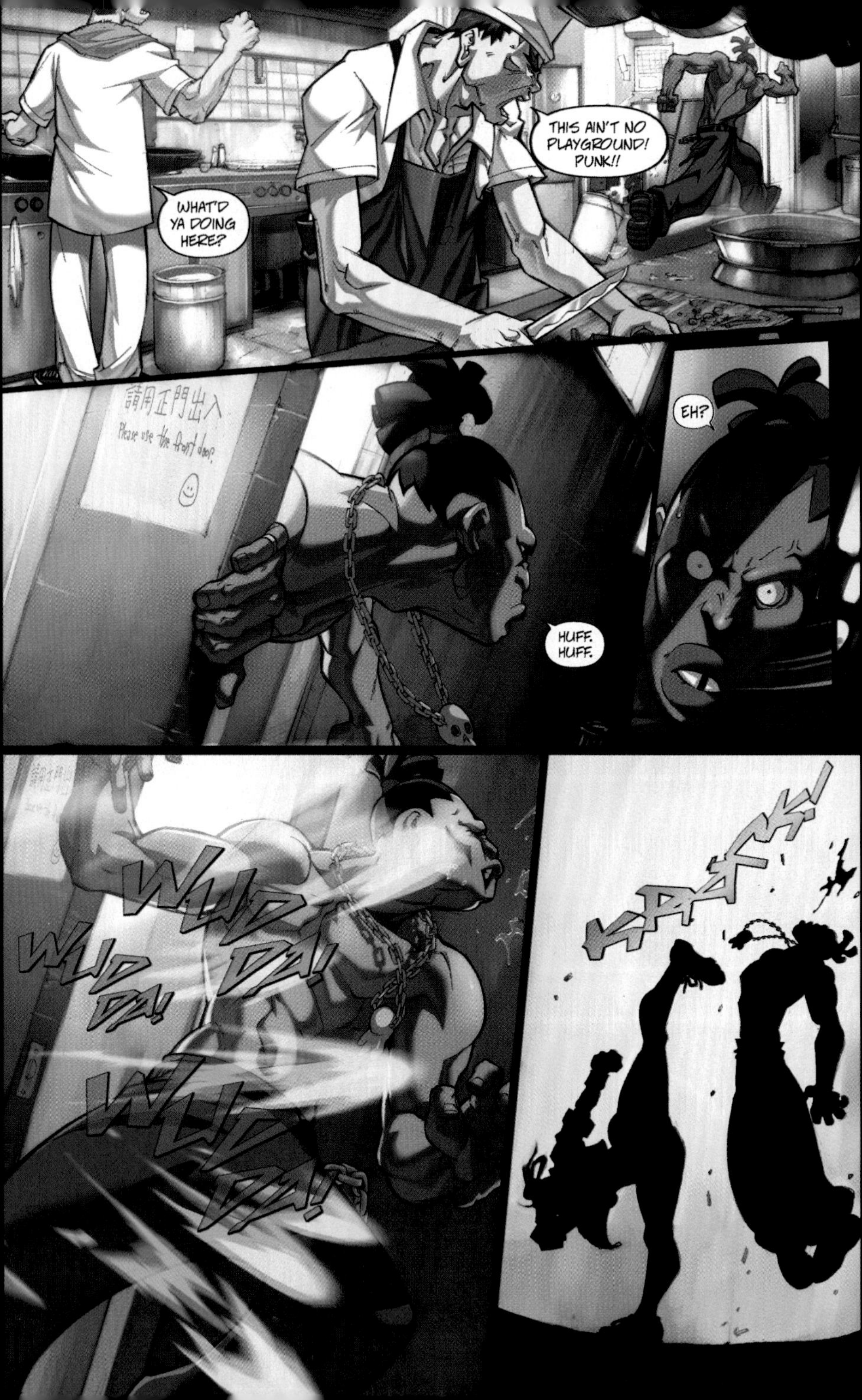
WHAT'D YA DOING HERE?
THIS AIN'T NO PLAYGROUND! PUNK!!
請用正門出入
Please use the front door.
HUFF. HUFF.
EH?
WUD-DA!
WUD-DA!
WUD-DA!
KRAK!

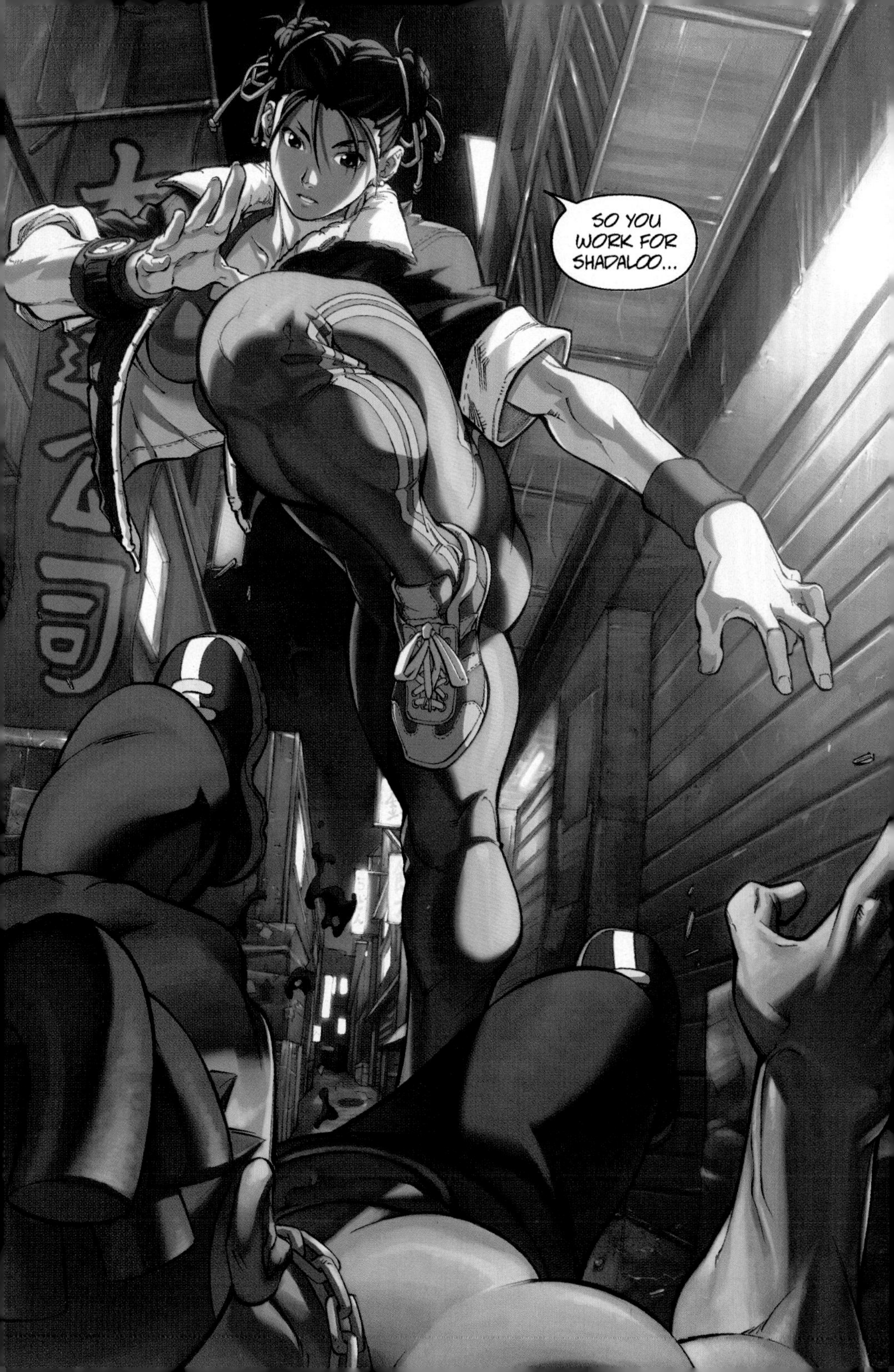
SO YOU WORK FOR SHADALOO...

Cover Art by: Arnold Tsang

Chapter 02: JAPAN

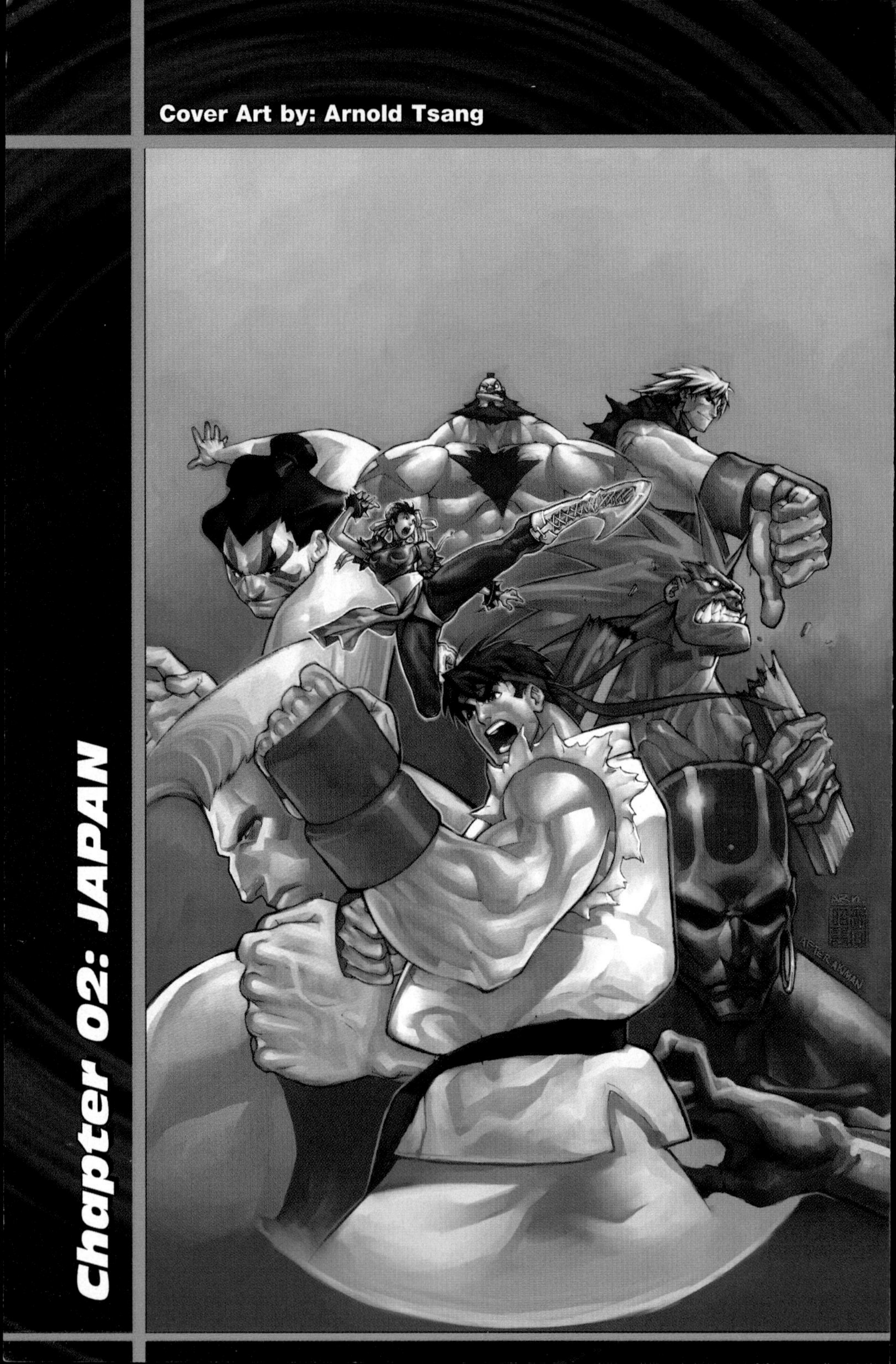
AFTER AKIMAN

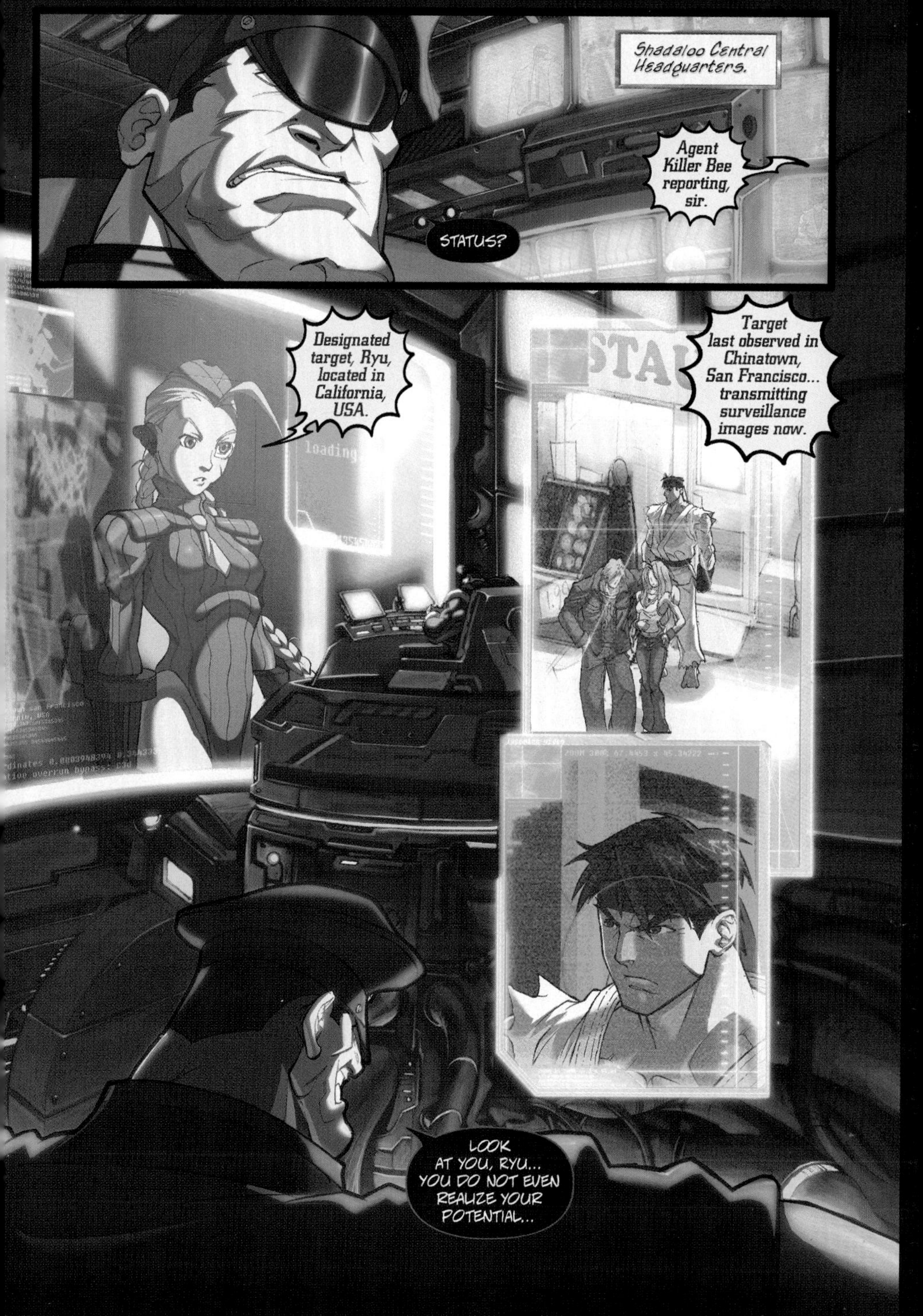
Shadaloo Central Headquarters.
Agent Killer Bee reporting, sir.
STATUS?
Designated target, Ryu, located in California, USA.
Target last observed in Chinatown, San Francisco... transmitting surveillance images now.
LOOK AT YOU, RYU... YOU DO NOT EVEN REALIZE YOUR POTENTIAL...

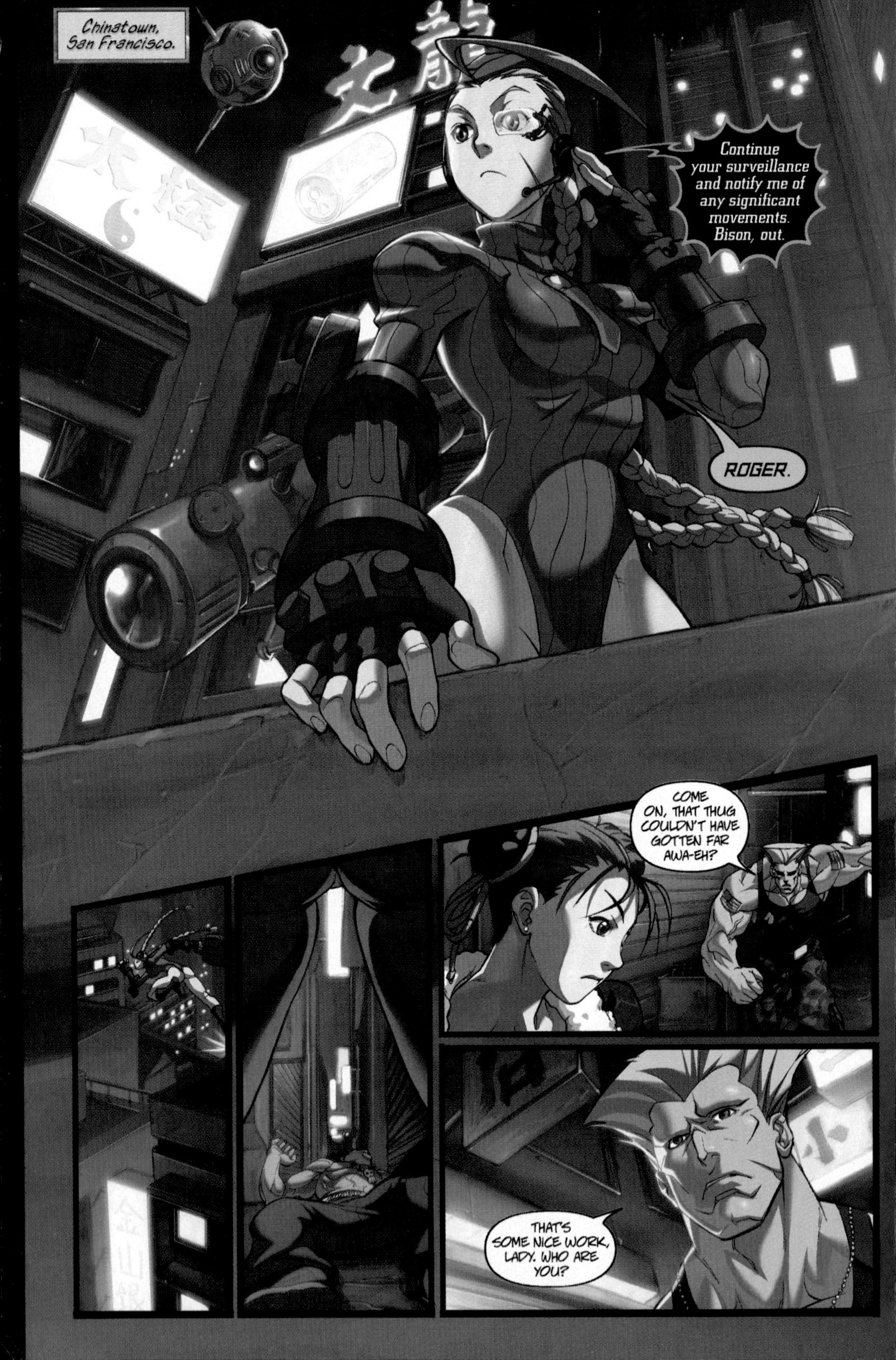
Chinatown, San Francisco.
Continue your surveillance and notify me of any significant movements. Bison, out.
ROGER.
COME ON, THAT THUG COULDN'T HAVE GOTTEN FAR AWA-EH?
THAT'S SOME NICE WORK, LADY. WHO ARE YOU?

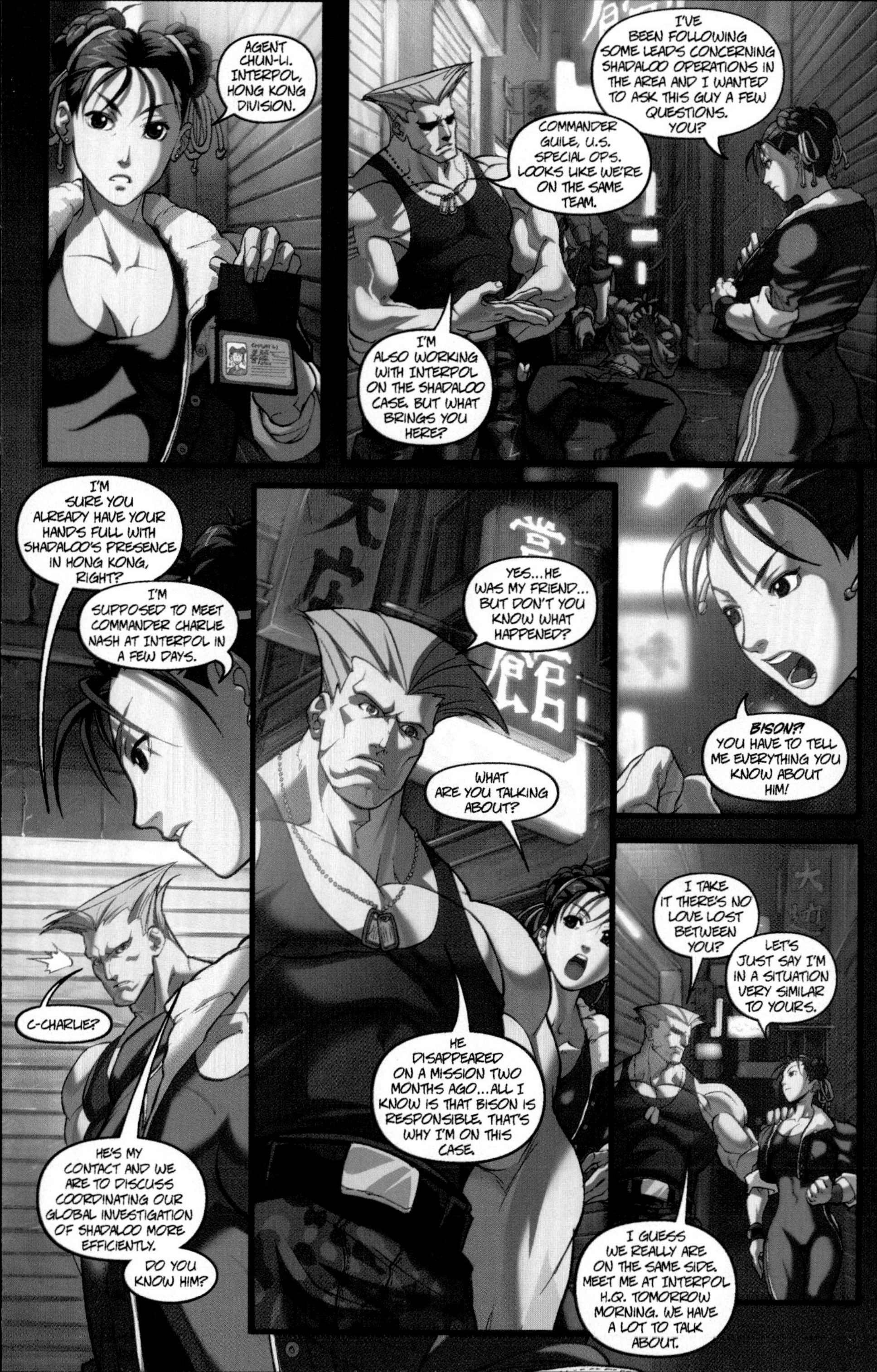
AGENT CHUN-LI. INTERPOL, HONG KONG DIVISION.
COMMANDER GUILE, U.S. SPECIAL OPS. LOOKS LIKE WE'RE ON THE SAME TEAM.
I'M ALSO WORKING WITH INTERPOL ON THE SHADALOO CASE. BUT WHAT BRINGS YOU HERE?
I'VE BEEN FOLLOWING SOME LEADS CONCERNING SHADALOO OPERATIONS IN THE AREA AND I WANTED TO ASK THIS GUY A FEW QUESTIONS. YOU?
I'M SURE YOU ALREADY HAVE YOUR HANDS FULL WITH SHADALOO'S PRESENCE IN HONG KONG, RIGHT?
I'M SUPPOSED TO MEET COMMANDER CHARLIE NASH AT INTERPOL IN A FEW DAYS.
C-CHARLIE?
HE'S MY CONTACT AND WE ARE TO DISCUSS COORDINATING OUR GLOBAL INVESTIGATION OF SHADALOO MORE EFFICIENTLY.
DO YOU KNOW HIM?
YES...HE WAS MY FRIEND... BUT DON'T YOU KNOW WHAT HAPPENED?
WHAT ARE YOU TALKING ABOUT?
HE DISAPPEARED ON A MISSION TWO MONTHS AGO...ALL I KNOW IS THAT BISON IS RESPONSIBLE. THAT'S WHY I'M ON THIS CASE.
BISON?! YOU HAVE TO TELL ME EVERYTHING YOU KNOW ABOUT HIM!
I TAKE IT THERE'S NO LOVE LOST BETWEEN YOU?
LET'S JUST SAY I'M IN A SITUATION VERY SIMILAR TO YOURS.
I GUESS WE REALLY ARE ON THE SAME SIDE. MEET ME AT INTERPOL H.Q. TOMORROW MORNING. WE HAVE A LOT TO TALK ABOUT.

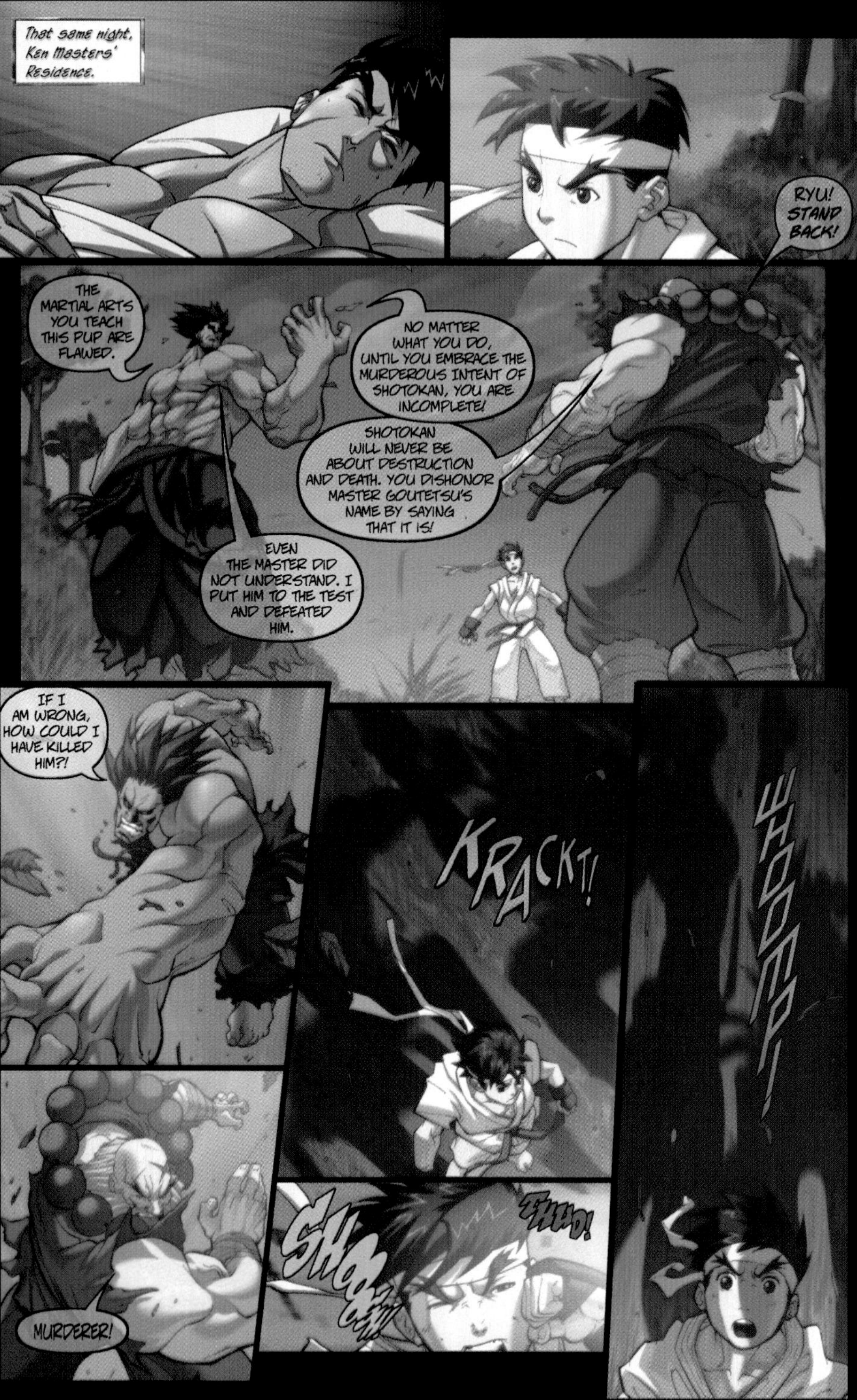
That same night, Ken Masters' Residence.
RYU! STAND BACK!
THE MARTIAL ARTS YOU TEACH THIS PUP ARE FLAWED.
NO MATTER WHAT YOU DO, UNTIL YOU EMBRACE THE MURDEROUS INTENT OF SHOTOKAN, YOU ARE INCOMPLETE!
SHOTOKAN WILL NEVER BE ABOUT DESTRUCTION AND DEATH. YOU DISHONOR MASTER GOUTETSU'S NAME BY SAYING THAT IT IS!
EVEN THE MASTER DID NOT UNDERSTAND. I PUT HIM TO THE TEST AND DEFEATED HIM.
IF I AM WRONG, HOW COULD I HAVE KILLED HIM?!
KRACKT!
WHOOMP!
MURDERER!
SHOOOM!
THUD!

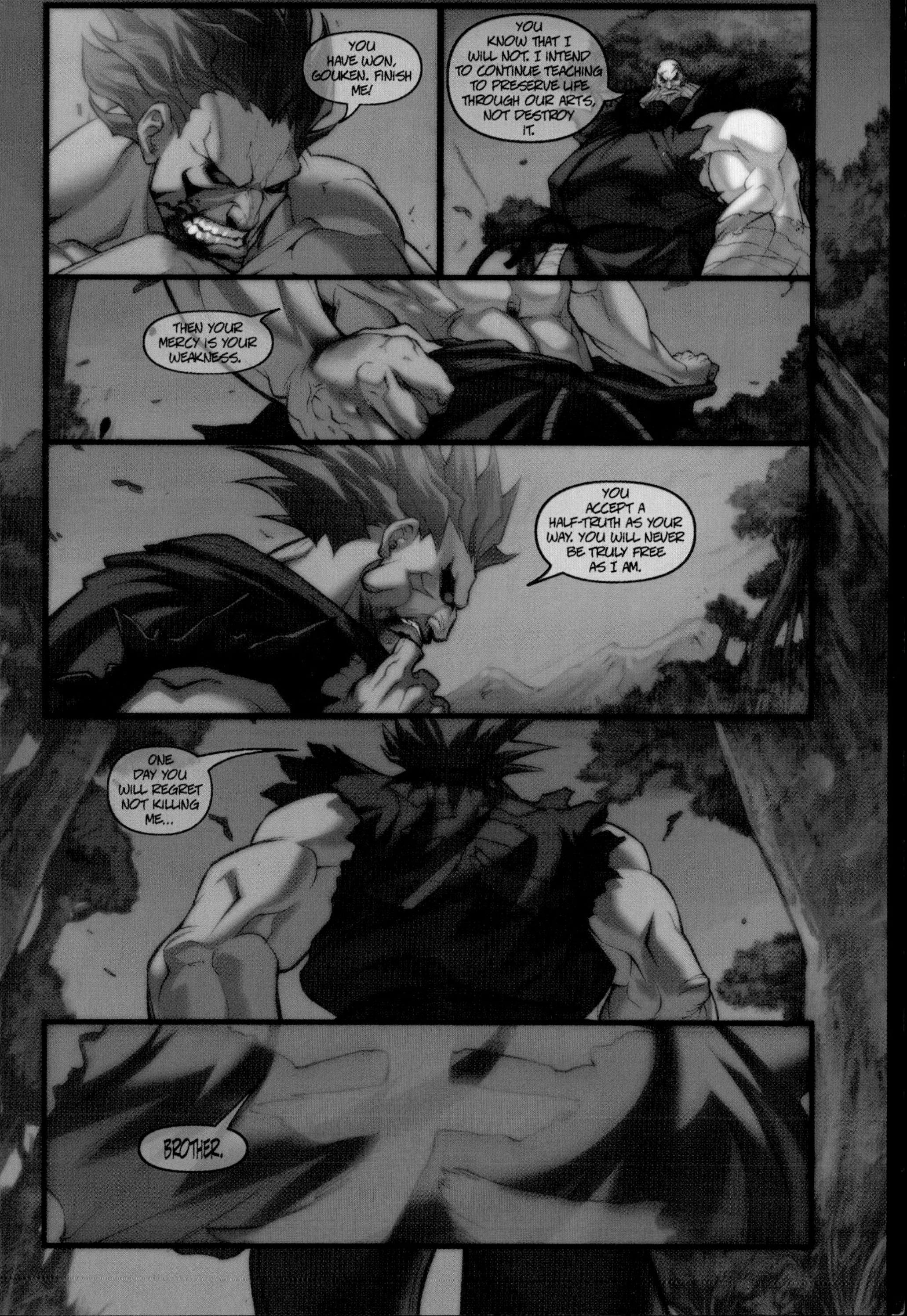
YOU HAVE WON, GOUKEN. FINISH ME!
YOU KNOW THAT I WILL NOT. I INTEND TO CONTINUE TEACHING TO PRESERVE LIFE THROUGH OUR ARTS, NOT DESTROY IT.
THEN YOUR MERCY IS YOUR WEAKNESS.
YOU ACCEPT A HALF-TRUTH AS YOUR WAY. YOU WILL NEVER BE TRULY FREE AS I AM.
ONE DAY YOU WILL REGRET NOT KILLING ME...
BROTHER.

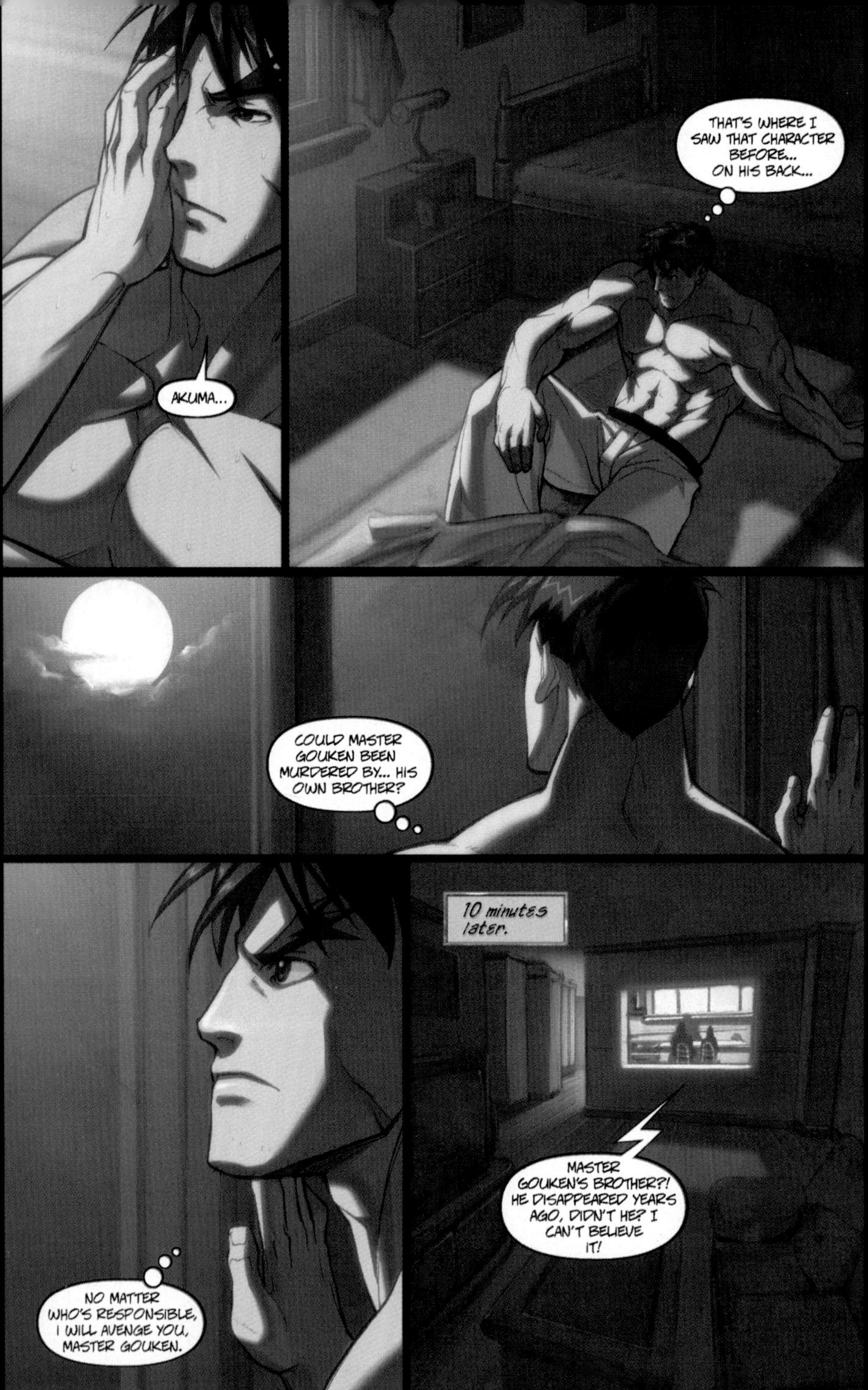
AKUMA...
THAT'S WHERE I SAW THAT CHARACTER BEFORE... ON HIS BACK...
COULD MASTER GOUKEN BEEN MURDERED BY... HIS OWN BROTHER?
NO MATTER WHO'S RESPONSIBLE, I WILL AVENGE YOU, MASTER GOUKEN.
10 minutes later.
MASTER GOUKEN'S BROTHER?! HE DISAPPEARED YEARS AGO, DIDN'T HE? I CAN'T BELIEVE IT!

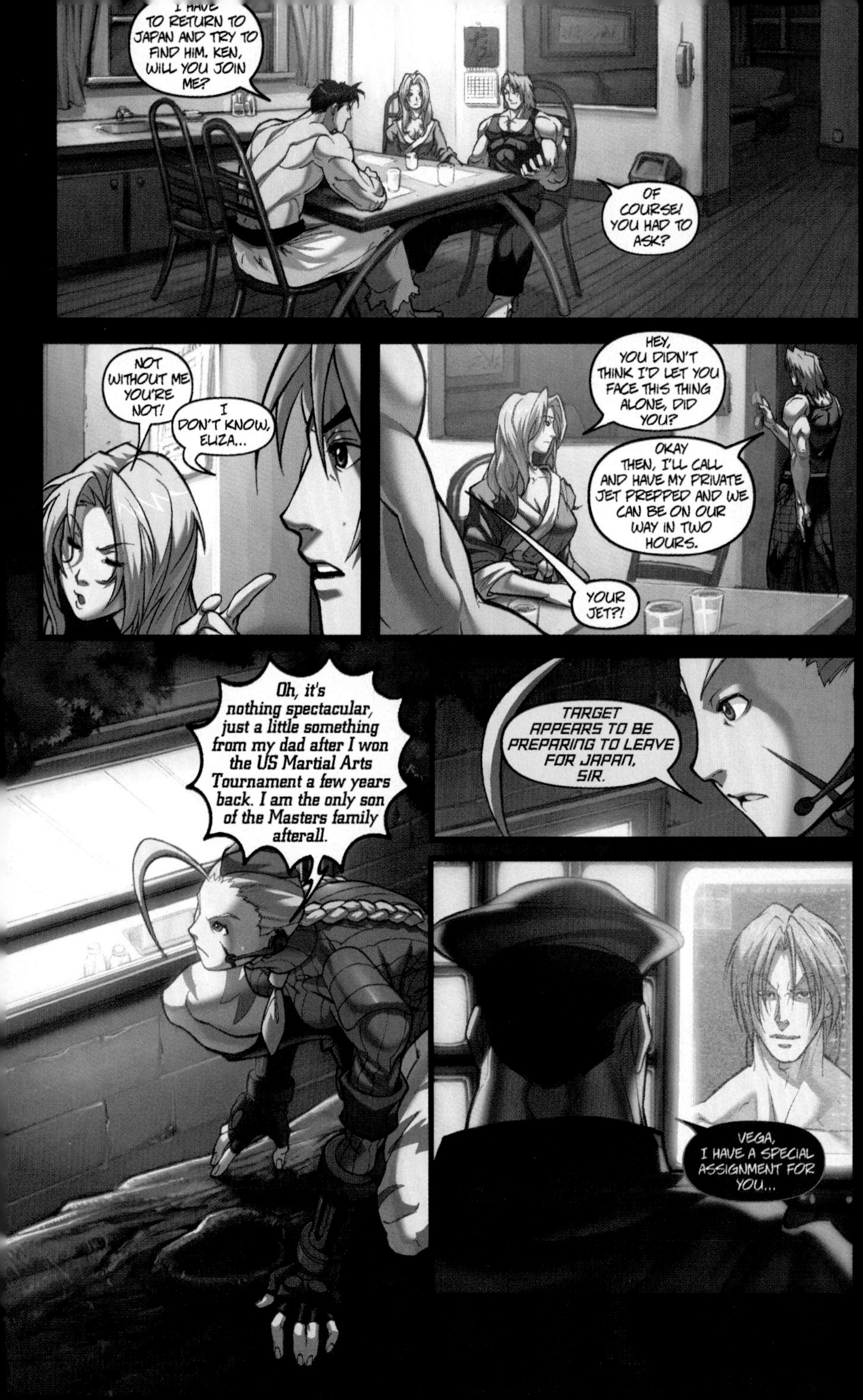
I HAVE TO RETURN TO JAPAN AND TRY TO FIND HIM. KEN, WILL YOU JOIN ME?
OF COURSE! YOU HAD TO ASK?
NOT WITHOUT ME YOU'RE NOT!
I DON'T KNOW, ELIZA...
HEY, YOU DIDN'T THINK I'D LET YOU FACE THIS THING ALONE, DID YOU?
OKAY THEN, I'LL CALL AND HAVE MY PRIVATE JET PREPPED AND WE CAN BE ON OUR WAY IN TWO HOURS.
YOUR JET?!
Oh, it's nothing spectacular, just a little something from my dad after I won the US Martial Arts Tournament a few years back. I am the only son of the Masters family afterall.
TARGET APPEARS TO BE PREPARING TO LEAVE FOR JAPAN, SIR.
VEGA, I HAVE A SPECIAL ASSIGNMENT FOR YOU...

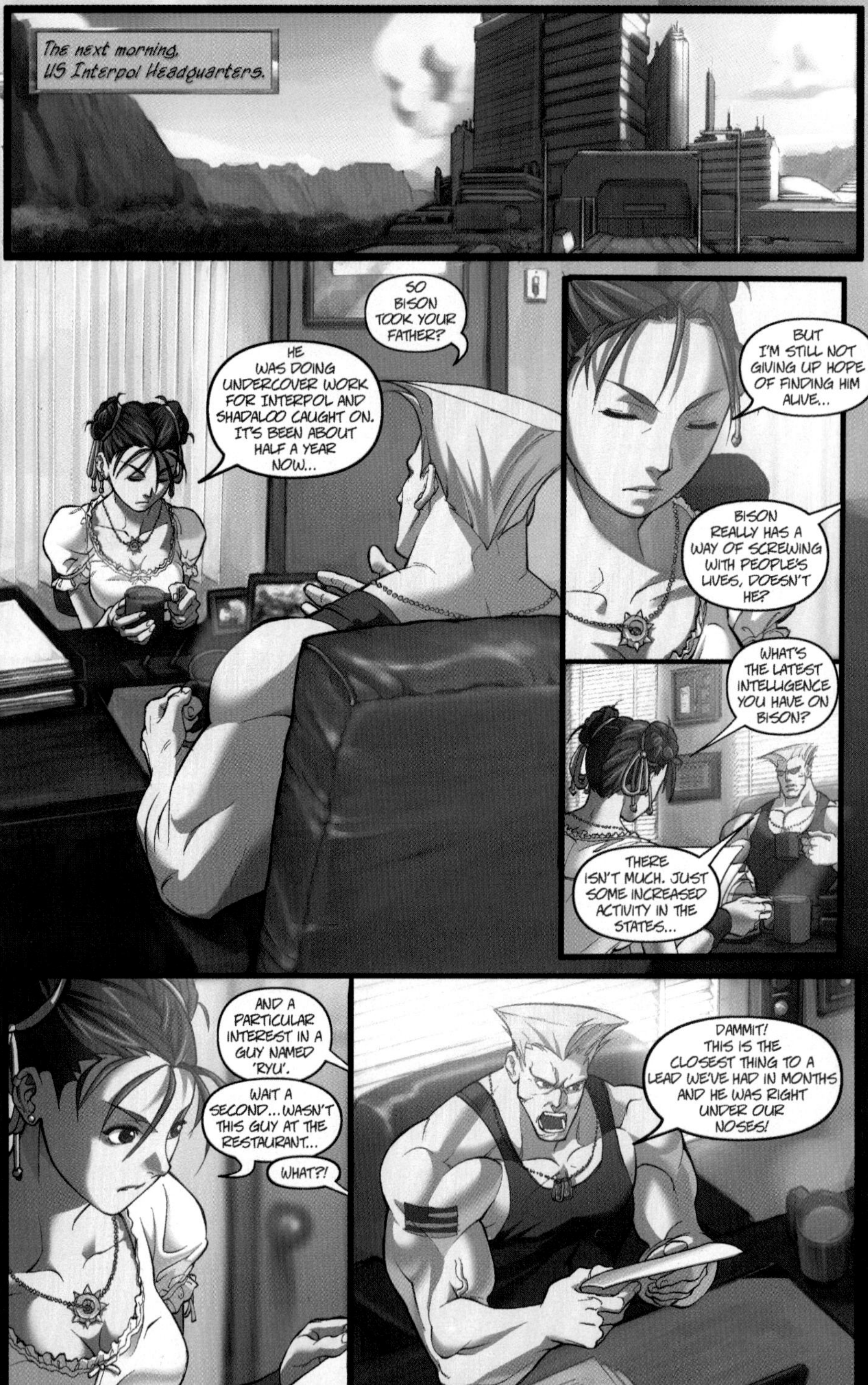
The next morning, US Interpol Headquarters.
SO BISON TOOK YOUR FATHER?
HE WAS DOING UNDERCOVER WORK FOR INTERPOL AND SHADALOO CAUGHT ON. IT'S BEEN ABOUT HALF A YEAR NOW...
BUT I'M STILL NOT GIVING UP HOPE OF FINDING HIM ALIVE...
BISON REALLY HAS A WAY OF SCREWING WITH PEOPLE'S LIVES, DOESN'T HE?
WHAT'S THE LATEST INTELLIGENCE YOU HAVE ON BISON?
THERE ISN'T MUCH. JUST SOME INCREASED ACTIVITY IN THE STATES...
AND A PARTICULAR INTEREST IN A GUY NAMED 'RYU'.
WAIT A SECOND...WASN'T THIS GUY AT THE RESTAURANT...
WHAT?!
DAMMIT! THIS IS THE CLOSEST THING TO A LEAD WE'VE HAD IN MONTHS AND HE WAS RIGHT UNDER OUR NOSES!

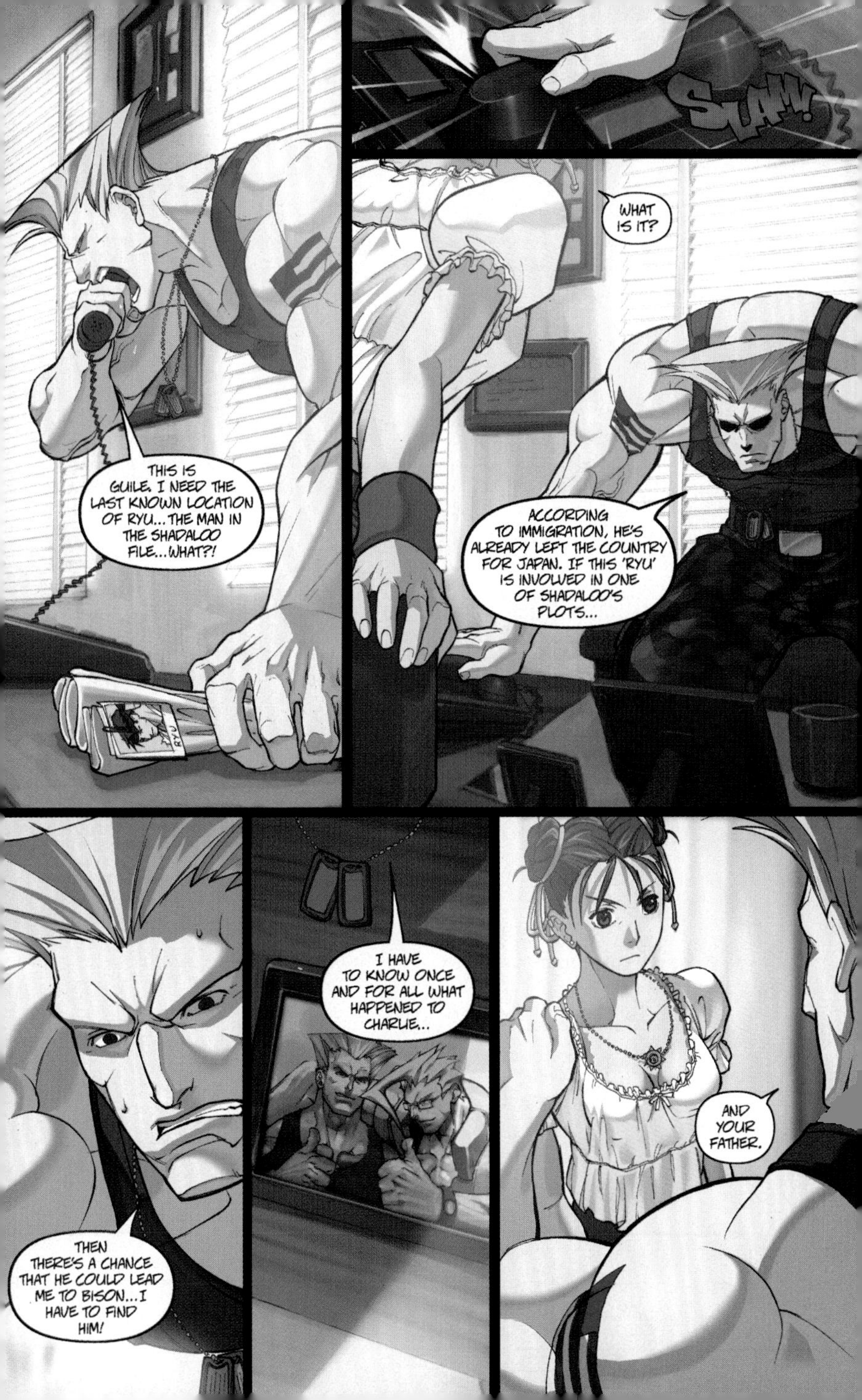
SLAM!
THIS IS GUILE. I NEED THE LAST KNOWN LOCATION OF RYU... THE MAN IN THE SHADALOO FILE... WHAT?!
RYU
WHAT IS IT?
ACCORDING TO IMMIGRATION, HE'S ALREADY LEFT THE COUNTRY FOR JAPAN. IF THIS 'RYU' IS INVOLVED IN ONE OF SHADALOO'S PLOTS...
THEN THERE'S A CHANCE THAT HE COULD LEAD ME TO BISON... I HAVE TO FIND HIM!
I HAVE TO KNOW ONCE AND FOR ALL WHAT HAPPENED TO CHARLIE...
AND YOUR FATHER.

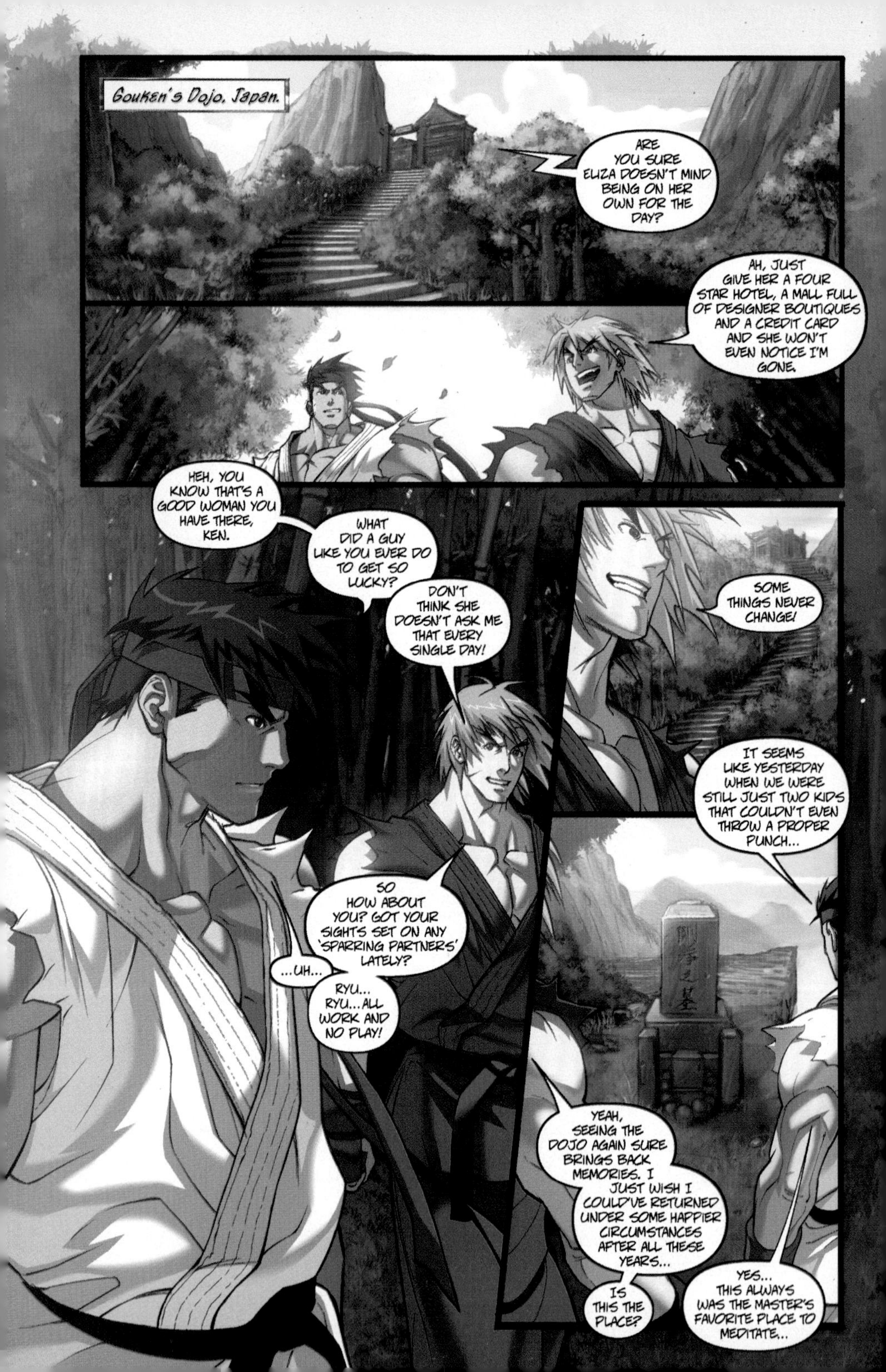
Gouken's Dojo, Japan.
ARE YOU SURE ELIZA DOESN'T MIND BEING ON HER OWN FOR THE DAY?
AH, JUST GIVE HER A FOUR STAR HOTEL, A MALL FULL OF DESIGNER BOUTIQUES AND A CREDIT CARD AND SHE WON'T EVEN NOTICE I'M GONE.
HEH, YOU KNOW THAT'S A GOOD WOMAN YOU HAVE THERE, KEN.
WHAT DID A GUY LIKE YOU EVER DO TO GET SO LUCKY?
DON'T THINK SHE DOESN'T ASK ME THAT EVERY SINGLE DAY!
SO HOW ABOUT YOU? GOT YOUR SIGHTS SET ON ANY 'SPARRING PARTNERS' LATELY?
...UH...
RYU... RYU...ALL WORK AND NO PLAY!
SOME THINGS NEVER CHANGE!
IT SEEMS LIKE YESTERDAY WHEN WE WERE STILL JUST TWO KIDS THAT COULDN'T EVEN THROW A PROPER PUNCH...
YEAH, SEEING THE DOJO AGAIN SURE BRINGS BACK MEMORIES. I JUST WISH I COULD'VE RETURNED UNDER SOME HAPPIER CIRCUMSTANCES AFTER ALL THESE YEARS...
IS THIS THE PLACE?
YES... THIS ALWAYS WAS THE MASTER'S FAVORITE PLACE TO MEDITATE...

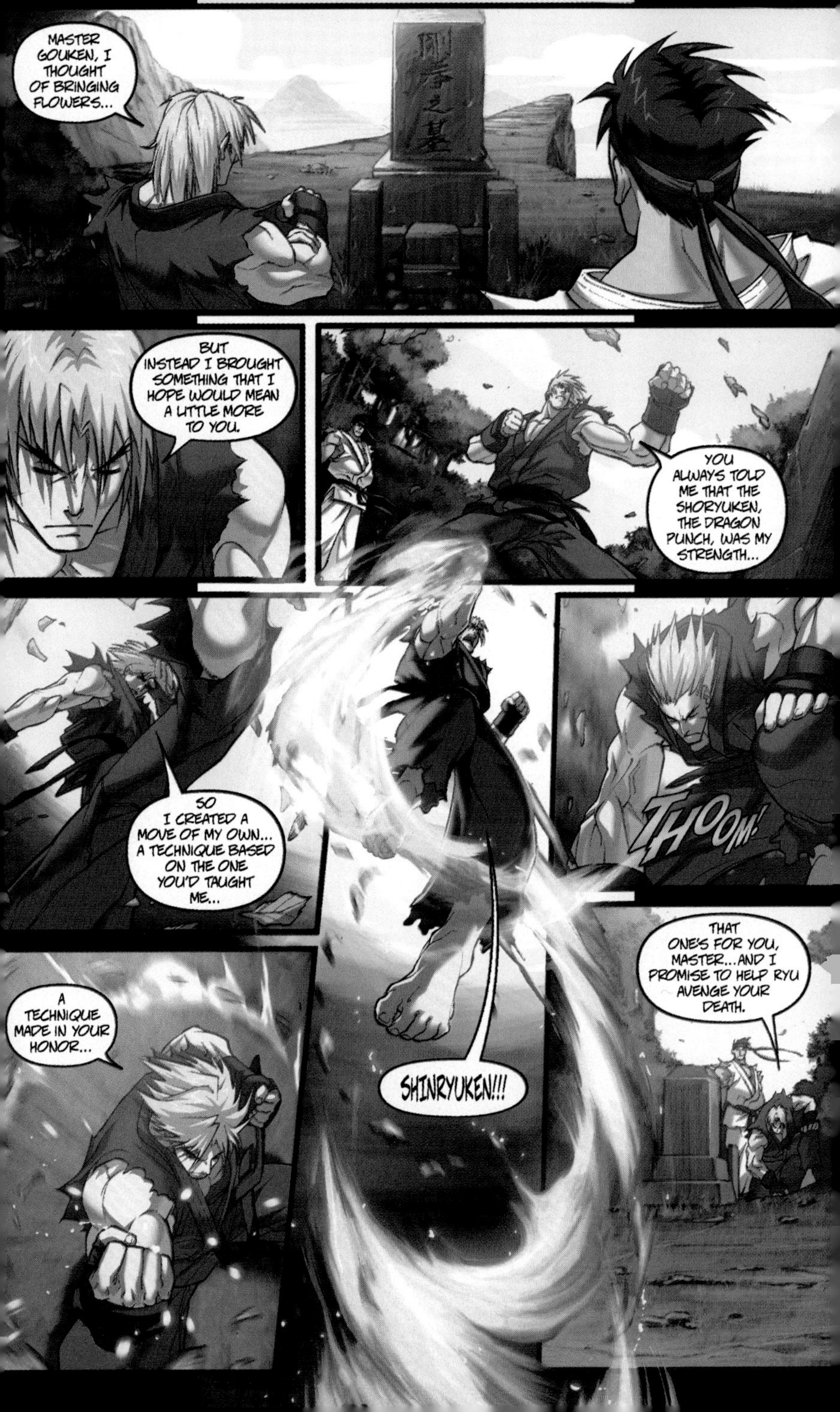

MASTER GOUKEN, I THOUGHT OF BRINGING FLOWERS...
BUT INSTEAD I BROUGHT SOMETHING THAT I HOPE WOULD MEAN A LITTLE MORE TO YOU.
YOU ALWAYS TOLD ME THAT THE SHORYUKEN, THE DRAGON PUNCH, WAS MY STRENGTH...
SO I CREATED A MOVE OF MY OWN... A TECHNIQUE BASED ON THE ONE YOU'D TAUGHT ME...
THOOM!
A TECHNIQUE MADE IN YOUR HONOR...
SHINRYUKEN!!!
THAT ONE'S FOR YOU, MASTER...AND I PROMISE TO HELP RYU AVENGE YOUR DEATH.

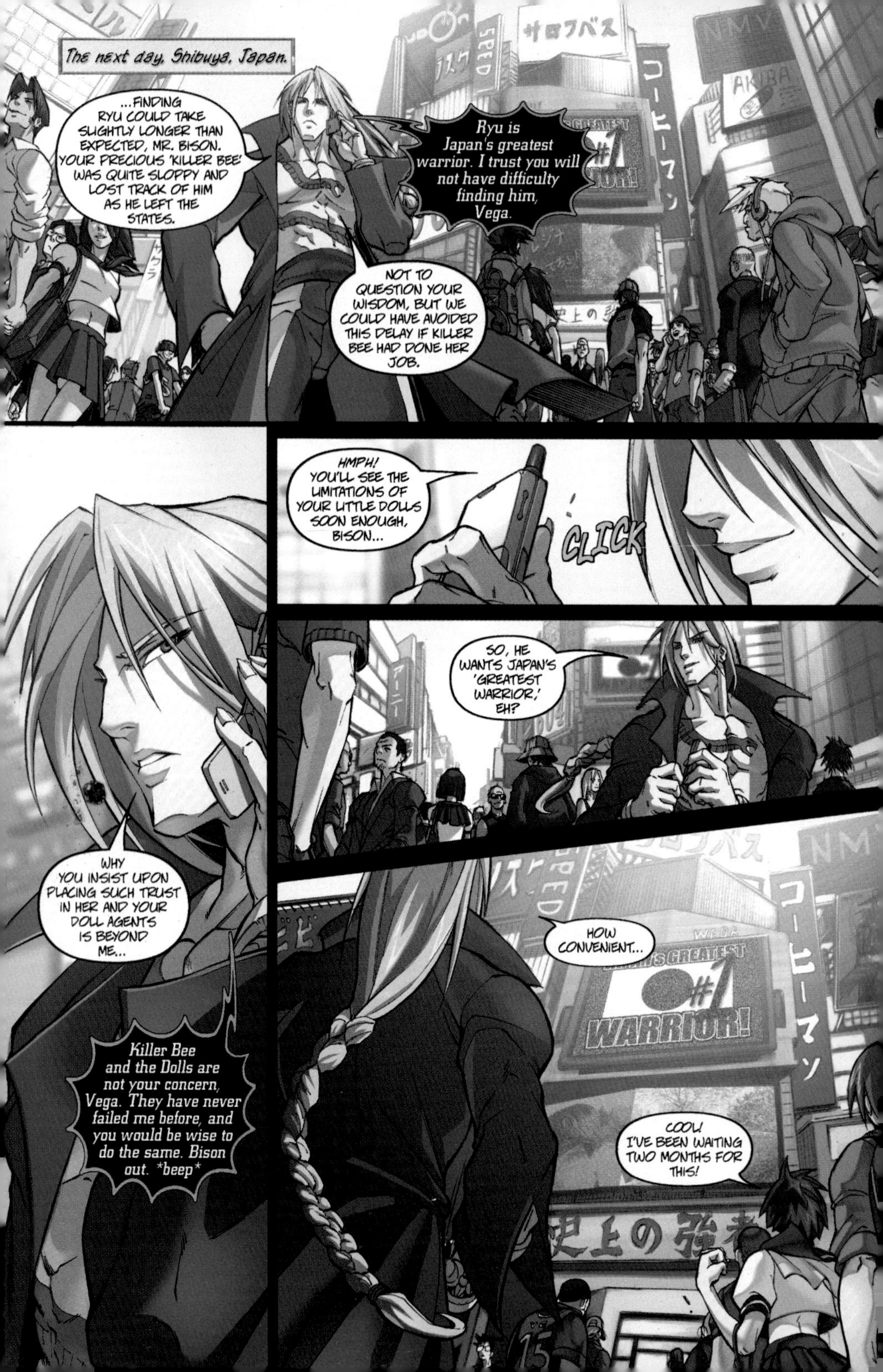
The next day, Shibuya, Japan.
...FINDING RYU COULD TAKE SLIGHTLY LONGER THAN EXPECTED, MR. BISON. YOUR PRECIOUS 'KILLER BEE' WAS QUITE SLOPPY AND LOST TRACK OF HIM AS HE LEFT THE STATES.
Ryu is Japan's greatest warrior. I trust you will not have difficulty finding him, Vega.
NOT TO QUESTION YOUR WISDOM, BUT WE COULD HAVE AVOIDED THIS DELAY IF KILLER BEE HAD DONE HER JOB.
WHY YOU INSIST UPON PLACING SUCH TRUST IN HER AND YOUR DOLL AGENTS IS BEYOND ME...
Killer Bee and the Dolls are not your concern, Vega. They have never failed me before, and you would be wise to do the same. Bison out. *beep*
HMPH! YOU'LL SEE THE LIMITATIONS OF YOUR LITTLE DOLLS SOON ENOUGH, BISON...
CLICK
SO, HE WANT'S JAPAN'S 'GREATEST WARRIOR,' EH?
HOW CONVENIENT...
#1 WARRIOR!
COOL! I'VE BEEN WAITING TWO MONTHS FOR THIS!

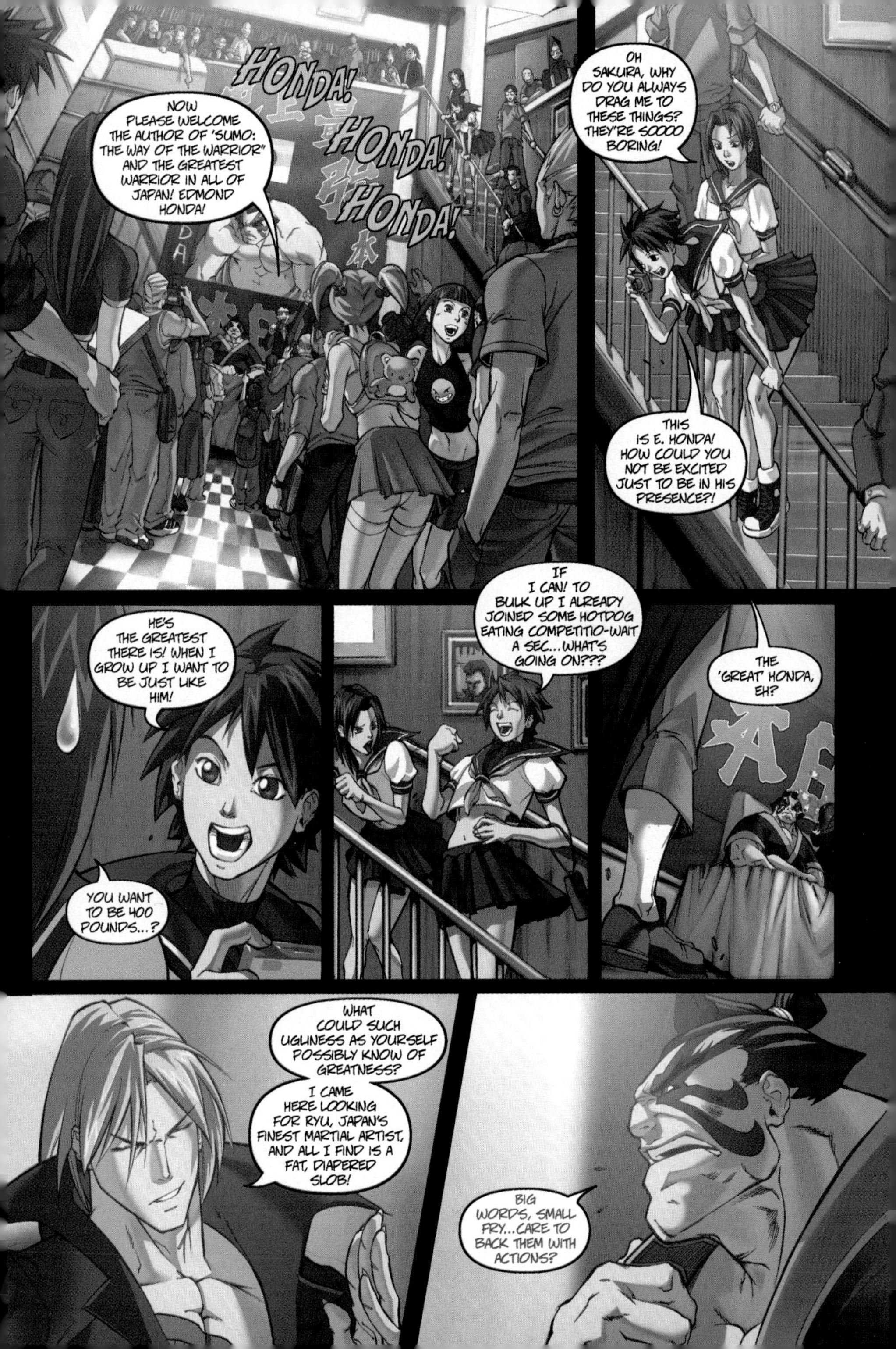
NOW PLEASE WELCOME THE AUTHOR OF 'SUMO: THE WAY OF THE WARRIOR" AND THE GREATEST WARRIOR IN ALL OF JAPAN! EDMOND HONDA!
HONDA! HONDA! HONDA!
OH SAKURA, WHY DO YOU ALWAYS DRAG ME TO THESE THINGS? THEY'RE SOOOO BORING!
THIS IS E. HONDA! HOW COULD YOU NOT BE EXCITED JUST TO BE IN HIS PRESENCE?!
HE'S THE GREATEST THERE IS! WHEN I GROW UP I WANT TO BE JUST LIKE HIM!
YOU WANT TO BE 400 POUNDS...?
IF I CAN! TO BULK UP I ALREADY JOINED SOME HOTDOG EATING COMPETITIO-WAIT A SEC...WHAT'S GOING ON???
THE 'GREAT' HONDA, EH?
WHAT COULD SUCH UGLINESS AS YOURSELF POSSIBLY KNOW OF GREATNESS?
I CAME HERE LOOKING FOR RYU, JAPAN'S FINEST MARTIAL ARTIST, AND ALL I FIND IS A FAT, DIAPERED SLOB!
BIG WORDS, SMALL FRY...CARE TO BACK THEM WITH ACTIONS?

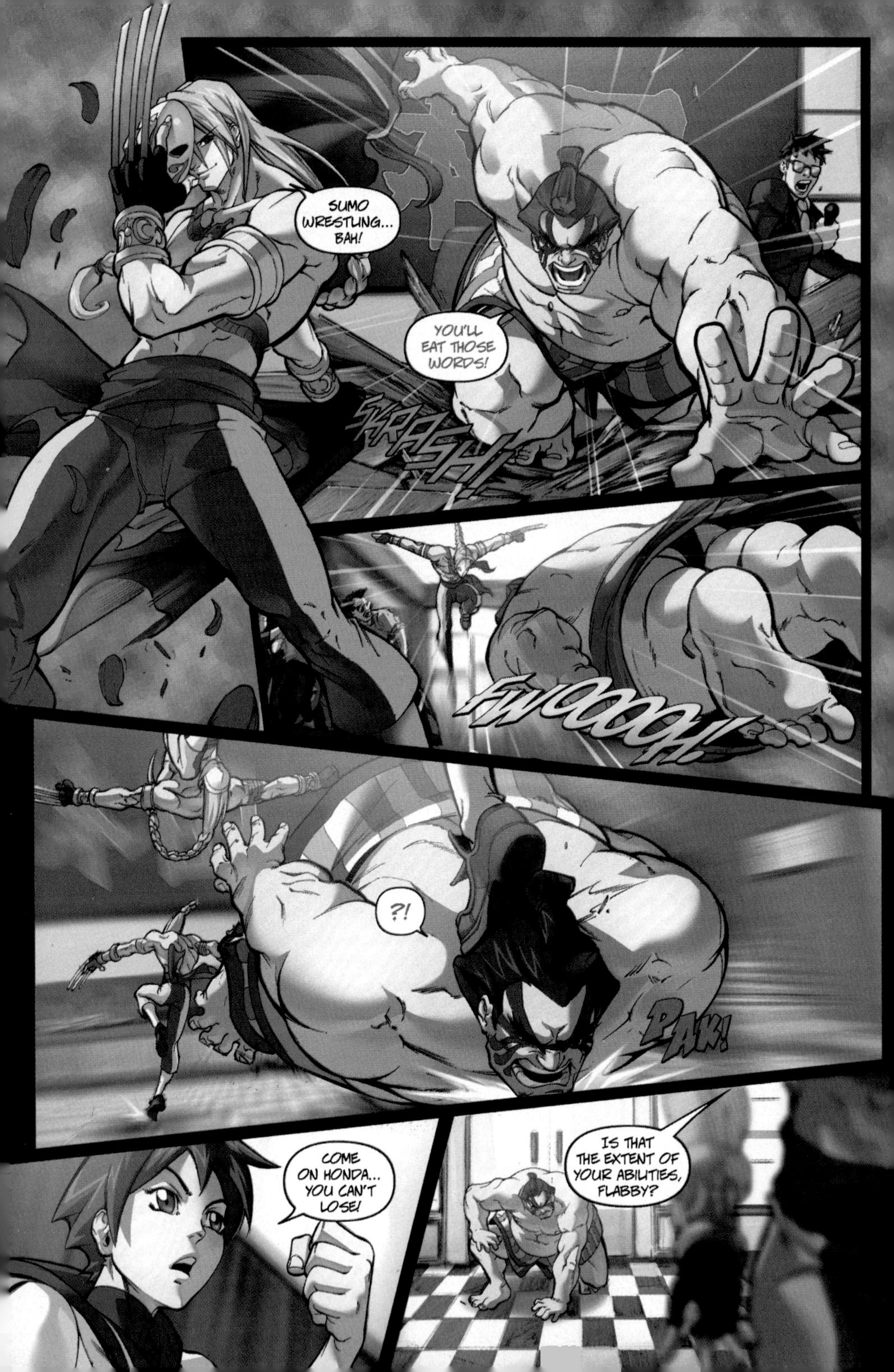

SUMO WRESTLING... BAH!
YOU'LL EAT THOSE WORDS!
SKRASH!
FWOOOOH!
?!
PAK!
COME ON HONDA... YOU CAN'T LOSE!
IS THAT THE EXTENT OF YOUR ABILITIES, FLABBY?

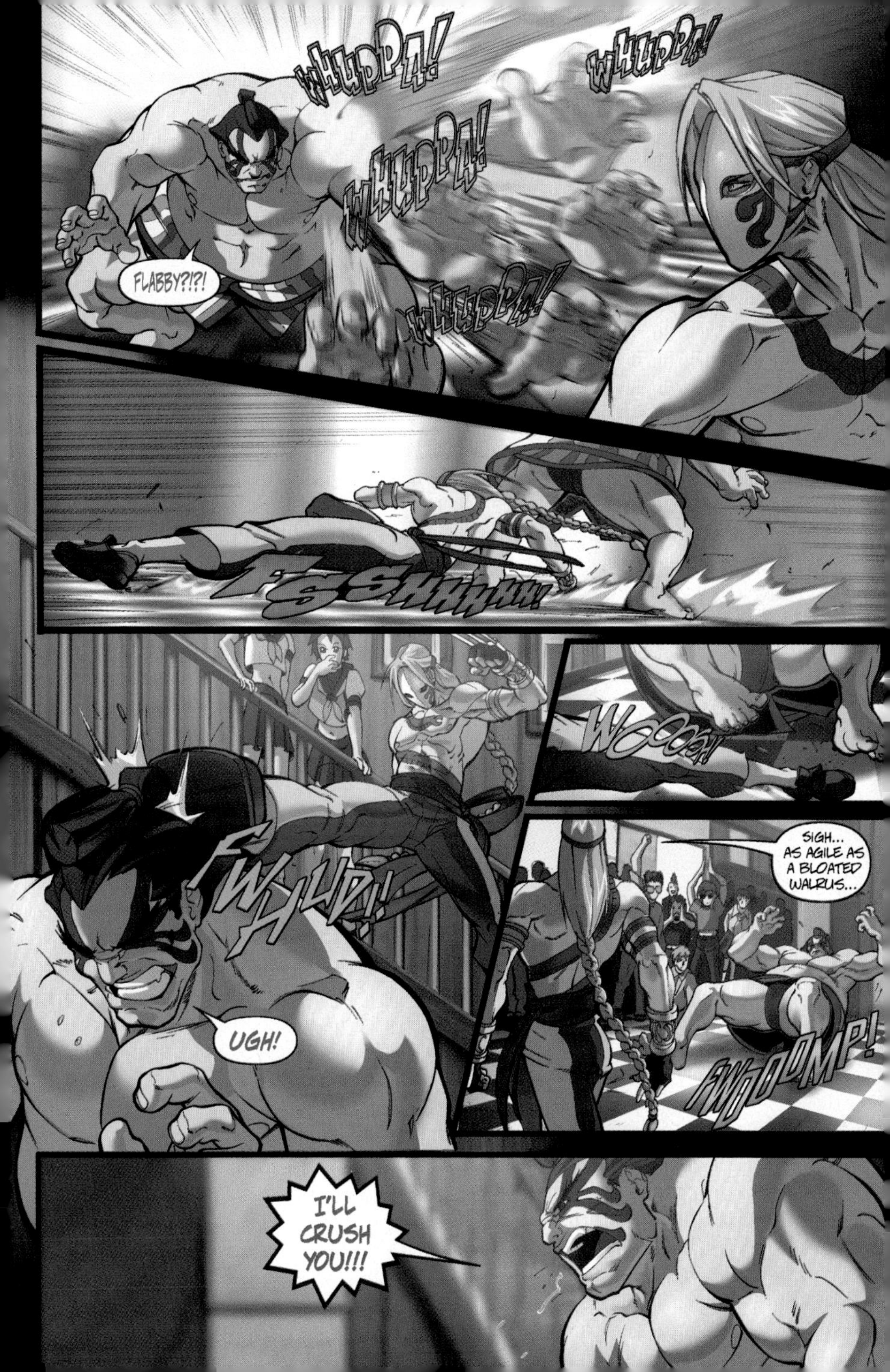
WHUPPA!
WHUPPA!
WHUPPA!
FLABBY?!?!
WHUPPA!
FSSHHHHH!
WOOOSH!
FWHUD!!
UGH!
SIGH... AS AGILE AS A BLOATED WALRUS...
FWHOOMP!
I'LL CRUSH YOU!!!

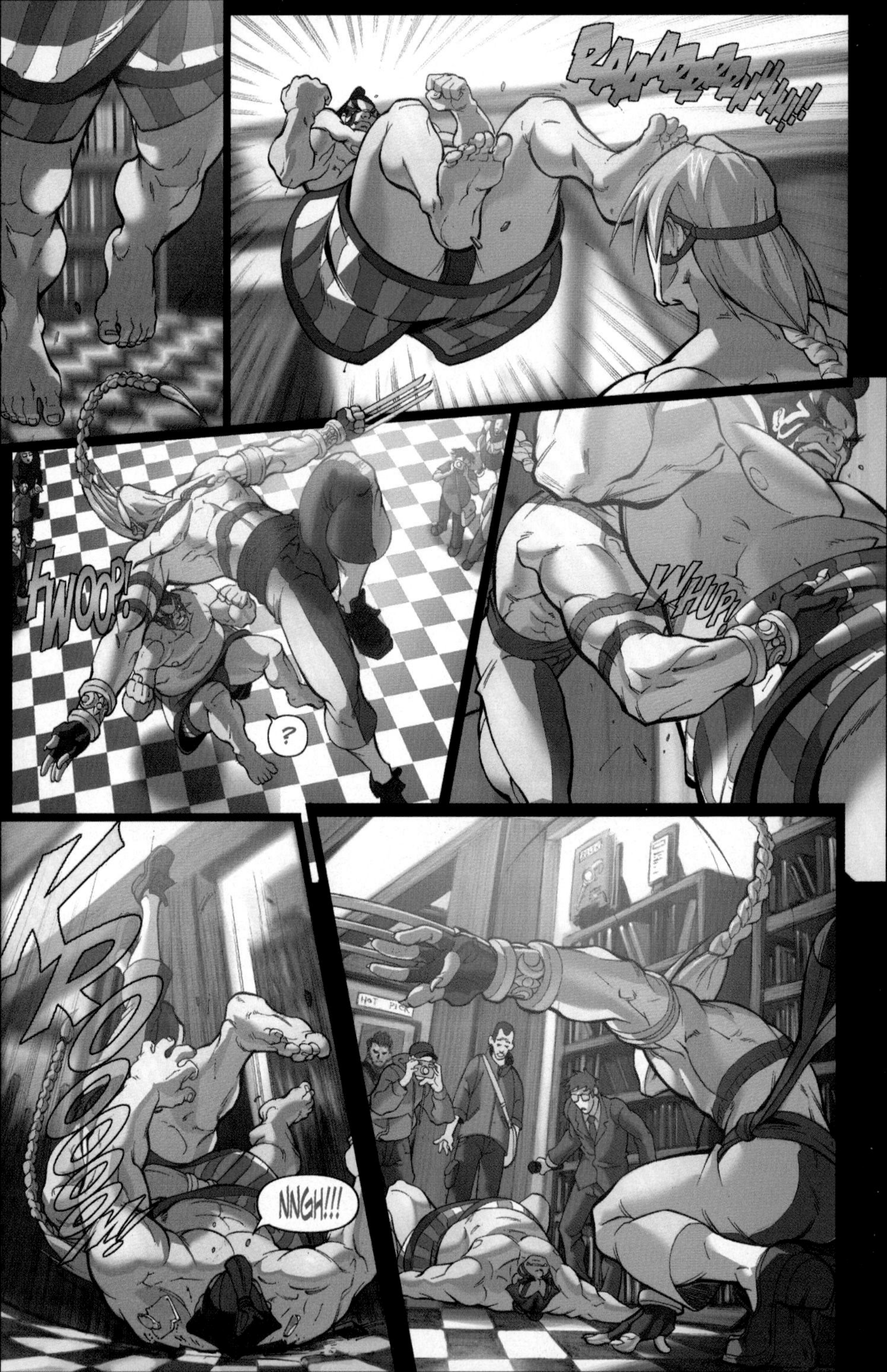
RAAARRGHHH!!
FWOOP!
?
WHUP!
KROOOOOOM!
NNGH!!!
HOT PICK

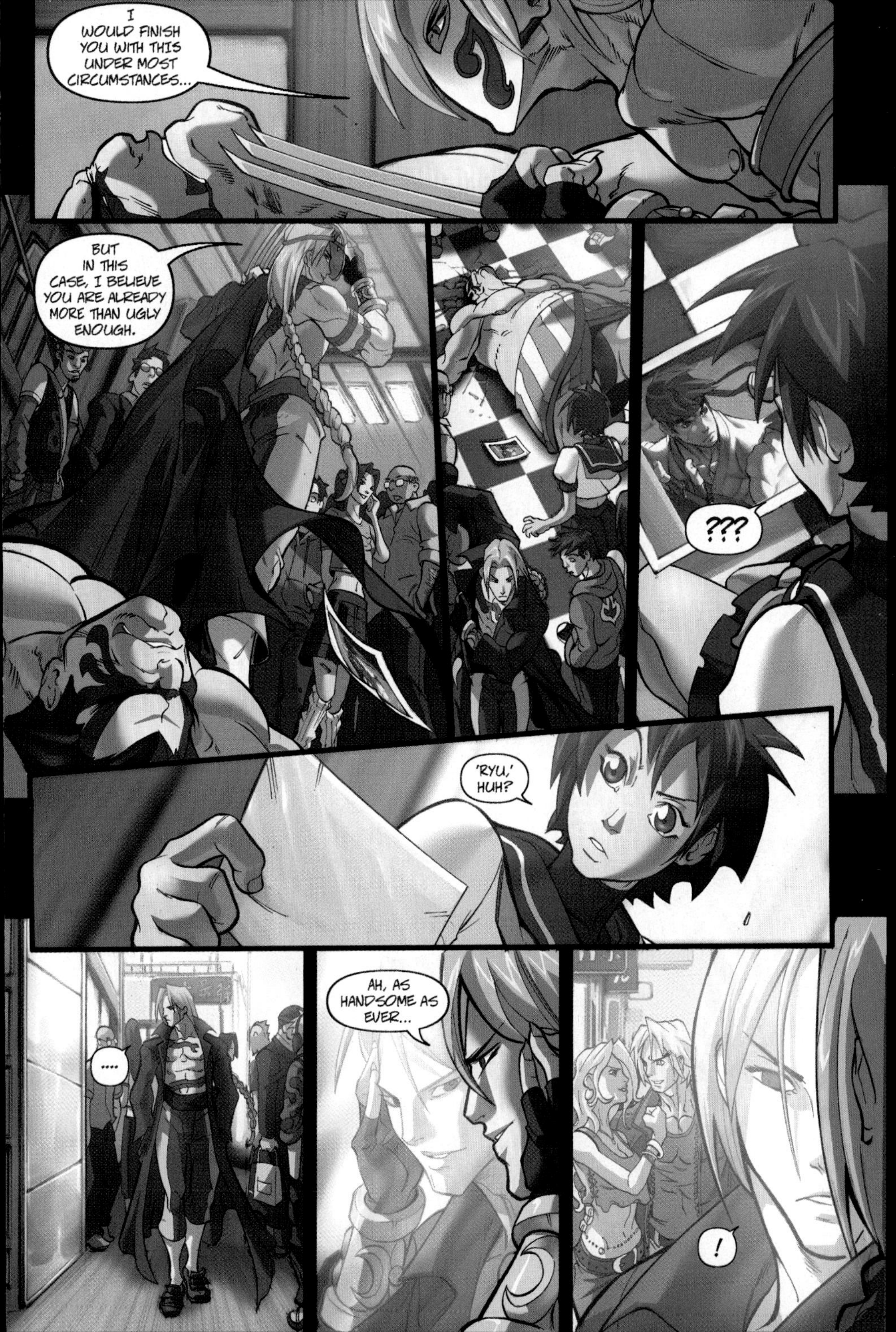
I WOULD FINISH YOU WITH THIS UNDER MOST CIRCUMSTANCES...
BUT IN THIS CASE, I BELIEVE YOU ARE ALREADY MORE THAN UGLY ENOUGH.
???
'RYU,' HUH?
....
AH, AS HANDSOME AS EVER...
!

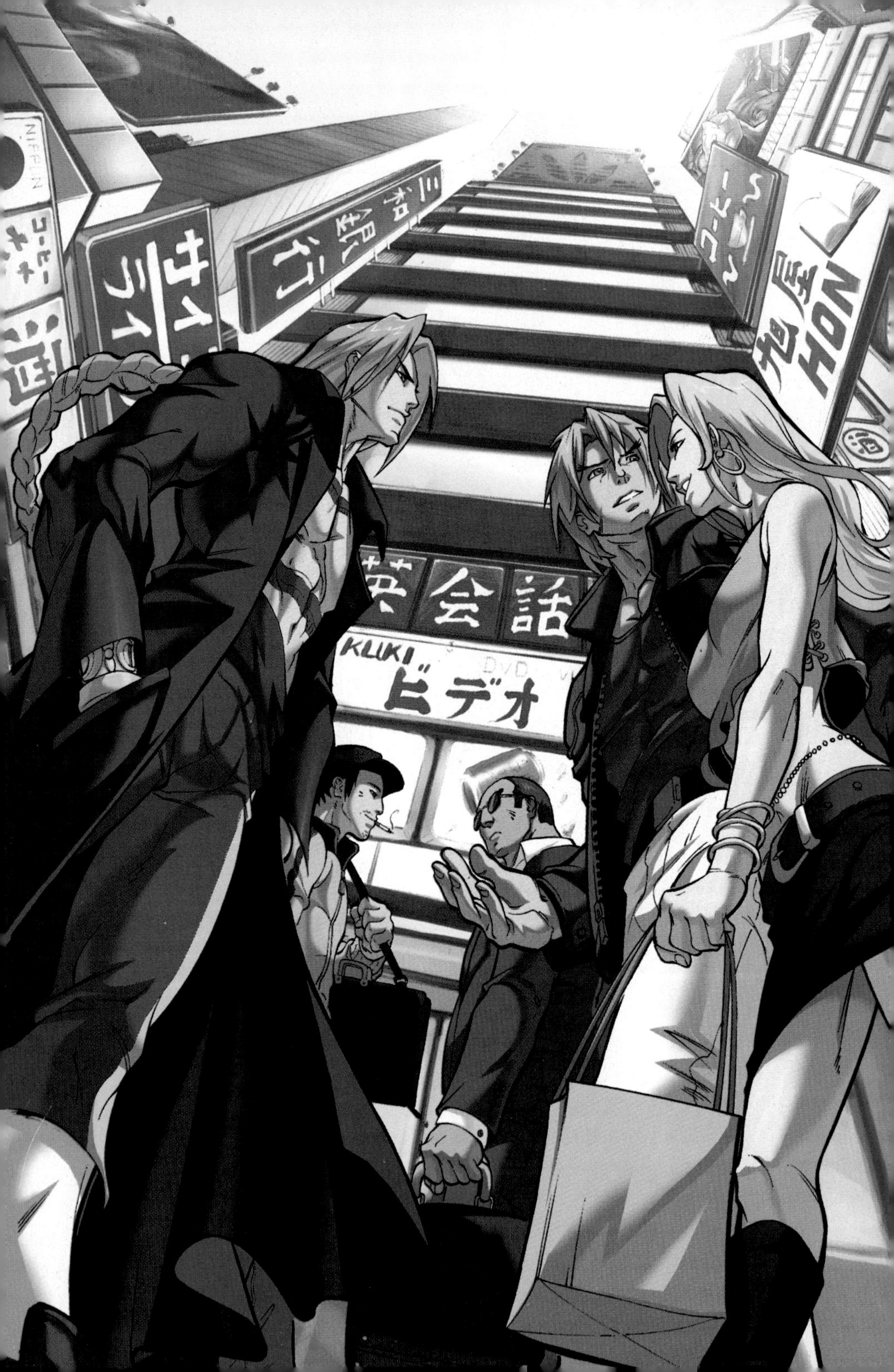
英会話
KUKI
DVD
ビデオ
HON

Cover Art by: Alvin Lee and Ramil Sunga

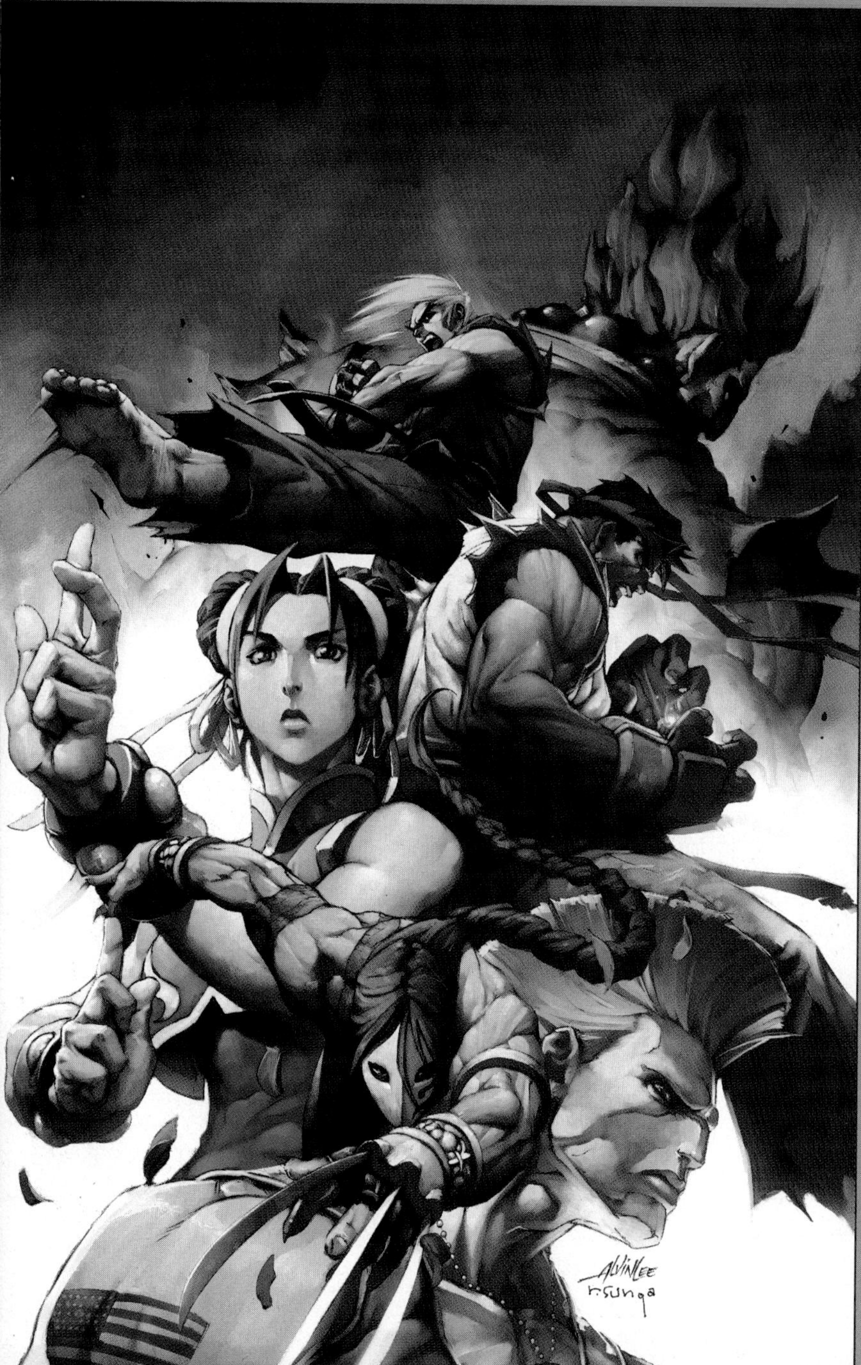
ALVINLEE
r.sunga

Chapter 03: VEGA ATTACKS

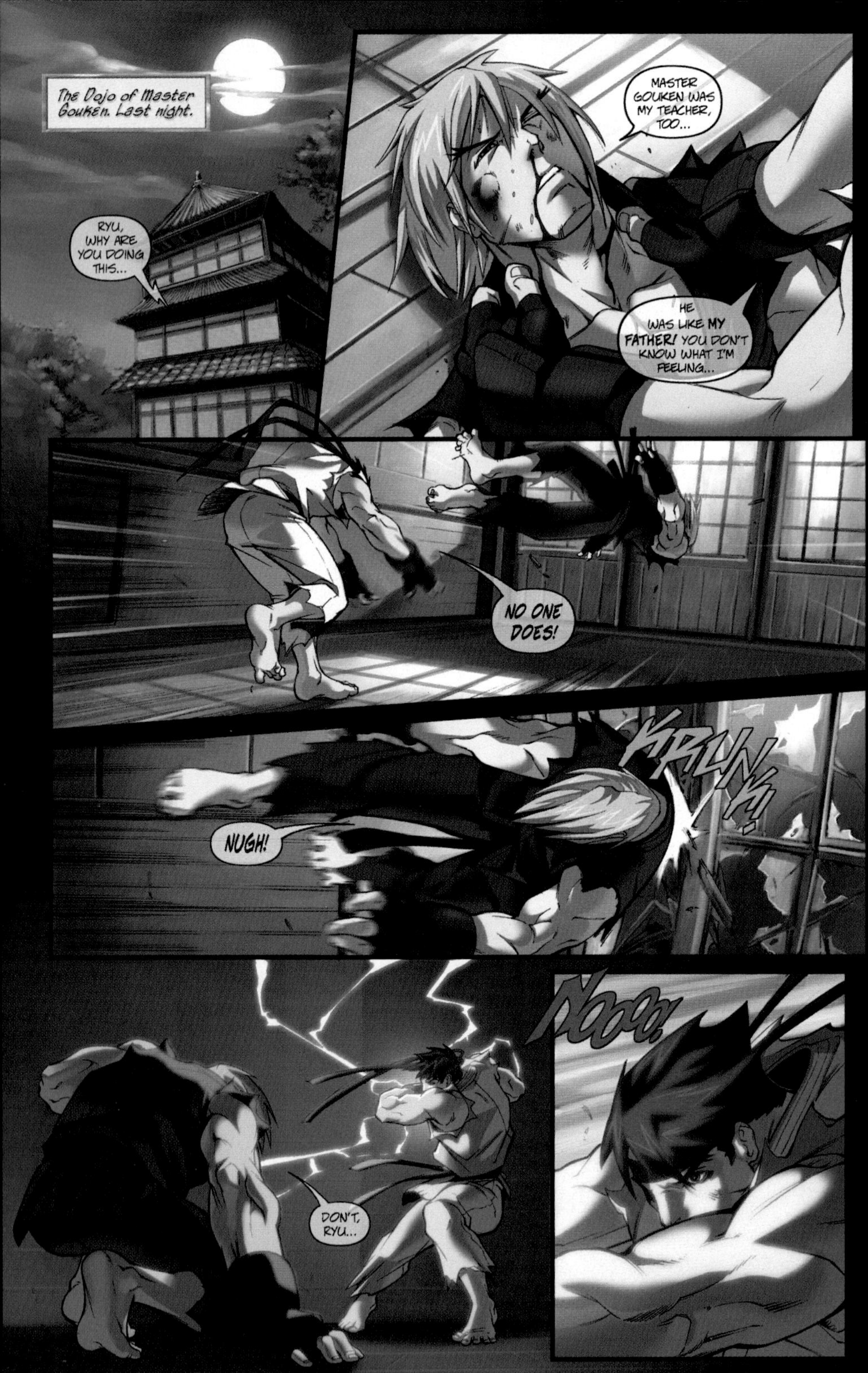
The Dojo of Master Gouken. Last night.
RYU, WHY ARE YOU DOING THIS...
MASTER GOUKEN WAS MY TEACHER, TOO...
HE WAS LIKE MY FATHER! YOU DON'T KNOW WHAT I'M FEELING...
NO ONE DOES!
KRUNK!
NUGH!
DON'T, RYU...
NOOOO!

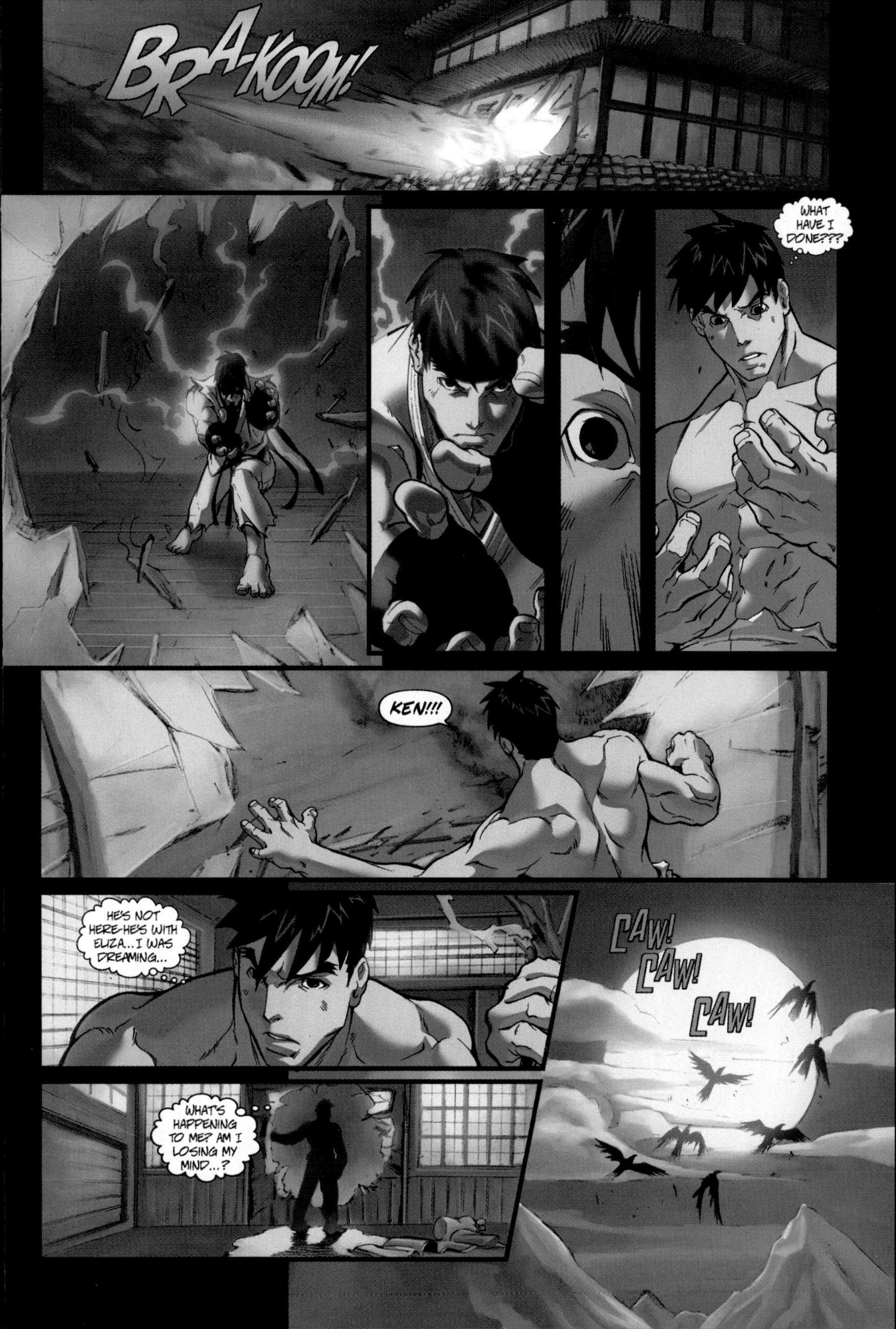
BRA-KOOM!
WHAT HAVE I DONE???
KEN!!!
HE'S NOT HERE-HE'S WITH ELIZA...I WAS DREAMING...
WHAT'S HAPPENING TO ME? AM I LOSING MY MIND...?
CAW! CAW! CAW!

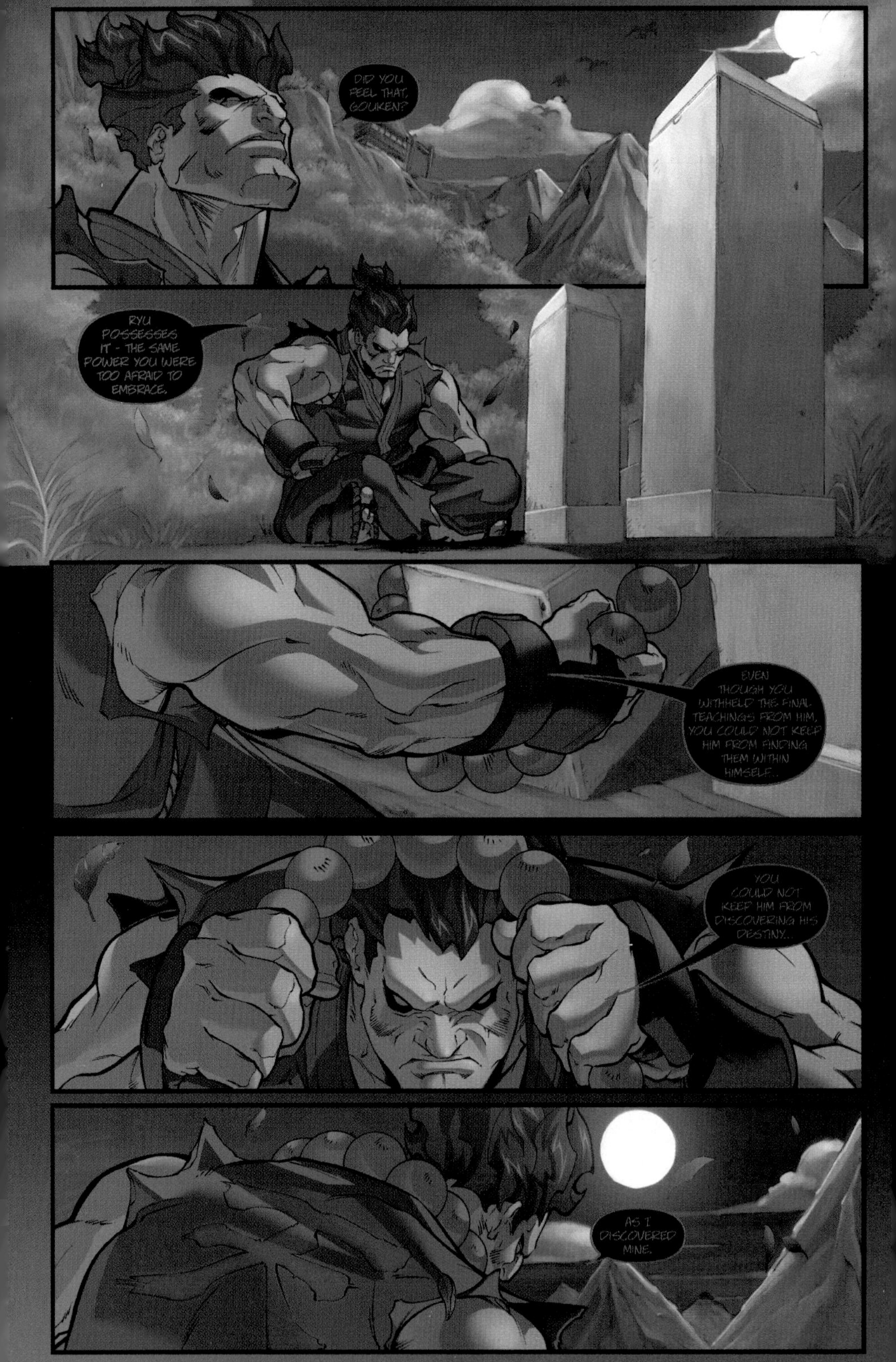
DID YOU FEEL THAT, GOUKEN?
RYU POSSESSES IT - THE SAME POWER YOU WERE TOO AFRAID TO EMBRACE.
EVEN THOUGH YOU WITHHELD THE FINAL TEACHINGS FROM HIM, YOU COULD NOT KEEP HIM FROM FINDING THEM WITHIN HIMSELF...
YOU COULD NOT KEEP HIM FROM DISCOVERING HIS DESTINY...
AS I DISCOVERED MINE.

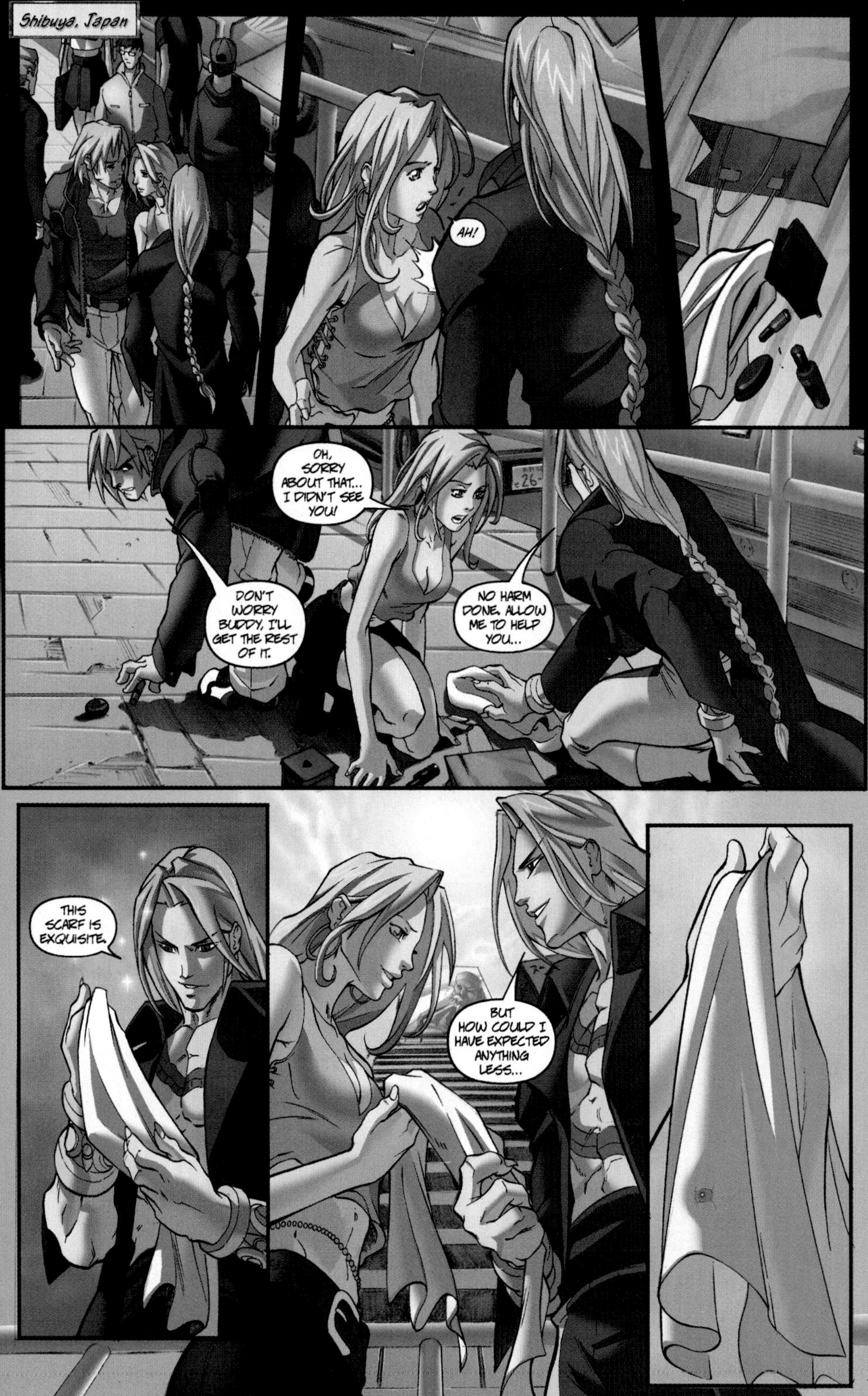
Shibuya, Japan
AH!
OH, SORRY ABOUT THAT... I DIDN'T SEE YOU!
DON'T WORRY BUDDY, I'LL GET THE REST OF IT.
NO HARM DONE. ALLOW ME TO HELP YOU...
THIS SCARF IS EXQUISITE.
BUT HOW COULD I HAVE EXPECTED ANYTHING LESS...

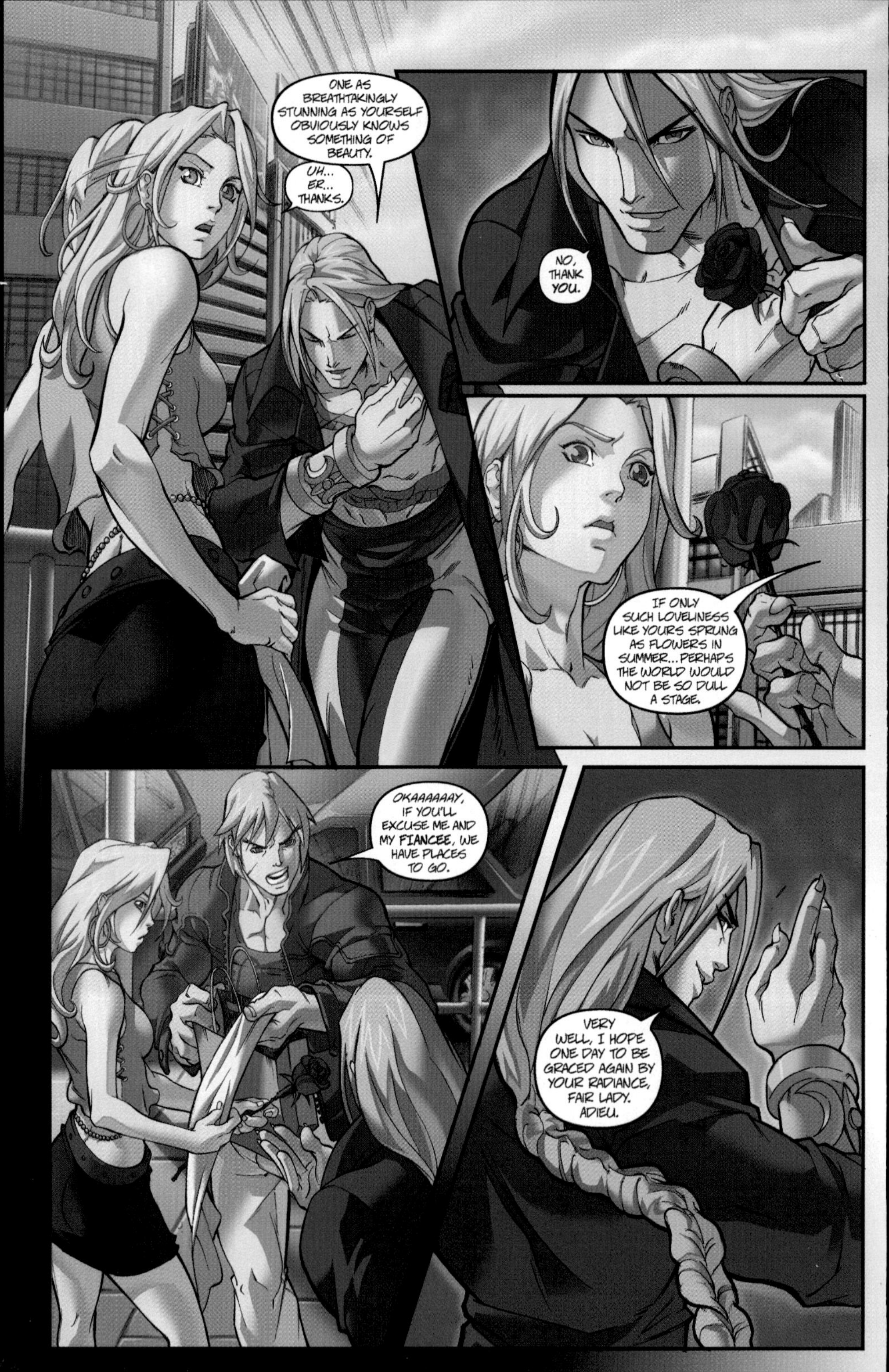
ONE AS BREATHTAKINGLY STUNNING AS YOURSELF OBUIOUSLY KNOWS SOMETHING OF BEAUTY.
UH... ER... THANKS.
NO, THANK YOU.
IF ONLY SUCH LOVELINESS LIKE YOURS SPRUNG AS FLOWERS IN SUMMER...PERHAPS THE WORLD WOULD NOT BE SO DULL A STAGE.
OKAAAAAAY, IF YOU'LL EXCUSE ME AND MY FIANCEE, WE HAVE PLACES TO GO.
VERY WELL, I HOPE ONE DAY TO BE GRACED AGAIN BY YOUR RADIANCE, FAIR LADY. ADIEU.

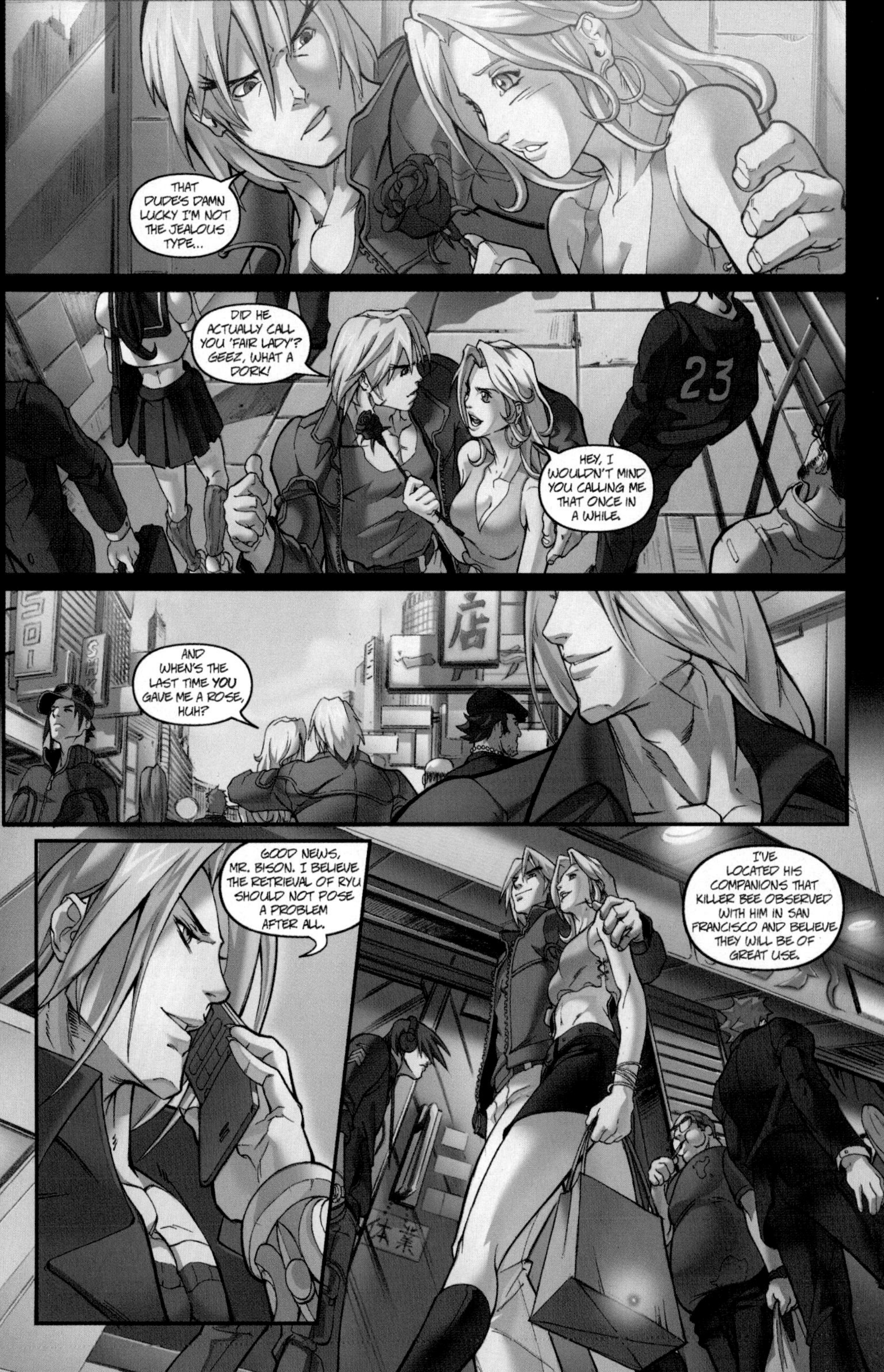
THAT DUDE'S DAMN LUCKY I'M NOT THE JEALOUS TYPE...
DID HE ACTUALLY CALL YOU 'FAIR LADY'? GEEZ, WHAT A DORK!
HEY, I WOULDN'T MIND YOU CALLING ME THAT ONCE IN A WHILE.
AND WHEN'S THE LAST TIME YOU GAVE ME A ROSE, HUH?
GOOD NEWS, MR. BISON. I BELIEVE THE RETRIEVAL OF RYU SHOULD NOT POSE A PROBLEM AFTER ALL.
I'VE LOCATED HIS COMPANIONS THAT KILLER BEE OBSERVED WITH HIM IN SAN FRANCISCO AND BELIEVE THEY WILL BE OF GREAT USE.

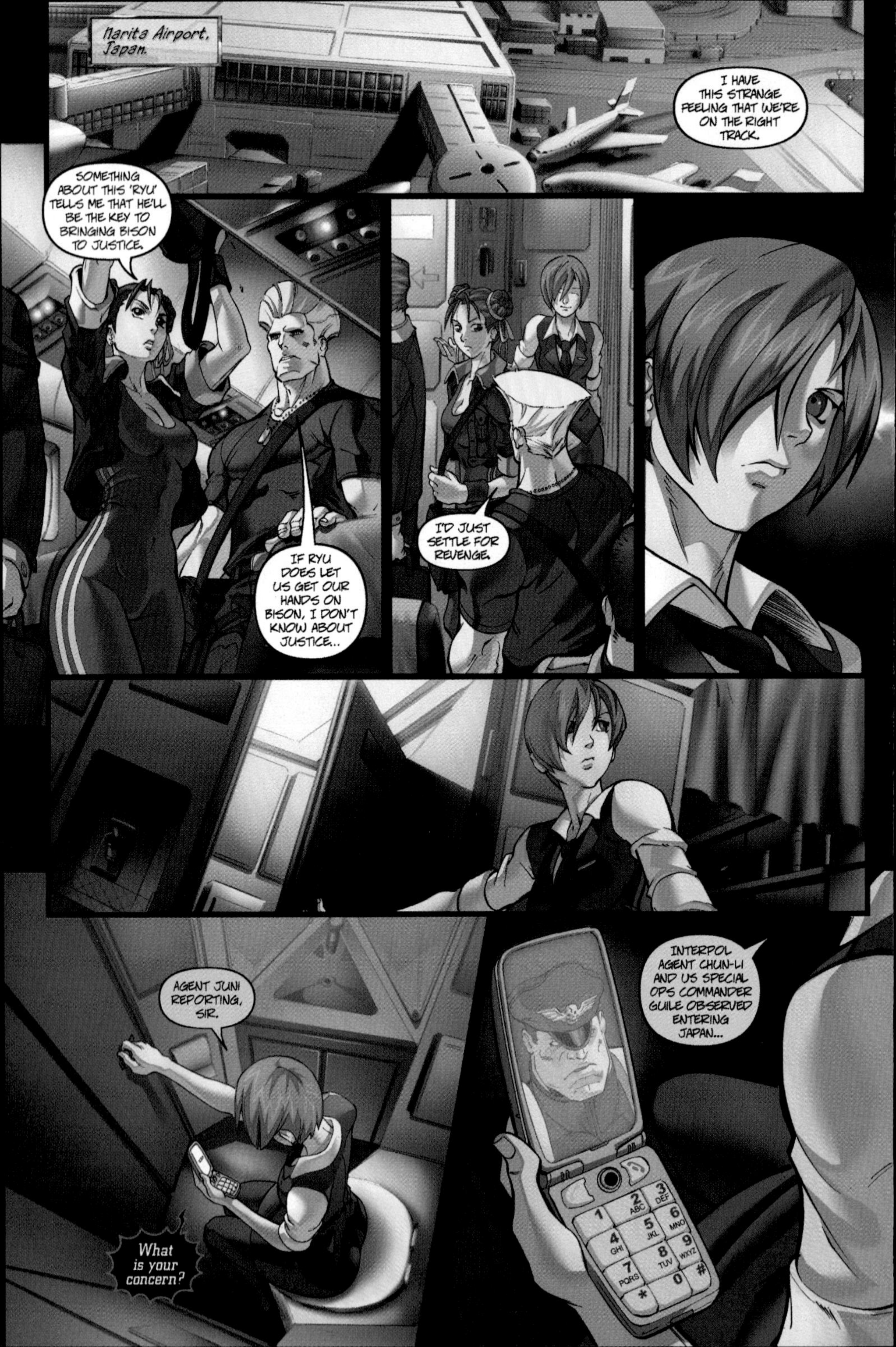
Narita Airport, Japan.
I HAVE THIS STRANGE FEELING THAT WE'RE ON THE RIGHT TRACK.
SOMETHING ABOUT THIS 'RYU' TELLS ME THAT HE'LL BE THE KEY TO BRINGING BISON TO JUSTICE.
IF RYU DOES LET US GET OUR HANDS ON BISON, I DON'T KNOW ABOUT JUSTICE...
I'D JUST SETTLE FOR REVENGE.
AGENT JUNI REPORTING, SIR.
What is your concern?
INTERPOL AGENT CHUN-LI AND US SPECIAL OPS COMMANDER GUILE OBSERVED ENTERING JAPAN...

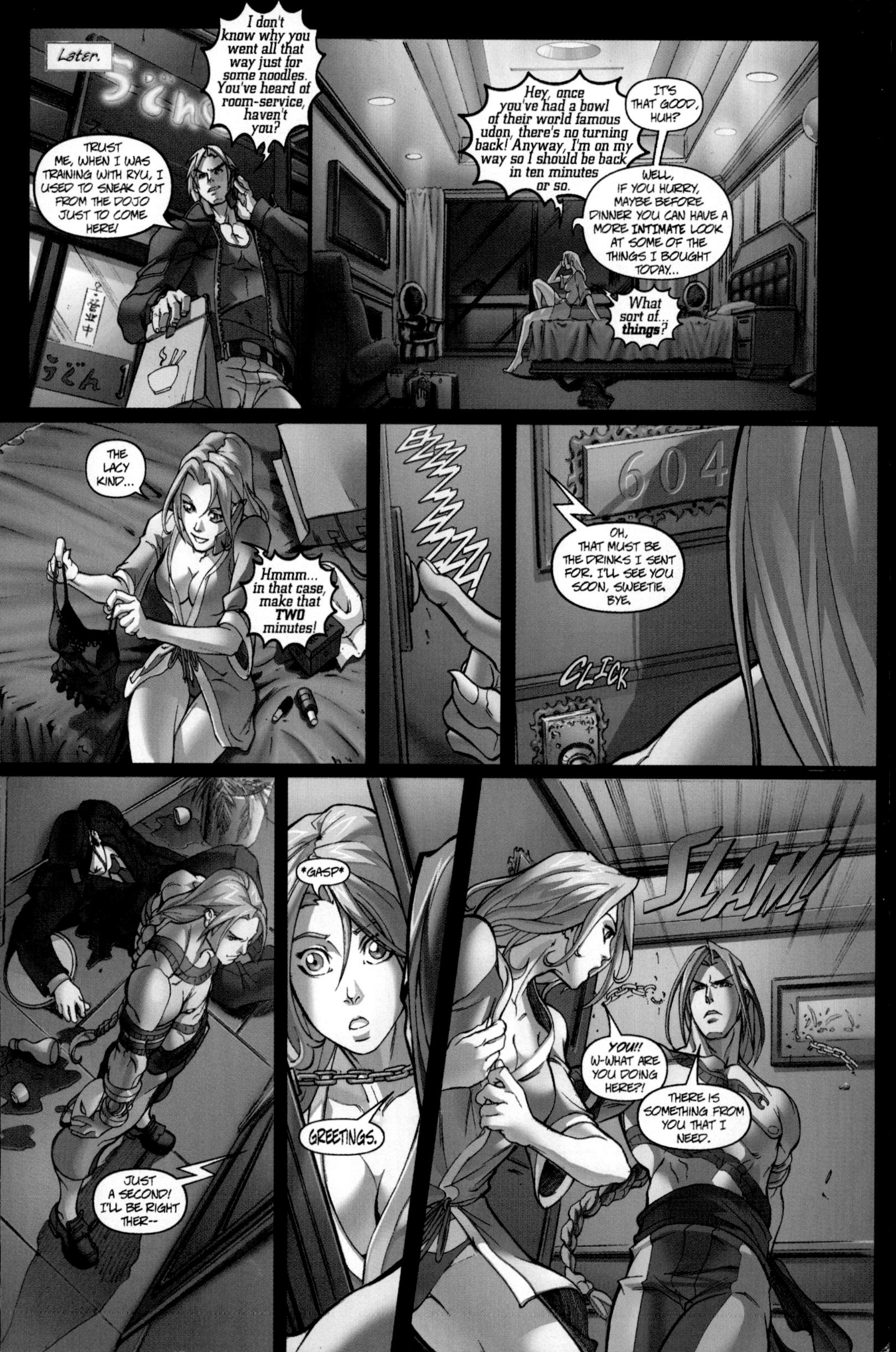
Later.
I don't know why you went all that way just for some noodles. You've heard of room-service, haven't you?
TRUST ME, WHEN I WAS TRAINING WITH RYU, I USED TO SNEAK OUT FROM THE DOJO JUST TO COME HERE!
Hey, once you've had a bowl of their world famous udon, there's no turning back! Anyway, I'm on my way so I should be back in ten minutes or so.
IT'S THAT GOOD, HUH?
WELL, IF YOU HURRY, MAYBE BEFORE DINNER YOU CAN HAVE A MORE INTIMATE LOOK AT SOME OF THE THINGS I BOUGHT TODAY...
What sort of... things?
THE LACY KIND...
Hmmm... in that case, make that TWO minutes!
604
OH, THAT MUST BE THE DRINKS I SENT FOR. I'LL SEE YOU SOON, SWEETIE. BYE.
CLICK
JUST A SECOND! I'LL BE RIGHT THER--
GASP
GREETINGS.
SLAM!
YOU!! W-WHAT ARE YOU DOING HERE?!
THERE IS SOMETHING FROM YOU THAT I NEED.

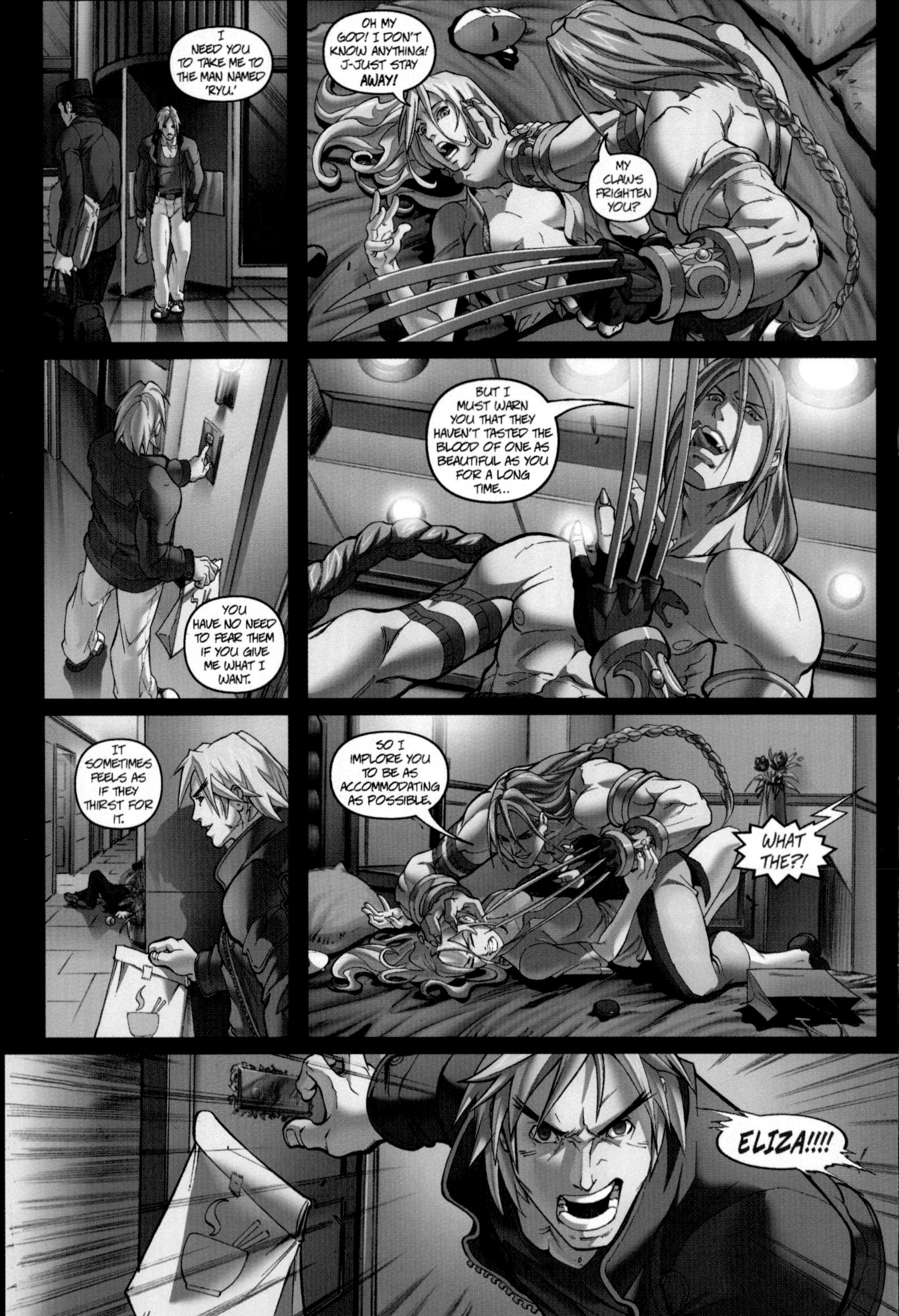
I NEED YOU TO TAKE ME TO THE MAN NAMED 'RYU.'
OH MY GOD! I DON'T KNOW ANYTHING! J-JUST STAY AWAY!
MY CLAWS FRIGHTEN YOU?
BUT I MUST WARN YOU THAT THEY HAVEN'T TASTED THE BLOOD OF ONE AS BEAUTIFUL AS YOU FOR A LONG TIME...
YOU HAVE NO NEED TO FEAR THEM IF YOU GIVE ME WHAT I WANT.
IT SOMETIMES FEELS AS IF THEY THIRST FOR IT.
SO I IMPLORE YOU TO BE AS ACCOMMODATING AS POSSIBLE.
WHAT THE?!
ELIZA!!!!

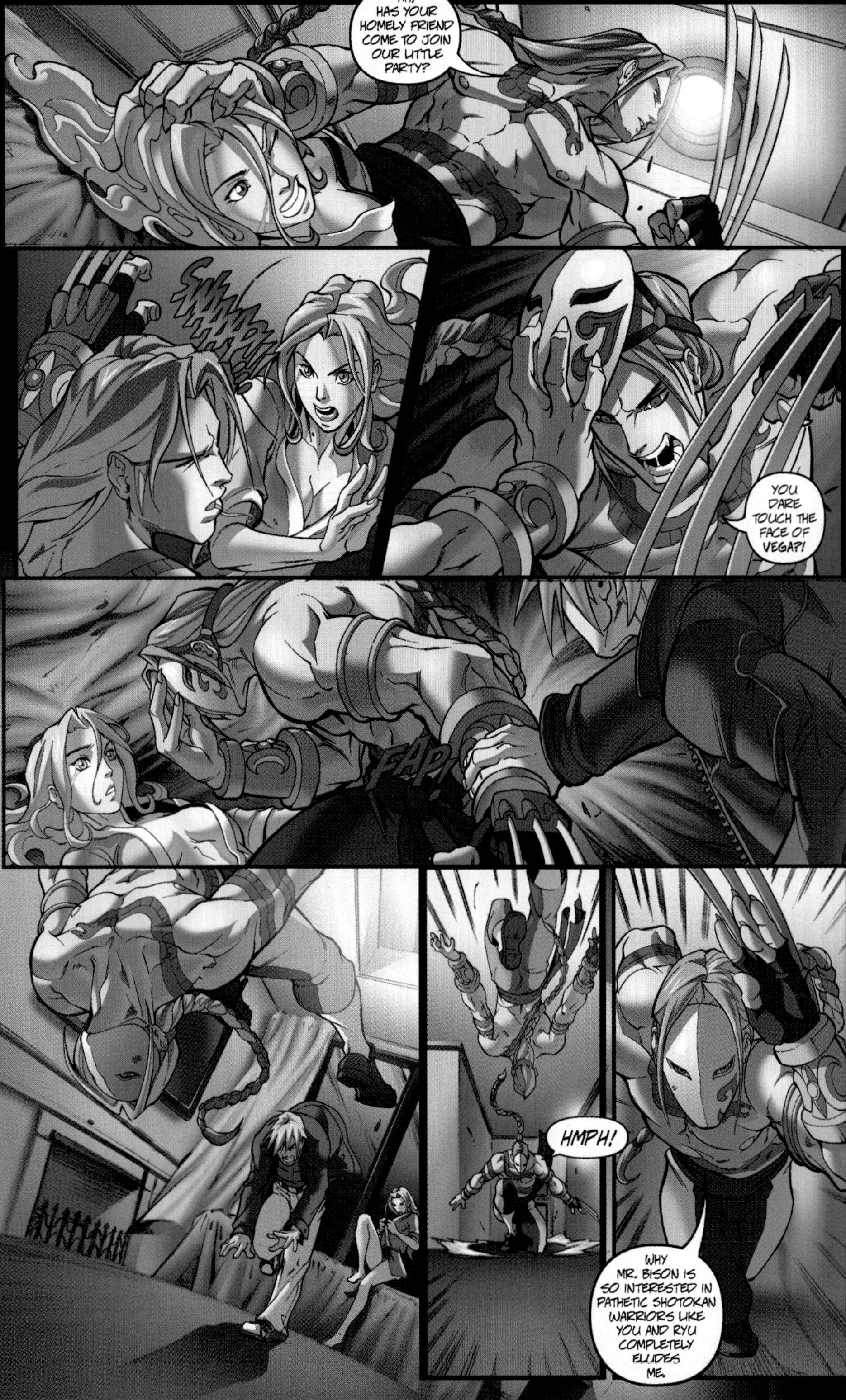
AH, HAS YOUR HOMELY FRIEND COME TO JOIN OUR LITTLE PARTY?
YOU DARE TOUCH THE FACE OF VEGA?!
FAP!
HMPH!
WHY MR. BISON IS SO INTERESTED IN PATHETIC SHOTOKAN WARRIORS LIKE YOU AND RYU COMPLETELY ELUDES ME.

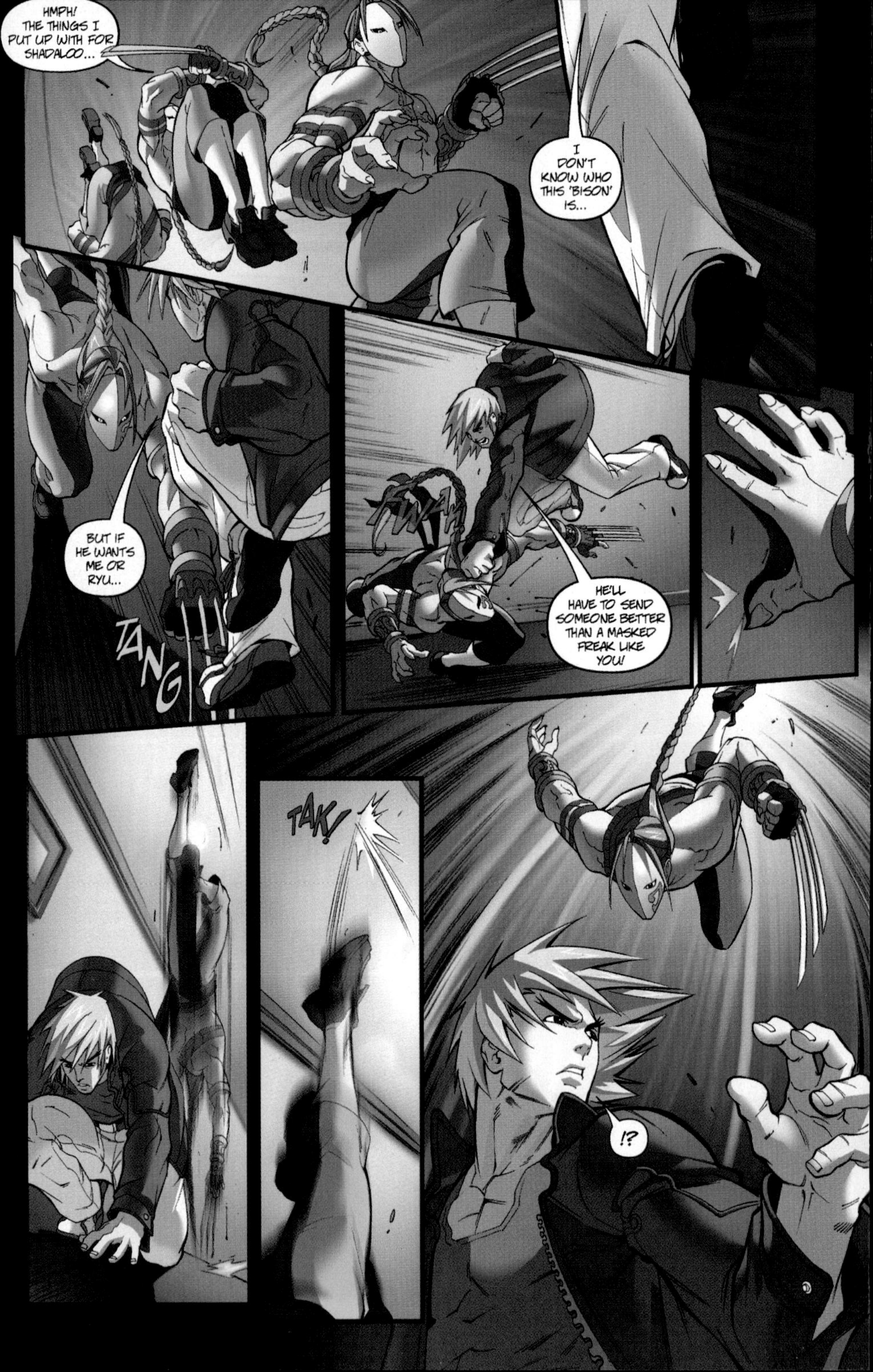
HMPH! THE THINGS I PUT UP WITH FOR SHADALOO...
I DON'T KNOW WHO THIS 'BISON' IS...
BUT IF HE WANTS ME OR RYU...
TANG
HE'LL HAVE TO SEND SOMEONE BETTER THAN A MASKED FREAK LIKE YOU!
TAK!
!?

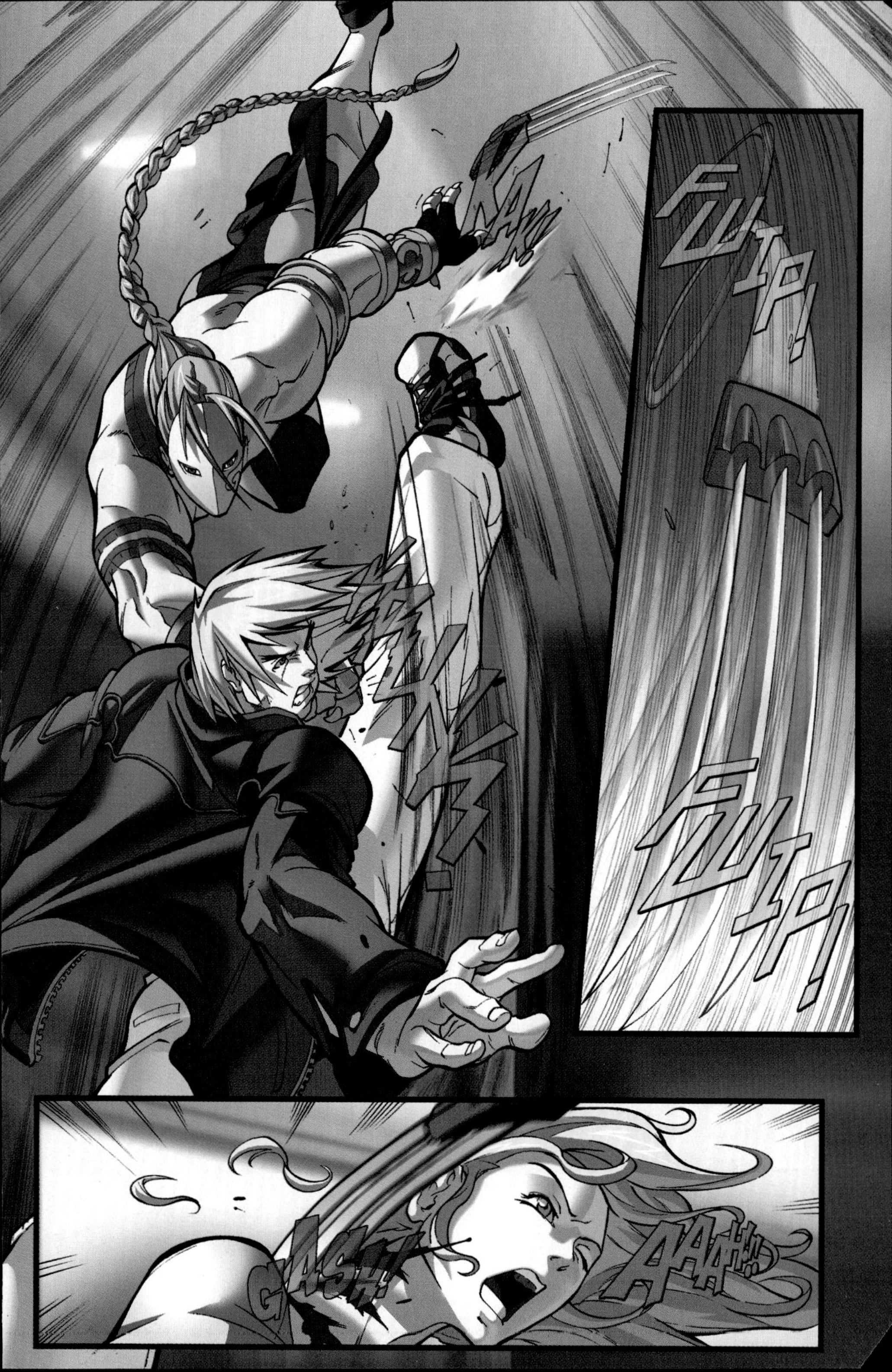

FWIP!
FWIP!
GASH!!
AAAH!!

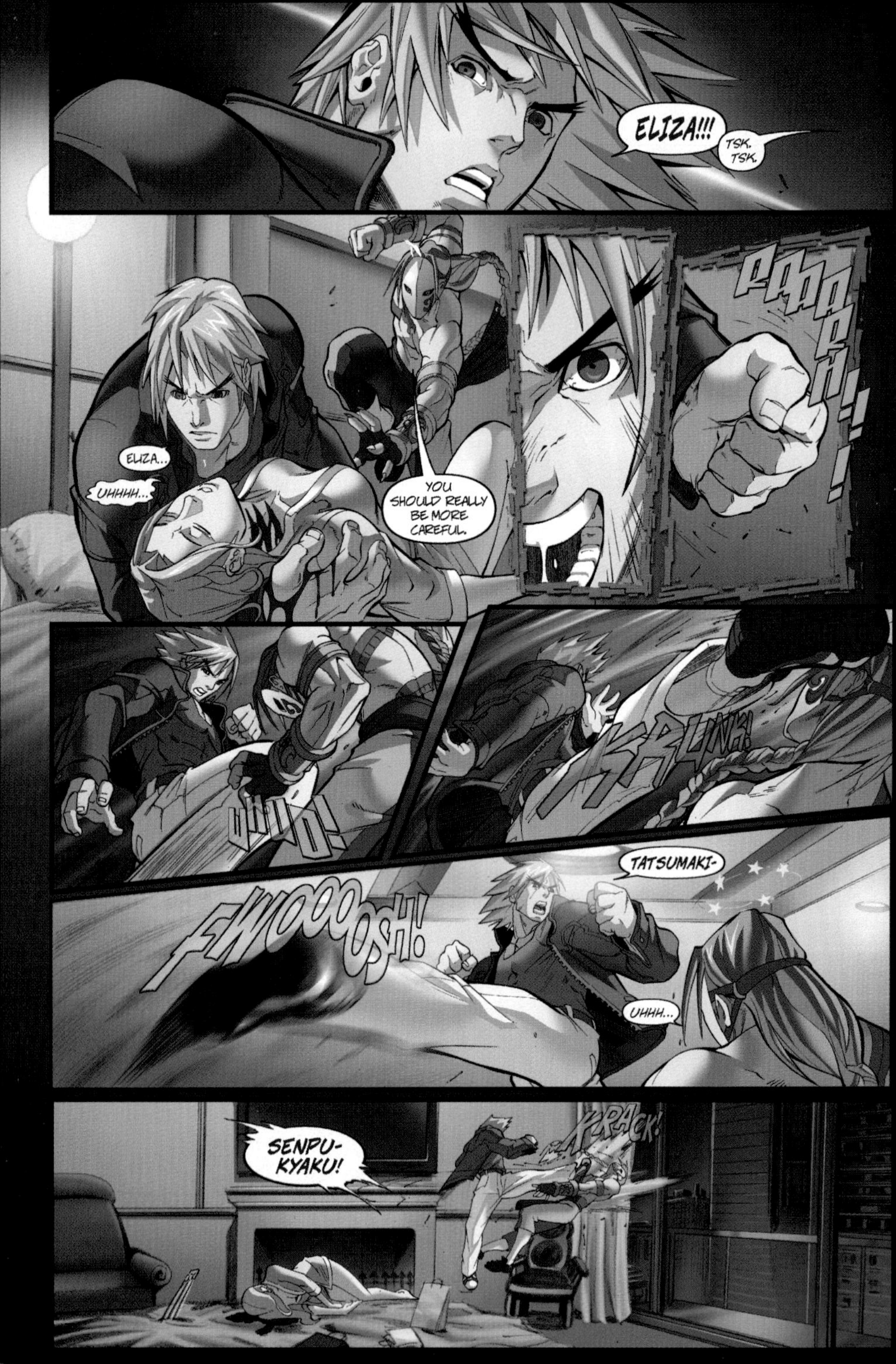
ELIZA!!!
TSK. TSK.
ELIZA...
UHHHH...
YOU SHOULD REALLY BE MORE CAREFUL.
RAAARH!!!
UMPD!
SBUNK!
FWOOOOSH!
TATSUMAKI-
UHHH...
SENPU-KYAKU!
KRACK!

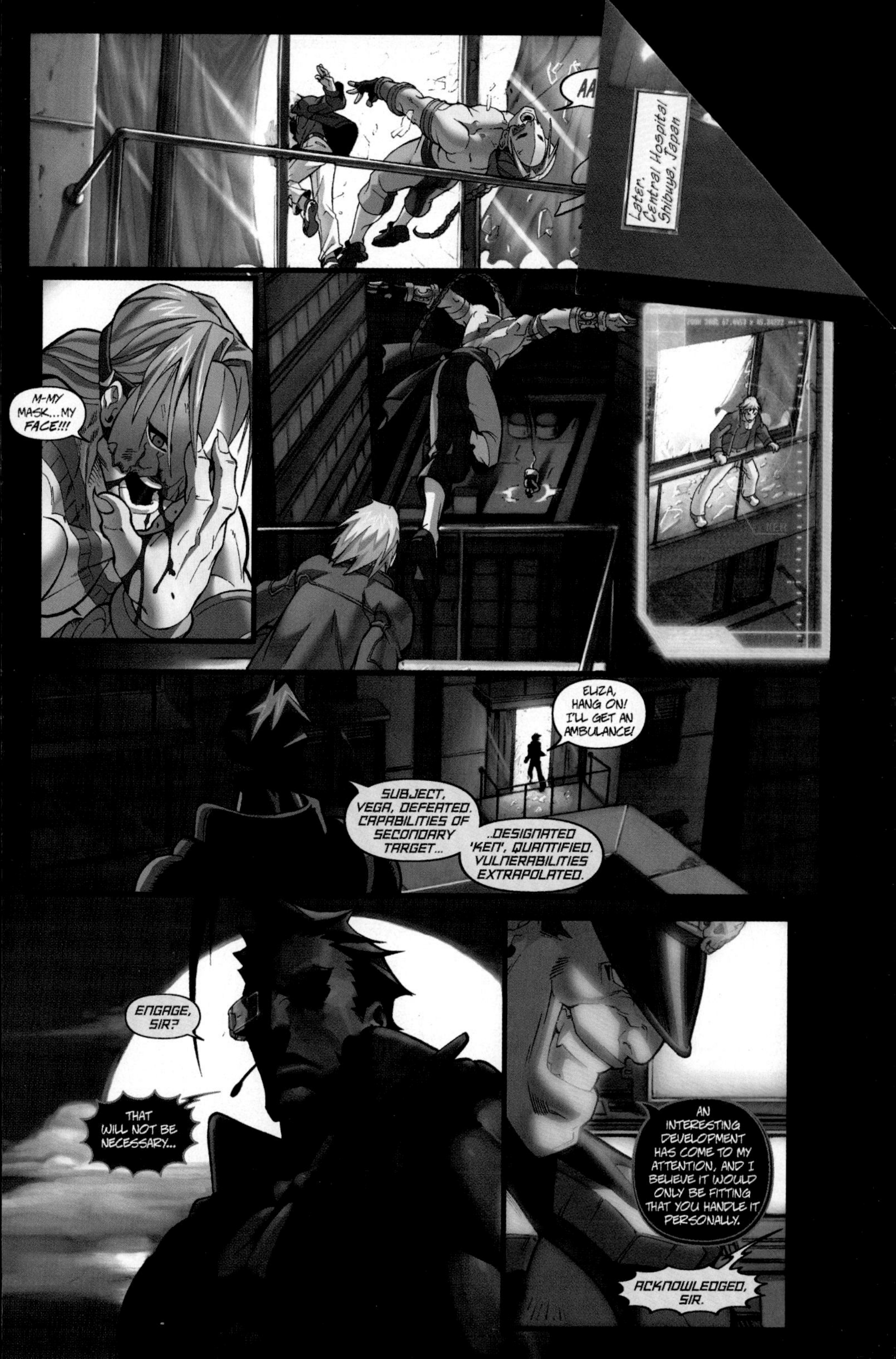
Later, Central Hospital Shibuya, Japan
M-MY MASK...MY FACE!!!
ELIZA, HANG ON! I'LL GET AN AMBULANCE!
SUBJECT, VEGA, DEFEATED. CAPABILITIES OF SECONDARY TARGET...
..DESIGNATED 'KEN', QUANTIFIED. VULNERABILITIES EXTRAPOLATED.
ENGAGE, SIR?
THAT WILL NOT BE NECESSARY...
AN INTERESTING DEVELOPMENT HAS COME TO MY ATTENTION, AND I BELIEVE IT WOULD ONLY BE FITTING THAT YOU HANDLE IT PERSONALLY.
ACKNOWLEDGED, SIR.

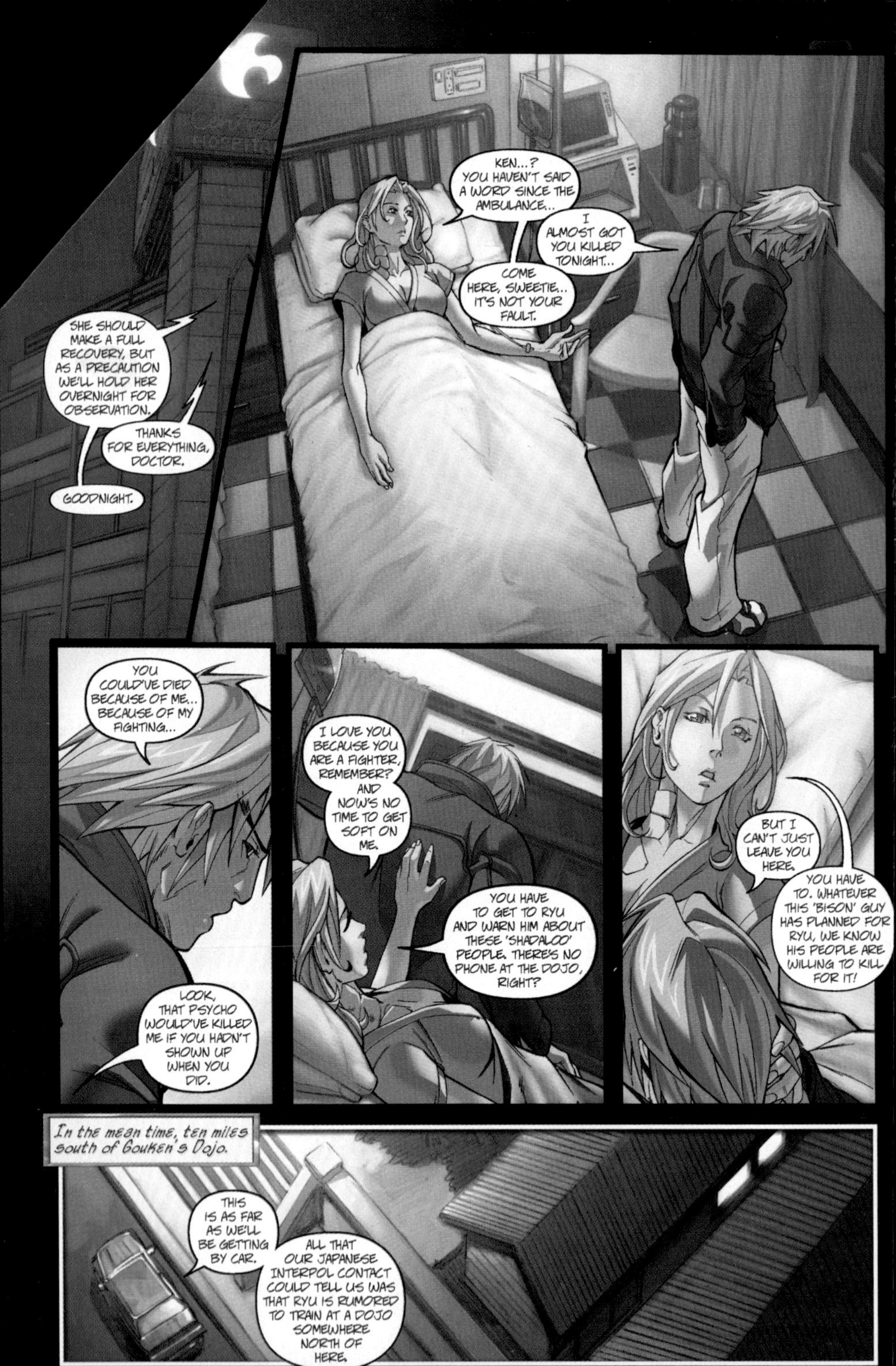
KEN...? YOU HAVEN'T SAID A WORD SINCE THE AMBULANCE...
I ALMOST GOT YOU KILLED TONIGHT...
COME HERE, SWEETIE... IT'S NOT YOUR FAULT.
SHE SHOULD MAKE A FULL RECOVERY, BUT AS A PRECAUTION WE'LL HOLD HER OVERNIGHT FOR OBSERVATION.
THANKS FOR EVERYTHING, DOCTOR.
GOODNIGHT.
YOU COULD'VE DIED BECAUSE OF ME... BECAUSE OF MY FIGHTING...
LOOK, THAT PSYCHO WOULD'VE KILLED ME IF YOU HADN'T SHOWN UP WHEN YOU DID.
I LOVE YOU BECAUSE YOU ARE A FIGHTER, REMEMBER? AND NOW'S NO TIME TO GET SOFT ON ME.
YOU HAVE TO GET TO RYU AND WARN HIM ABOUT THESE 'SHADALOO' PEOPLE. THERE'S NO PHONE AT THE DOJO, RIGHT?
BUT I CAN'T JUST LEAVE YOU HERE.
YOU HAVE TO. WHATEVER THIS 'BISON' GUY HAS PLANNED FOR RYU, WE KNOW HIS PEOPLE ARE WILLING TO KILL FOR IT!
In the mean time, ten miles south of Gouken's Dojo.
THIS IS AS FAR AS WE'LL BE GETTING BY CAR.
ALL THAT OUR JAPANESE INTERPOL CONTACT COULD TELL US WAS THAT RYU IS RUMORED TO TRAIN AT A DOJO SOMEWHERE NORTH OF HERE.

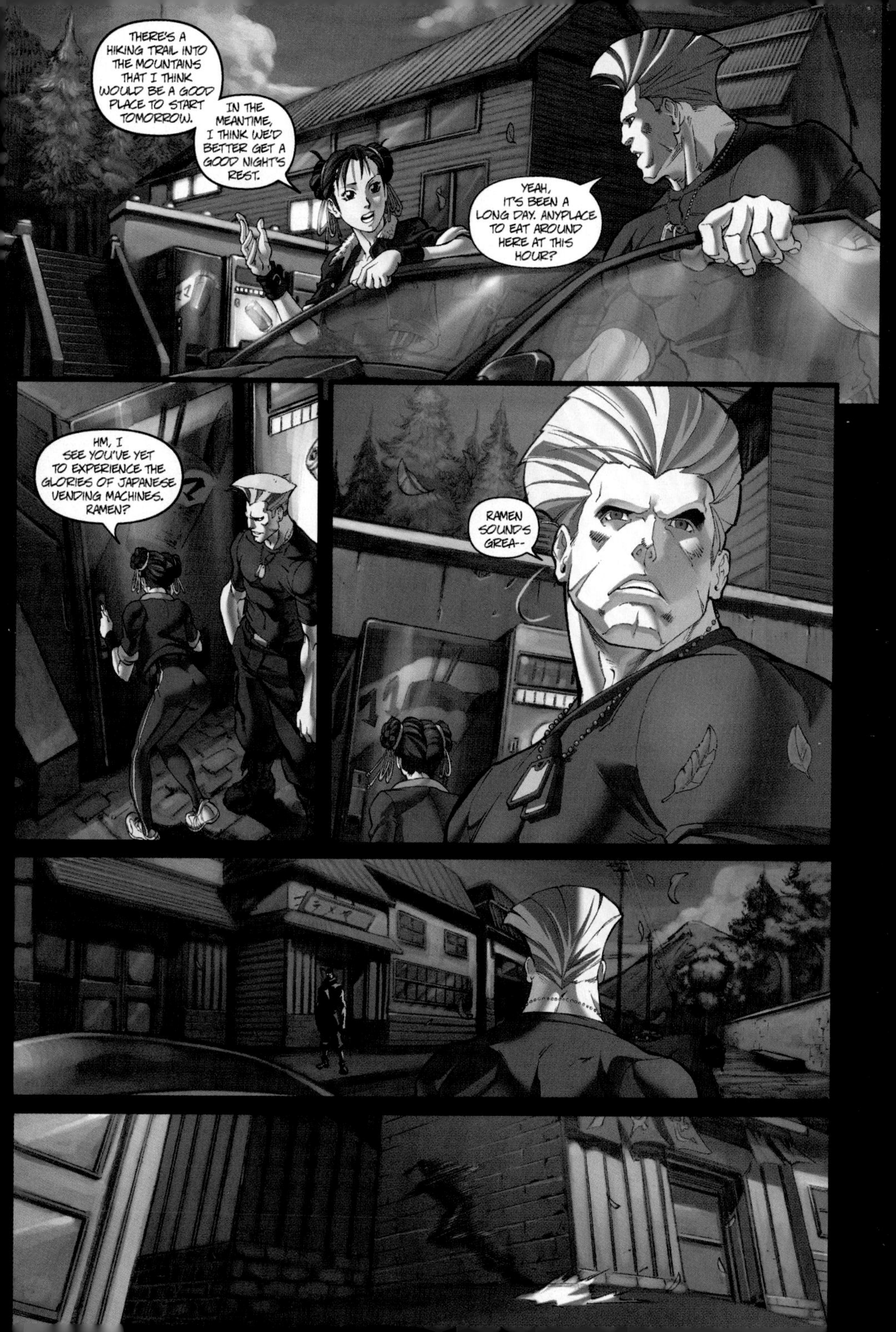
THERE'S A HIKING TRAIL INTO THE MOUNTAINS THAT I THINK WOULD BE A GOOD PLACE TO START TOMORROW.
IN THE MEANTIME, I THINK WE'D BETTER GET A GOOD NIGHT'S REST.
YEAH, IT'S BEEN A LONG DAY. ANYPLACE TO EAT AROUND HERE AT THIS HOUR?
HM, I SEE YOU'VE YET TO EXPERIENCE THE GLORIES OF JAPANESE VENDING MACHINES. RAMEN?
RAMEN SOUNDS GREA--

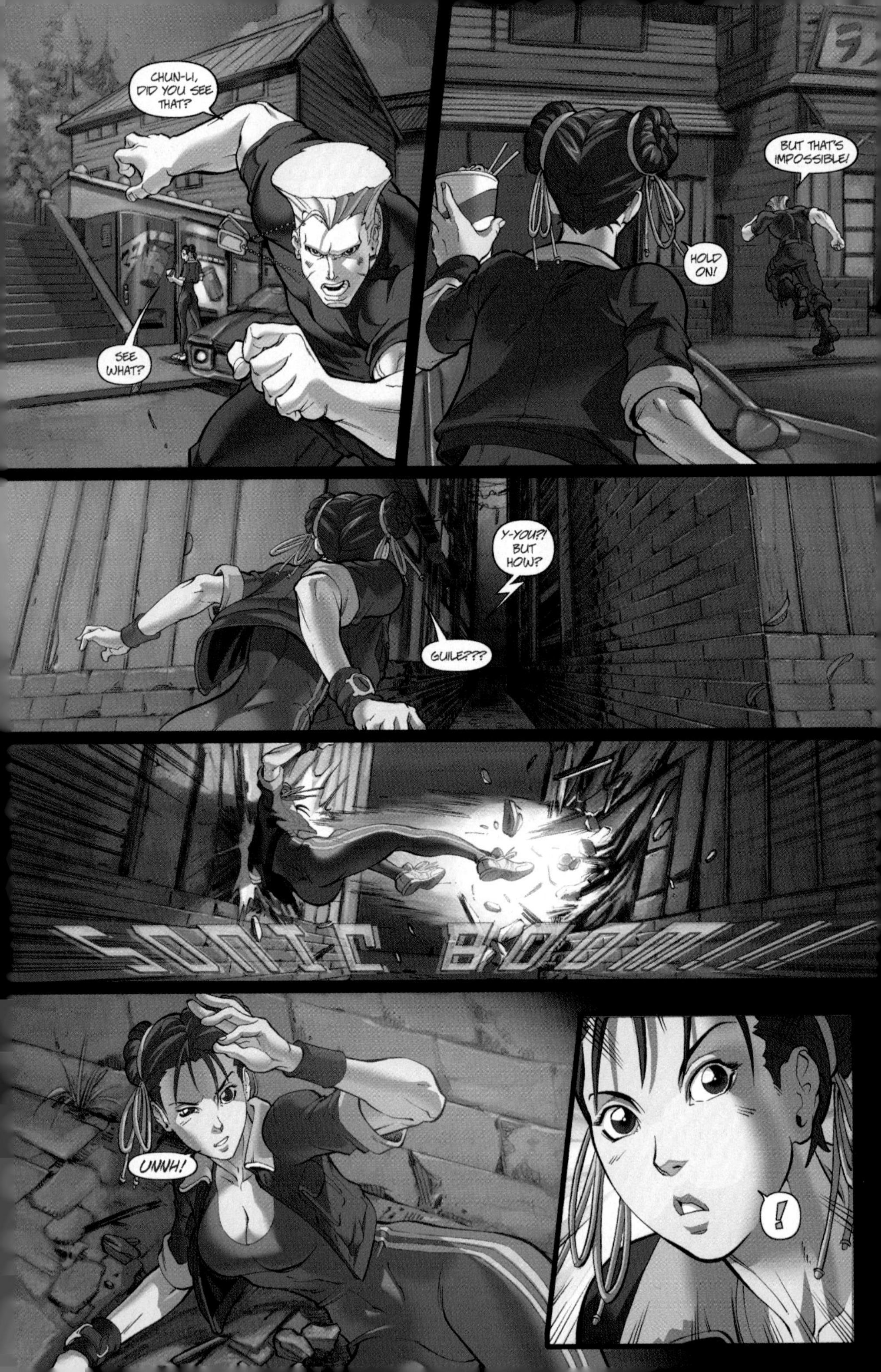
CHUN-LI, DID YOU SEE THAT?
SEE WHAT?
BUT THAT'S IMPOSSIBLE!
HOLD ON!
Y-YOU?! BUT HOW?
GUILE???
UNNH!
!

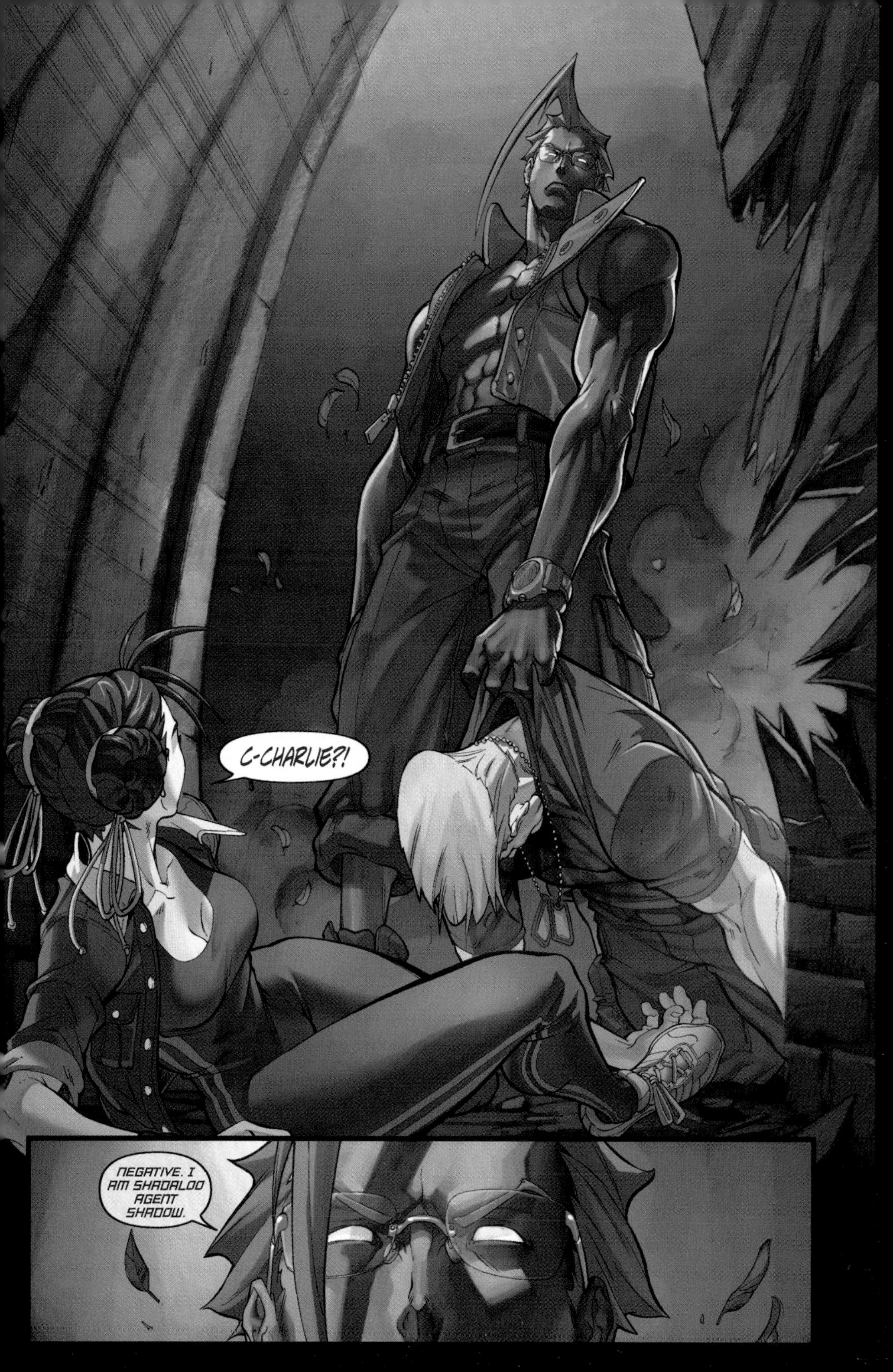
C-CHARLIE?!
NEGATIVE. I AM SHADALOO AGENT SHADOW.

Cover Art by: Alvin Lee and Arnold Tsang

Chapter 04: FROM THE SHADOWS

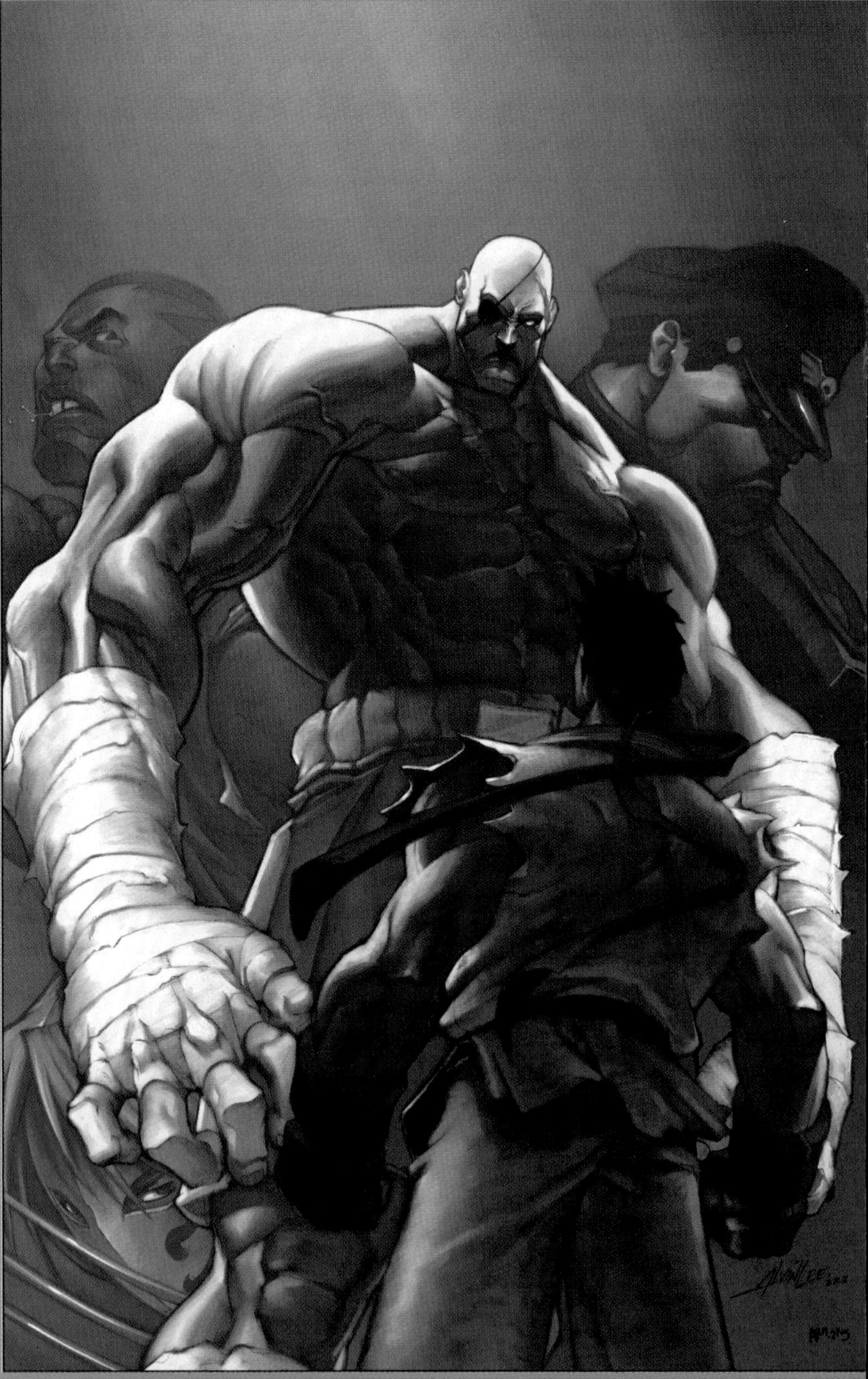

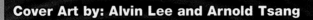

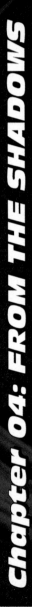

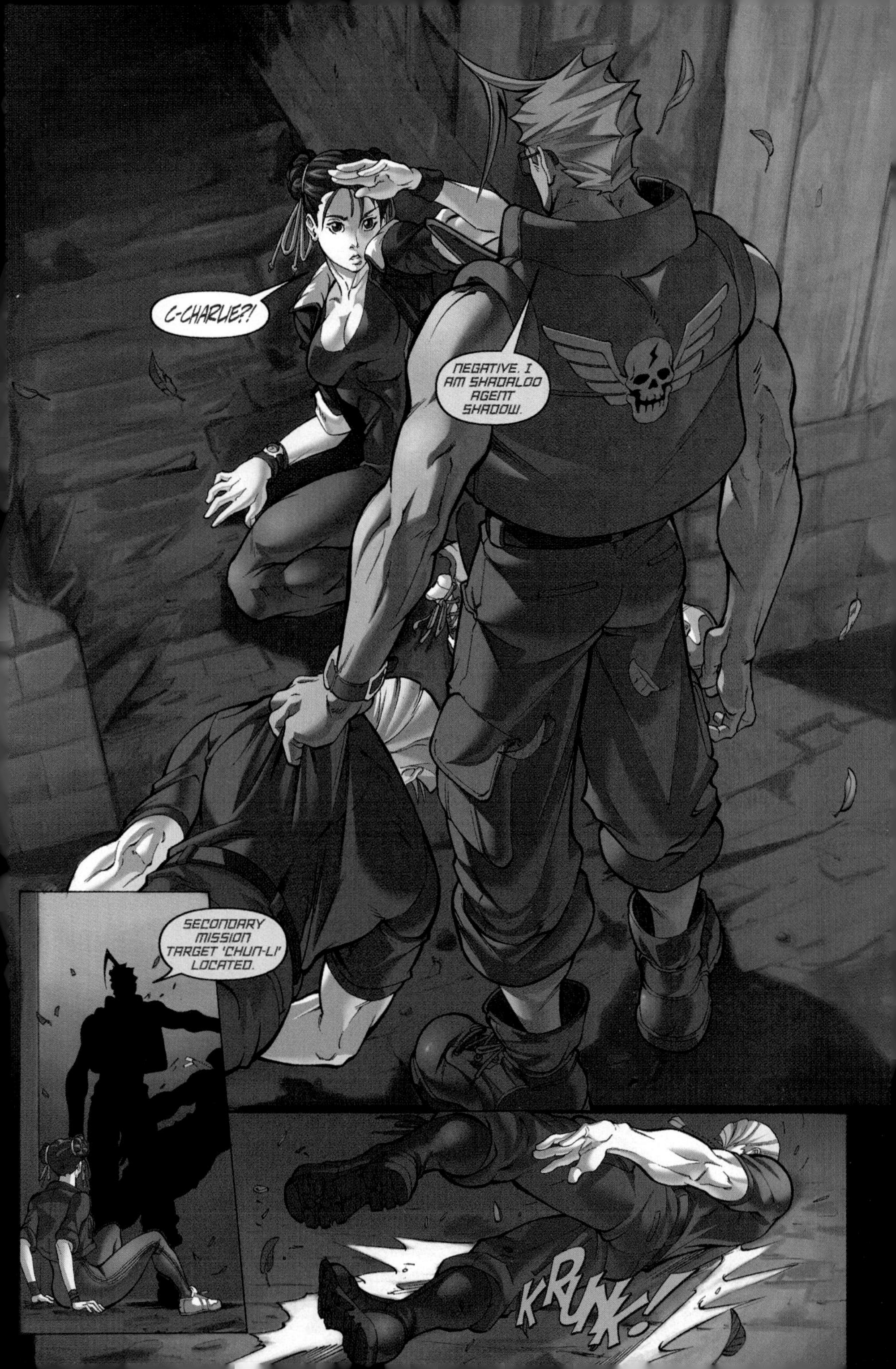
C-CHARLIE?!
NEGATIVE. I AM SHADALOO AGENT SHADOW.
SECONDARY MISSION TARGET 'CHUN-LI' LOCATED.
KRUNK!

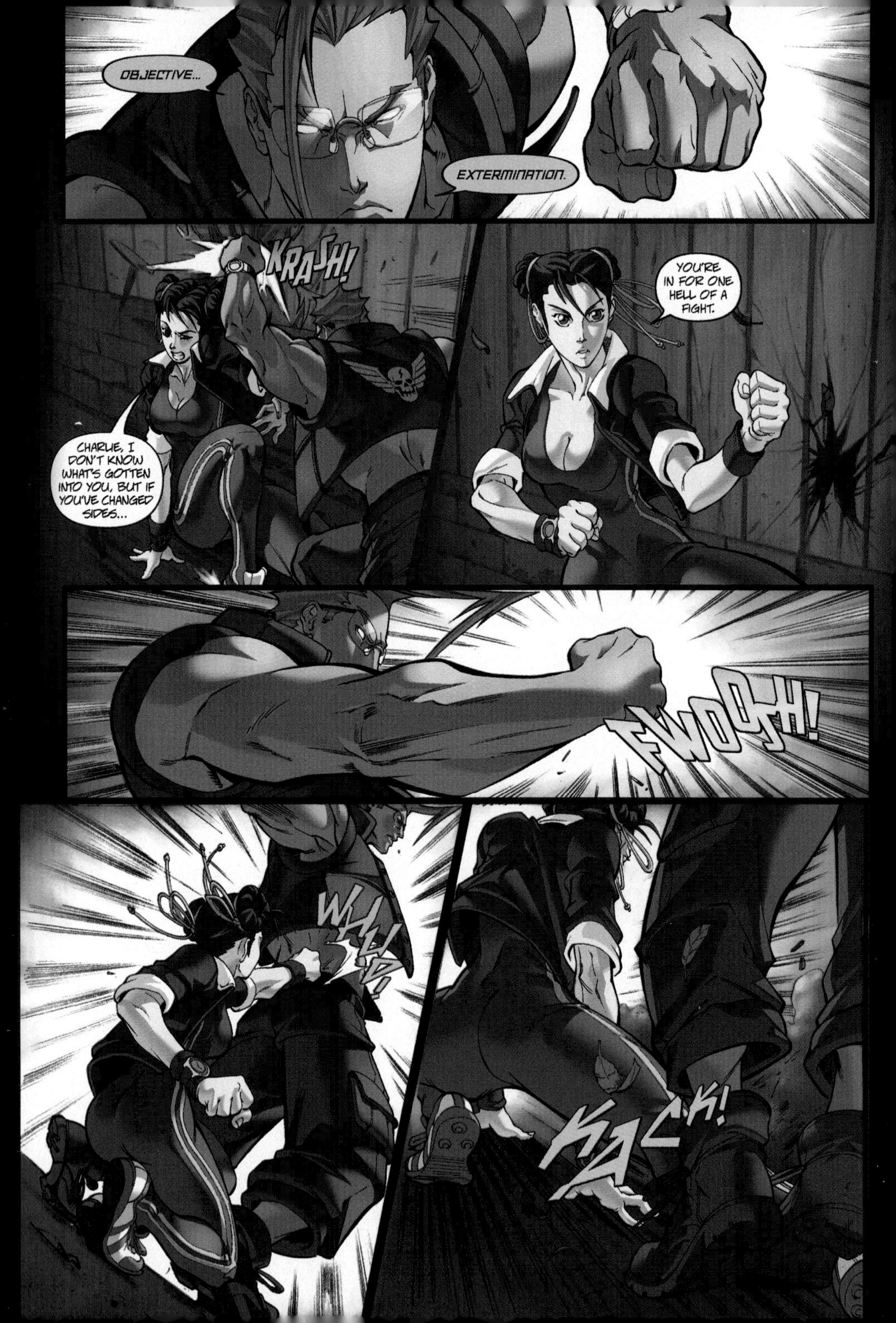
OBJECTIVE...
EXTERMINATION.
KRASH!
CHARLIE, I DON'T KNOW WHAT'S GOTTEN INTO YOU, BUT IF YOU'VE CHANGED SIDES...
YOU'RE IN FOR ONE HELL OF A FIGHT.
FWOOSH!
WHAM!
KRACK!

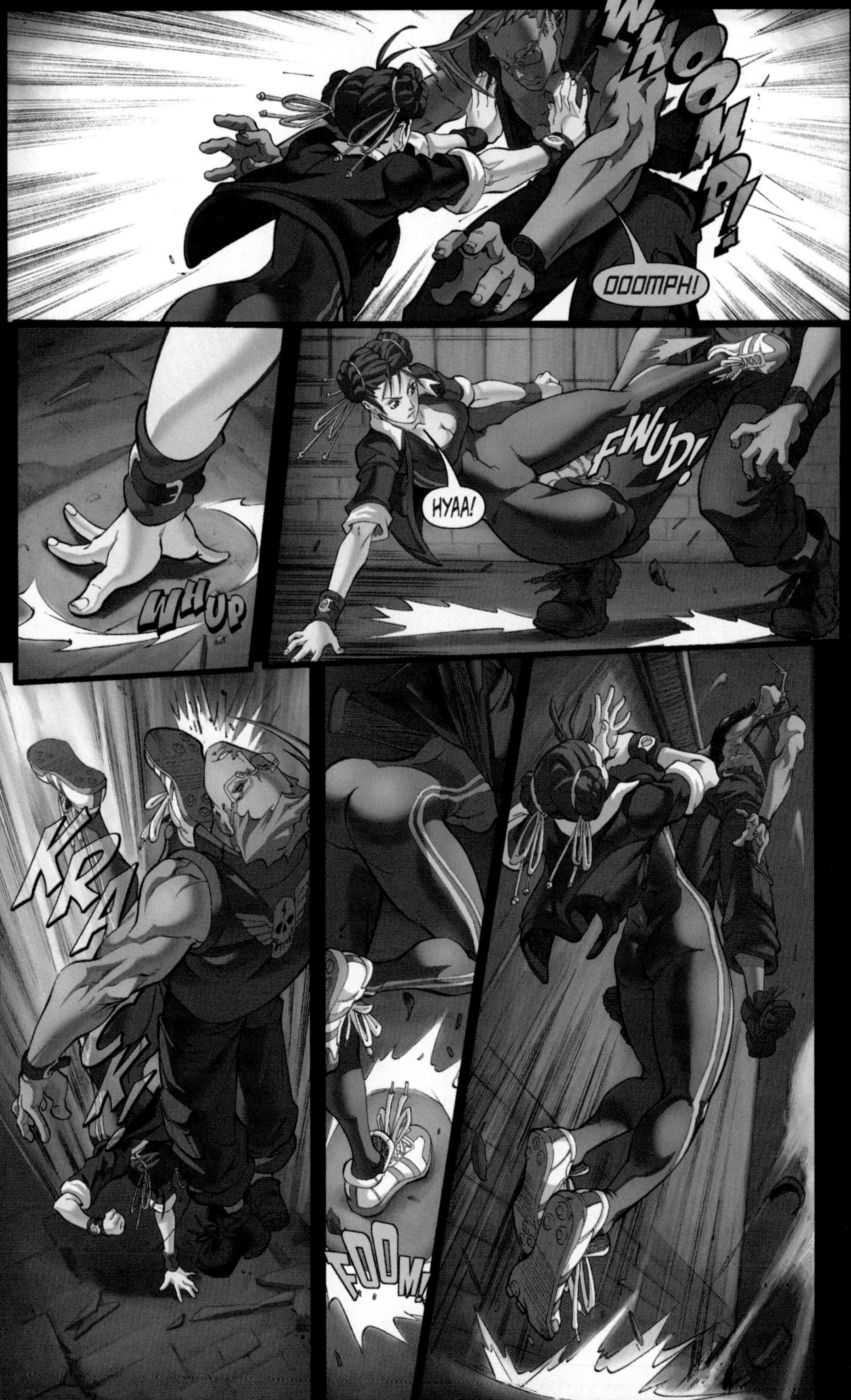
WHOOMP!
OOOMPH!
WHUP
HYAA!
FWUD!
FOOM!

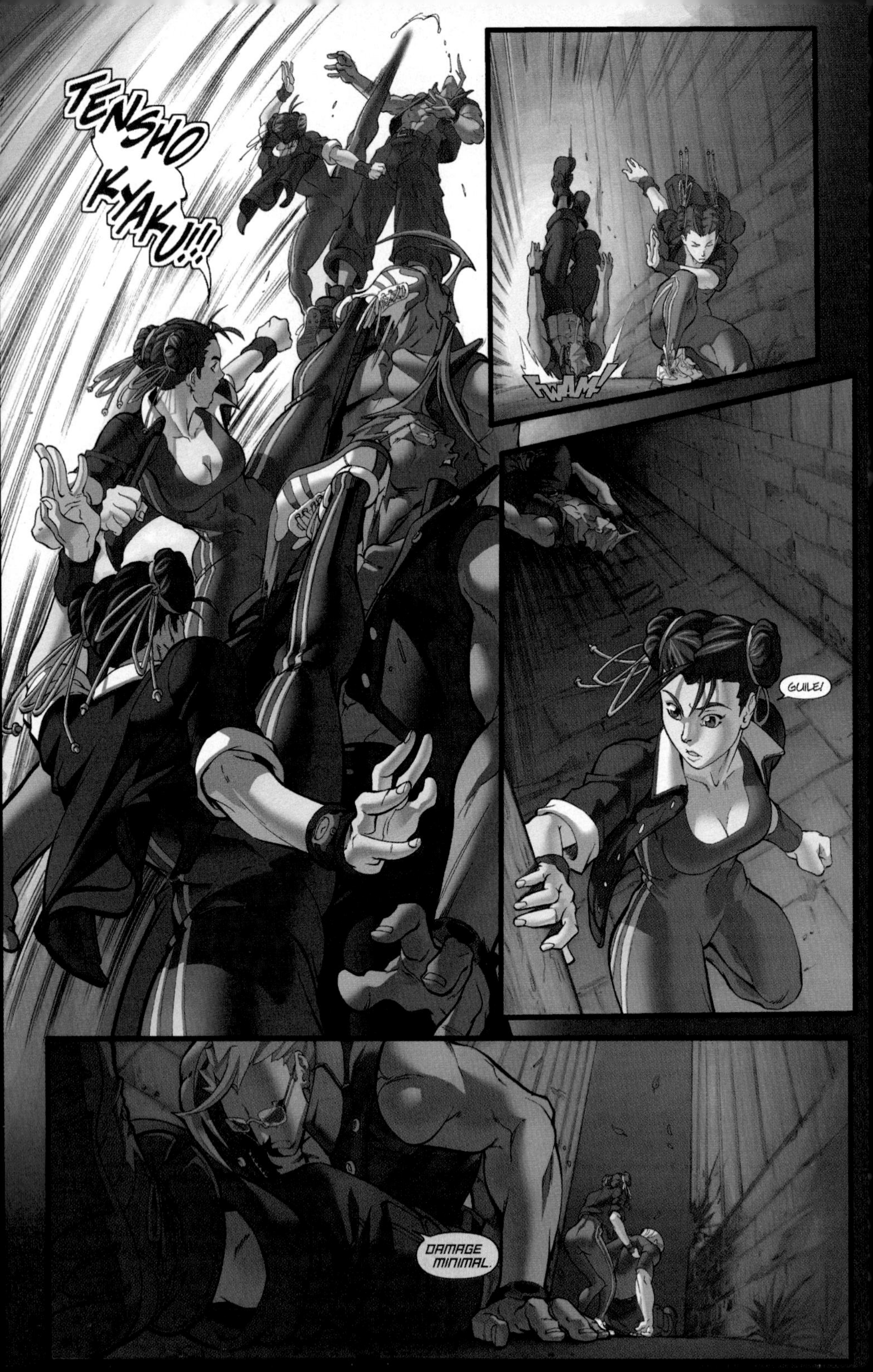
TENSHO KYAKU!!!
FWAM!
GUILE!
DAMAGE MINIMAL.

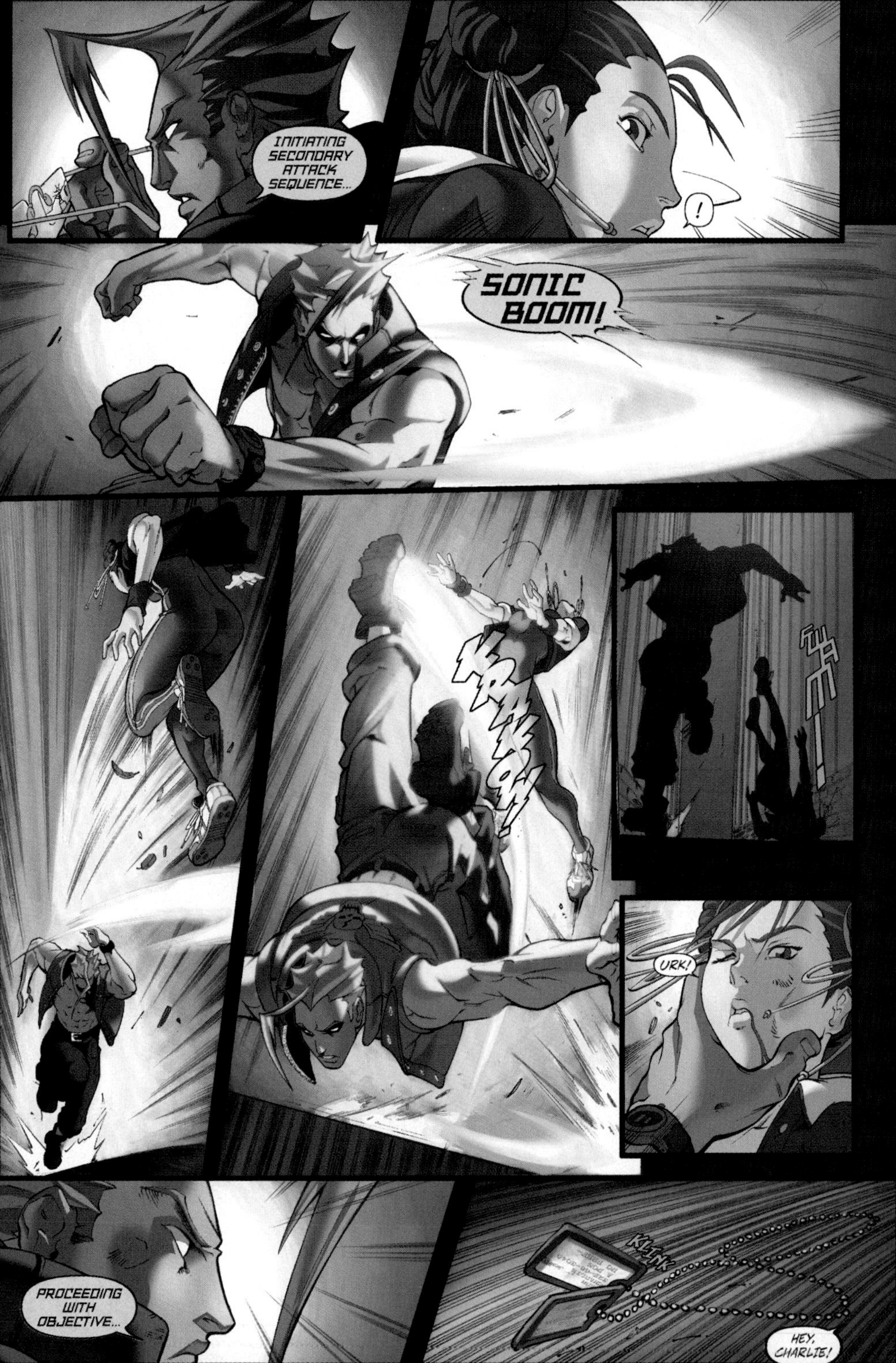
INITIATING SECONDARY ATTACK SEQUENCE...
!
SONIC BOOM!
KRAKOW!
URK!
PROCEEDING WITH OBJECTIVE...
KLINK
HEY, CHARLIE!

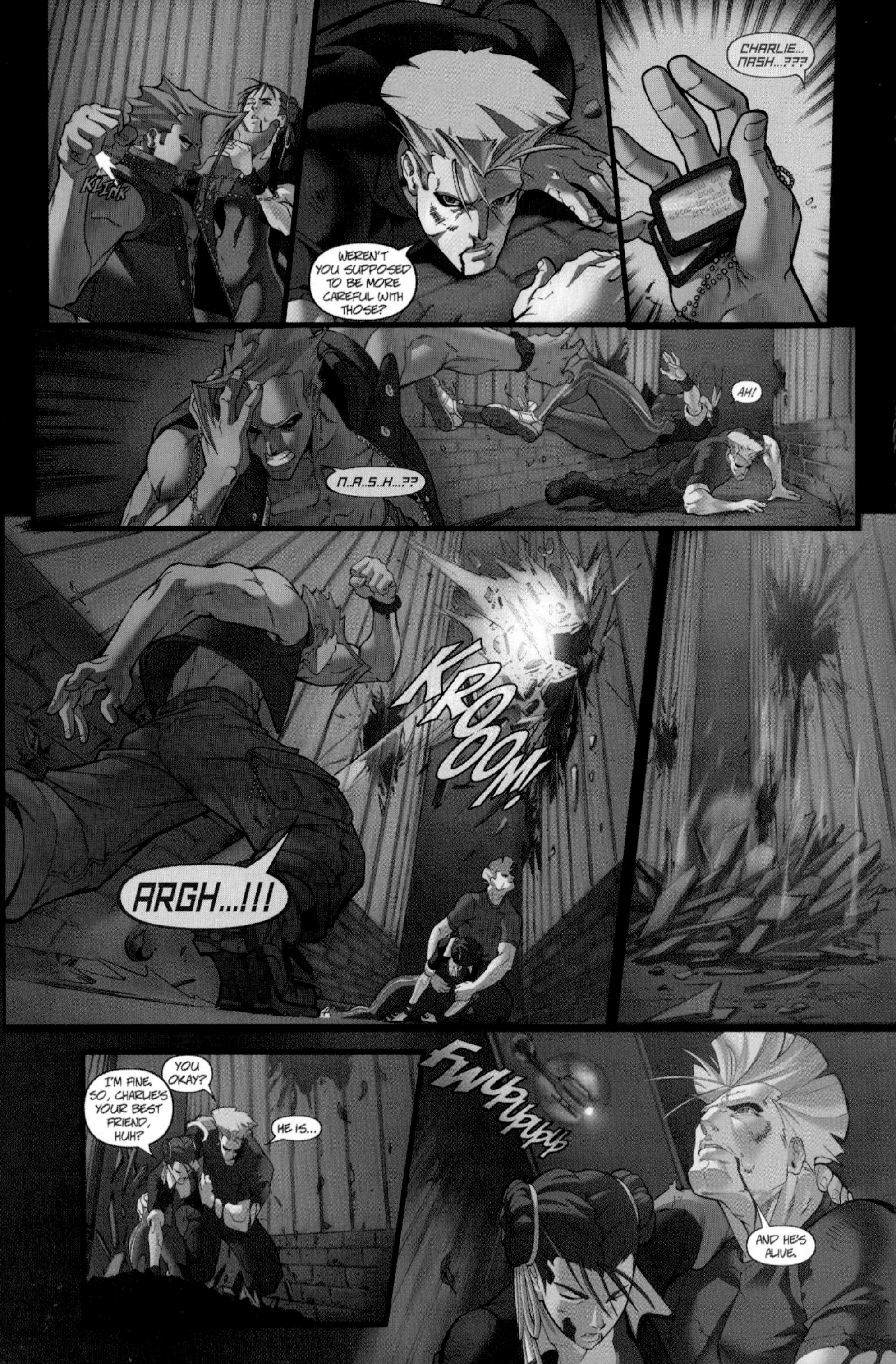

KLINK
WEREN'T YOU SUPPOSED TO BE MORE CAREFUL WITH THOSE?
CHARLIE... NASH...???
AH!
N.A.S.H...??
KROOOM!
ARGH...!!!
YOU OKAY?
I'M FINE. SO, CHARLIE'S YOUR BEST FRIEND, HUH?
HE IS...
FWUPUPUPUP
AND HE'S ALIVE.

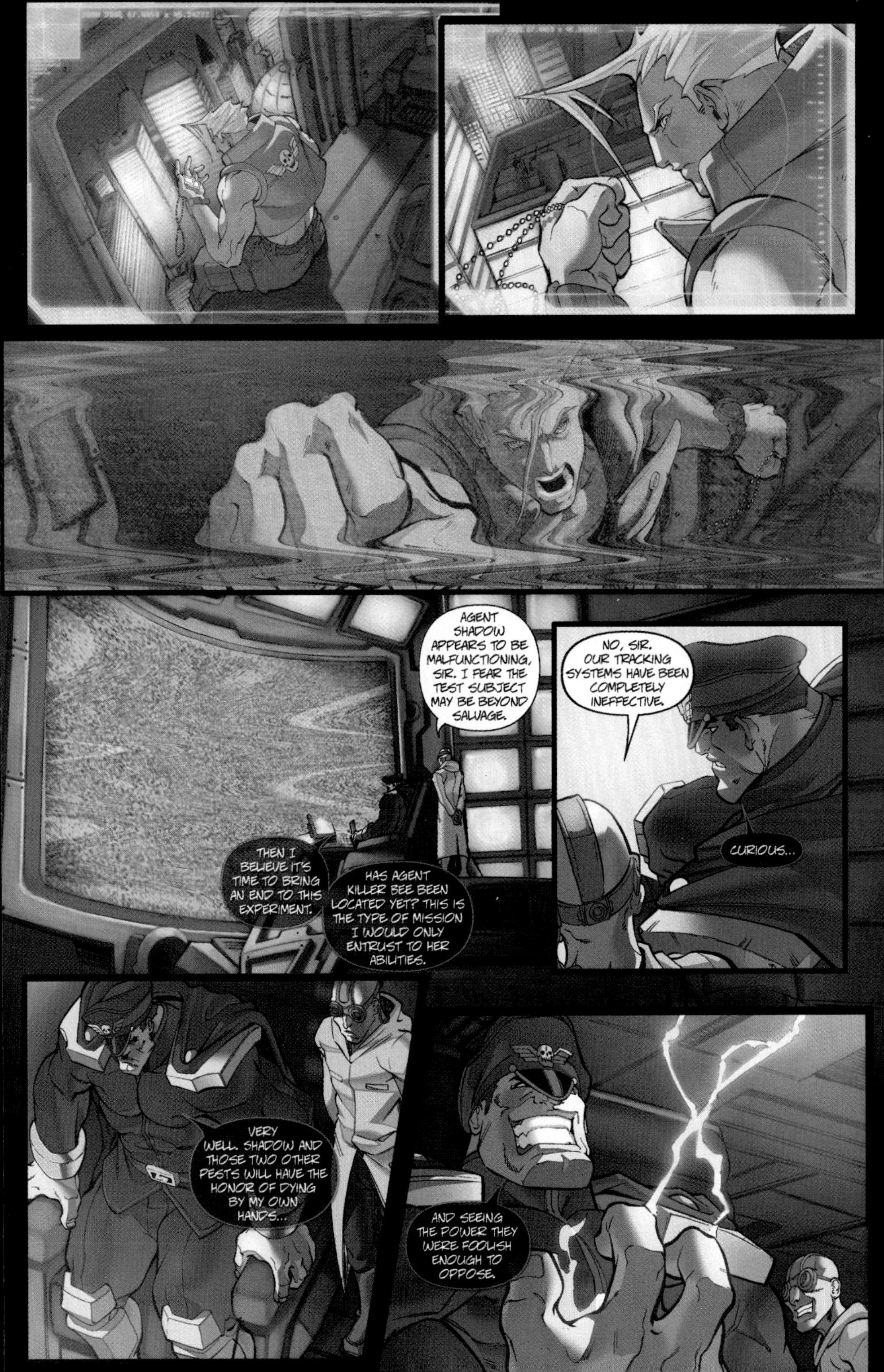
AGENT SHADOW APPEARS TO BE MALFUNCTIONING, SIR. I FEAR THE TEST SUBJECT MAY BE BEYOND SALVAGE.
THEN I BELIEVE IT'S TIME TO BRING AN END TO THIS EXPERIMENT.
HAS AGENT KILLER BEE BEEN LOCATED YET? THIS IS THE TYPE OF MISSION I WOULD ONLY ENTRUST TO HER ABILITIES.
NO, SIR. OUR TRACKING SYSTEMS HAVE BEEN COMPLETELY INEFFECTIVE.
CURIOUS...
VERY WELL. SHADOW AND THOSE TWO OTHER PESTS WILL HAVE THE HONOR OF DYING BY MY OWN HANDS...
AND SEEING THE POWER THEY WERE FOOLISH ENOUGH TO OPPOSE.

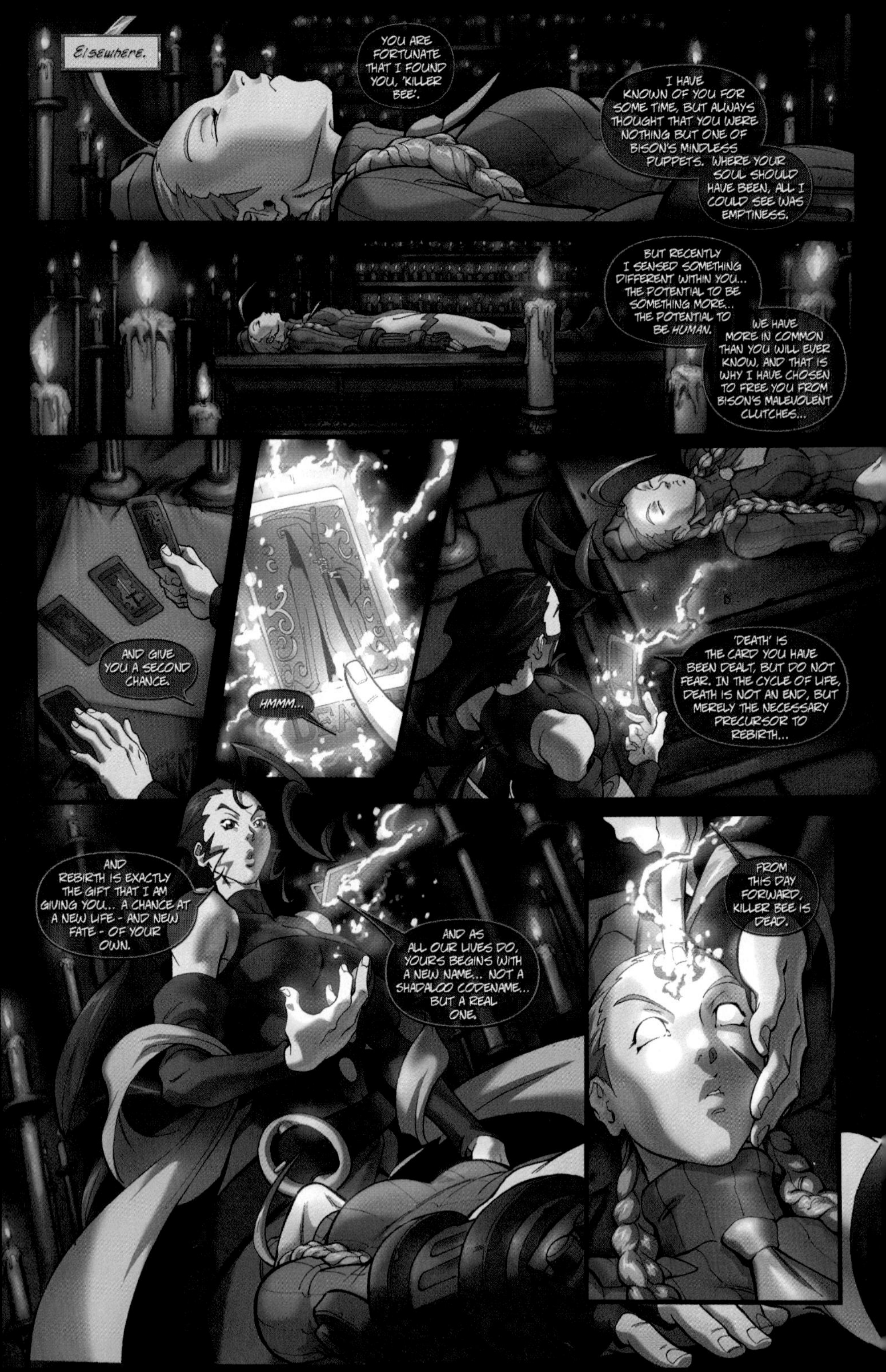
Elsewhere.
YOU ARE FORTUNATE THAT I FOUND YOU, 'KILLER BEE'.
I HAVE KNOWN OF YOU FOR SOME TIME, BUT ALWAYS THOUGHT THAT YOU WERE NOTHING BUT ONE OF BISON'S MINDLESS PUPPETS. WHERE YOUR SOUL SHOULD HAVE BEEN, ALL I COULD SEE WAS EMPTINESS.
BUT RECENTLY I SENSED SOMETHING DIFFERENT WITHIN YOU... THE POTENTIAL TO BE SOMETHING MORE... THE POTENTIAL TO BE HUMAN.
WE HAVE MORE IN COMMON THAN YOU WILL EVER KNOW, AND THAT IS WHY I HAVE CHOSEN TO FREE YOU FROM BISON'S MALEVOLENT CLUTCHES...
AND GIVE YOU A SECOND CHANCE.
HMMM...
'DEATH' IS THE CARD YOU HAVE BEEN DEALT, BUT DO NOT FEAR. IN THE CYCLE OF LIFE, DEATH IS NOT AN END, BUT MERELY THE NECESSARY PRECURSOR TO REBIRTH...
AND REBIRTH IS EXACTLY THE GIFT THAT I AM GIVING YOU... A CHANCE AT A NEW LIFE - AND NEW FATE - OF YOUR OWN.
AND AS ALL OUR LIVES DO, YOURS BEGINS WITH A NEW NAME... NOT A SHADALOO CODENAME... BUT A REAL ONE.
FROM THIS DAY FORWARD, KILLER BEE IS DEAD.

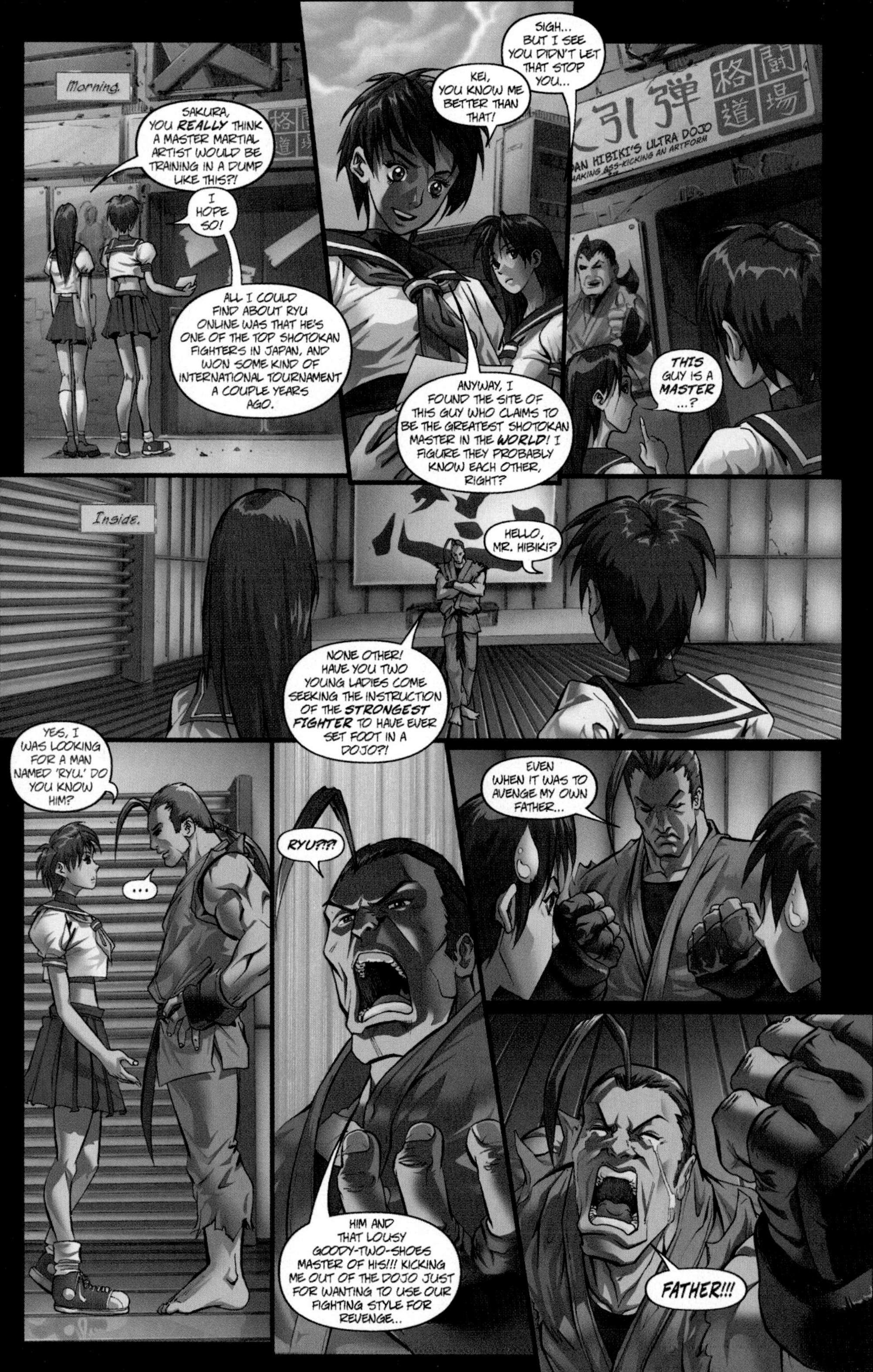

Morning.
SAKURA, YOU REALLY THINK A MASTER MARTIAL ARTIST WOULD BE TRAINING IN A DUMP LIKE THIS?!
I HOPE SO!
ALL I COULD FIND ABOUT RYU ONLINE WAS THAT HE'S ONE OF THE TOP SHOTOKAN FIGHTERS IN JAPAN, AND WON SOME KIND OF INTERNATIONAL TOURNAMENT A COUPLE YEARS AGO.
KEI, YOU KNOW ME BETTER THAN THAT!
SIGH... BUT I SEE YOU DIDN'T LET THAT STOP YOU...
ANYWAY, I FOUND THE SITE OF THIS GUY WHO CLAIMS TO BE THE GREATEST SHOTOKAN MASTER IN THE WORLD! I FIGURE THEY PROBABLY KNOW EACH OTHER, RIGHT?
格闘道場
DAN HIBIKI'S ULTRA DOJO
MAKING ASS-KICKING AN ARTFORM
THIS GUY IS A MASTER ...?
Inside.
HELLO, MR. HIBIKI?
NONE OTHER! HAVE YOU TWO YOUNG LADIES COME SEEKING THE INSTRUCTION OF THE STRONGEST FIGHTER TO HAVE EVER SET FOOT IN A DOJO?!
YES, I WAS LOOKING FOR A MAN NAMED 'RYU.' DO YOU KNOW HIM?
...
RYU?!?!
HIM AND THAT LOUSY GOODY-TWO-SHOES MASTER OF HIS!!! KICKING ME OUT OF THE DOJO JUST FOR WANTING TO USE OUR FIGHTING STYLE FOR REVENGE...
EVEN WHEN IT WAS TO AVENGE MY OWN FATHER...
FATHER!!!

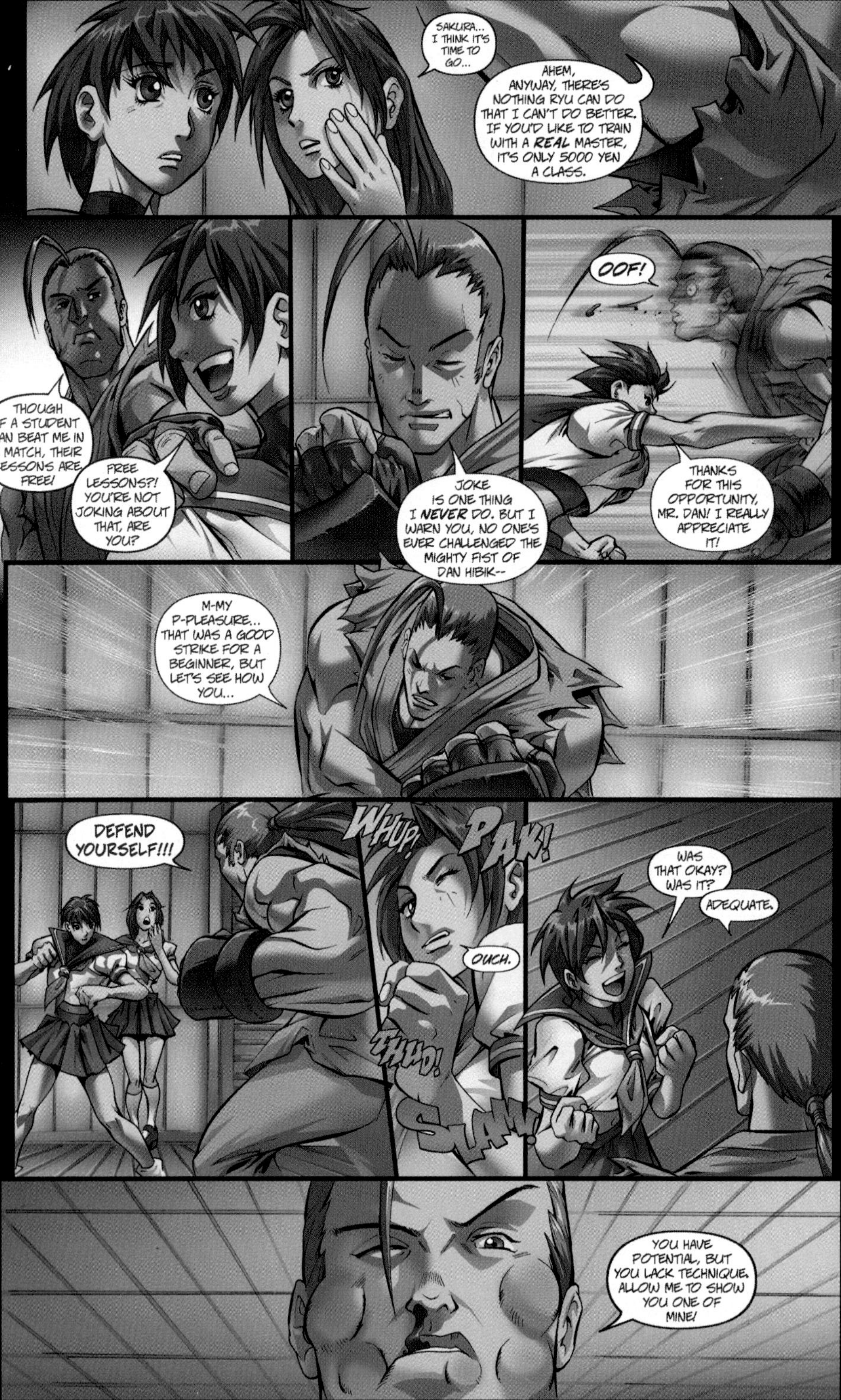
SAKURA... I THINK IT'S TIME TO GO...
AHEM, ANYWAY, THERE'S NOTHING RYU CAN DO THAT I CAN'T DO BETTER. IF YOU'D LIKE TO TRAIN WITH A REAL MASTER, IT'S ONLY 5000 YEN A CLASS.
THOUGH IF A STUDENT CAN BEAT ME IN A MATCH, THEIR LESSONS ARE FREE!
FREE LESSONS?! YOU'RE NOT JOKING ABOUT THAT, ARE YOU?
JOKE IS ONE THING I NEVER DO. BUT I WARN YOU, NO ONE'S EVER CHALLENGED THE MIGHTY FIST OF DAN HIBIK--
OOF!
THANKS FOR THIS OPPORTUNITY, MR. DAN! I REALLY APPRECIATE IT!
M-MY P-PLEASURE... THAT WAS A GOOD STRIKE FOR A BEGINNER, BUT LET'S SEE HOW YOU...
DEFEND YOURSELF!!!
WHUP!
PAK!
OUCH.
THUD!
SLAM!
WAS THAT OKAY? WAS IT?
ADEQUATE.
YOU HAVE POTENTIAL, BUT YOU LACK TECHNIQUE. ALLOW ME TO SHOW YOU ONE OF MINE!

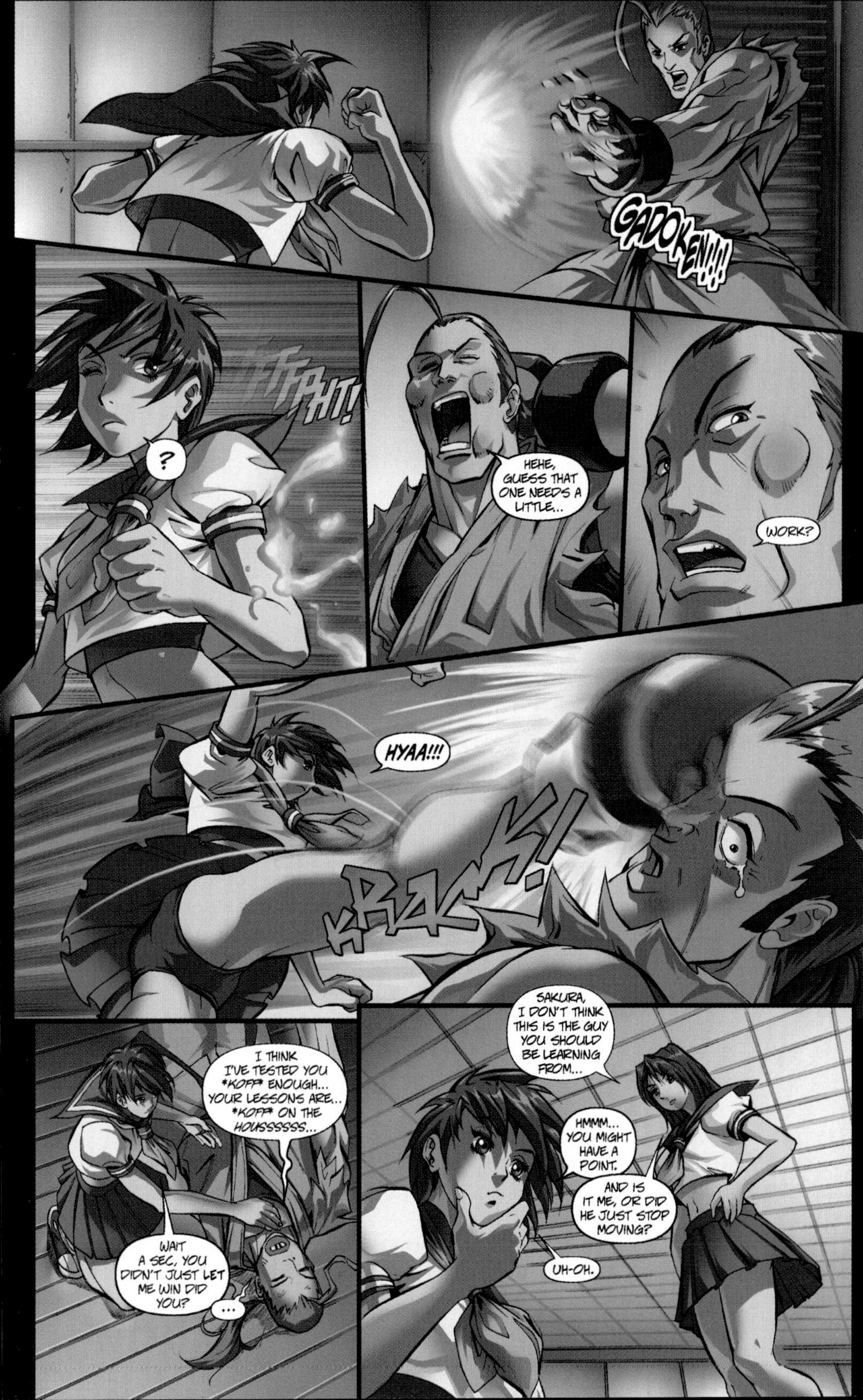
GADOKEN!!!
FFFPHT!
?
HEHE, GUESS THAT ONE NEEDS A LITTLE...
WORK?
HYAA!!!
KRAKK!
I THINK I'VE TESTED YOU *KOFF* ENOUGH... YOUR LESSONS ARE... *KOFF* ON THE HOUSSSSSS...
WAIT A SEC, YOU DIDN'T JUST LET ME WIN DID YOU?
...
SAKURA, I DON'T THINK THIS IS THE GUY YOU SHOULD BE LEARNING FROM...
HMMM... YOU MIGHT HAVE A POINT.
AND IS IT ME, OR DID HE JUST STOP MOVING?
UH-OH.

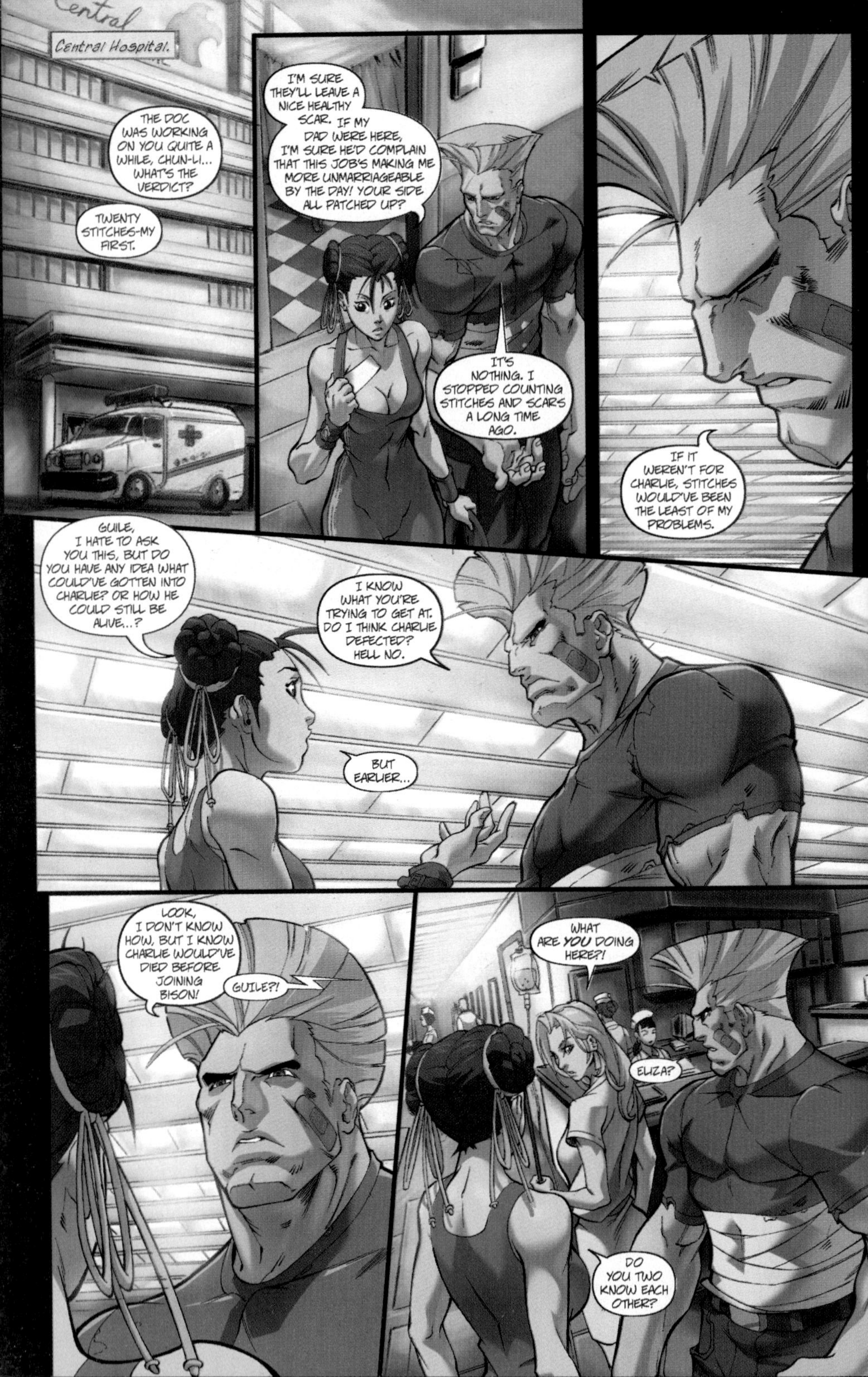
Central
Central Hospital.
THE DOC WAS WORKING ON YOU QUITE A WHILE, CHUN-LI... WHAT'S THE VERDICT?
TWENTY STITCHES-MY FIRST.
I'M SURE THEY'LL LEAVE A NICE HEALTHY SCAR. IF MY DAD WERE HERE, I'M SURE HE'D COMPLAIN THAT THIS JOB'S MAKING ME MORE UNMARRIAGEABLE BY THE DAY! YOUR SIDE ALL PATCHED UP?
IT'S NOTHING. I STOPPED COUNTING STITCHES AND SCARS A LONG TIME AGO.
IF IT WEREN'T FOR CHARLIE, STITCHES WOULD'VE BEEN THE LEAST OF MY PROBLEMS.
GUILE, I HATE TO ASK YOU THIS, BUT DO YOU HAVE ANY IDEA WHAT COULD'VE GOTTEN INTO CHARLIE? OR HOW HE COULD STILL BE ALIVE...?
I KNOW WHAT YOU'RE TRYING TO GET AT. DO I THINK CHARLIE DEFECTED? HELL NO.
BUT EARLIER...
LOOK, I DON'T KNOW HOW, BUT I KNOW CHARLIE WOULD'VE DIED BEFORE JOINING BISON!
GUILE?!
WHAT ARE YOU DOING HERE?!
ELIZA?
DO YOU TWO KNOW EACH OTHER?

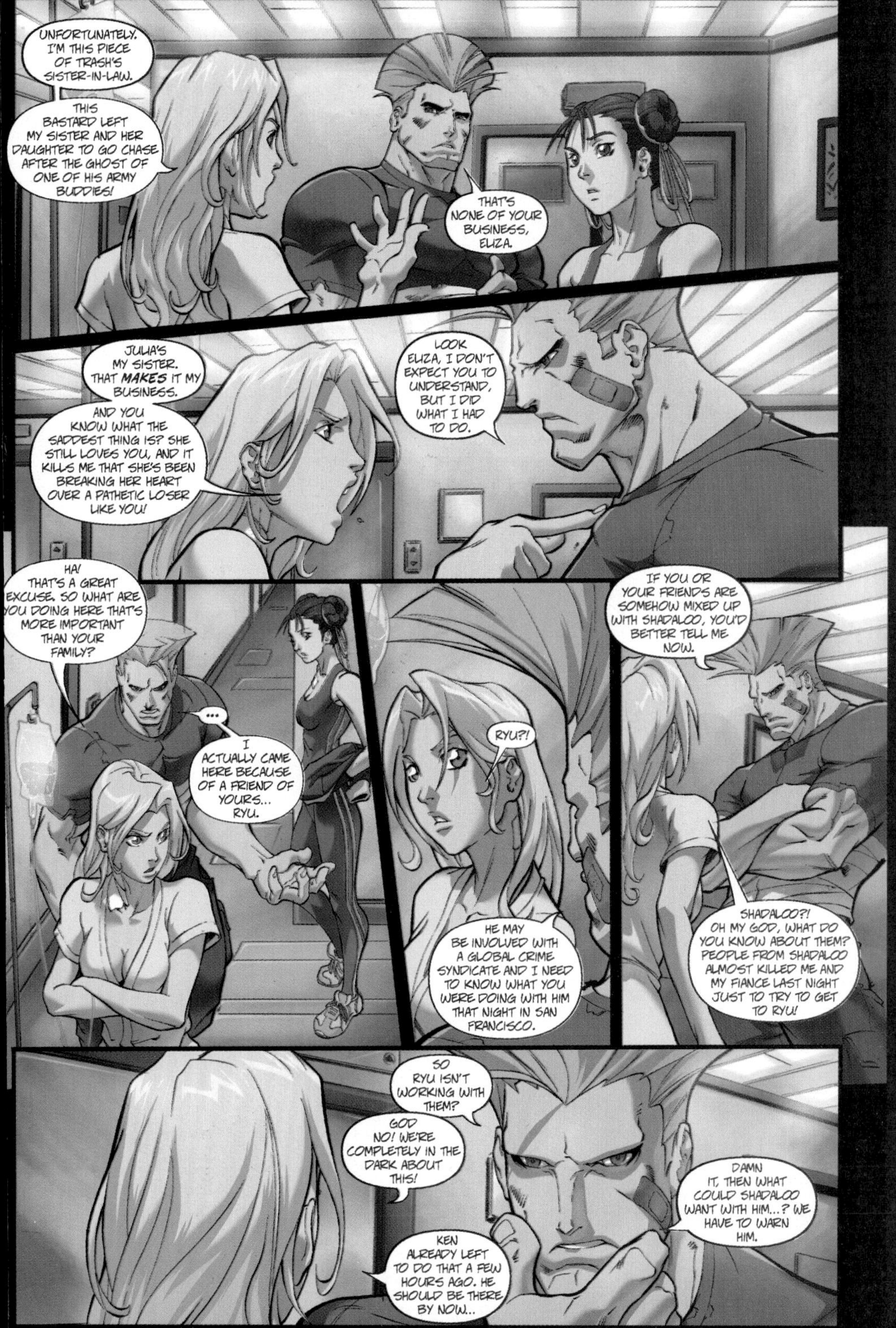
UNFORTUNATELY. I'M THIS PIECE OF TRASH'S SISTER-IN-LAW.
THIS BASTARD LEFT MY SISTER AND HER DAUGHTER TO GO CHASE AFTER THE GHOST OF ONE OF HIS ARMY BUDDIES!
THAT'S NONE OF YOUR BUSINESS, ELIZA.
JULIA'S MY SISTER. THAT *MAKES* IT MY BUSINESS.
AND YOU KNOW WHAT THE SADDEST THING IS? SHE STILL LOVES YOU, AND IT KILLS ME THAT SHE'S BEEN BREAKING HER HEART OVER A PATHETIC LOSER LIKE YOU!
LOOK ELIZA, I DON'T EXPECT YOU TO UNDERSTAND, BUT I DID WHAT I HAD TO DO.
HA! THAT'S A GREAT EXCUSE. SO WHAT ARE YOU DOING HERE THAT'S MORE IMPORTANT THAN YOUR FAMILY?
...
I ACTUALLY CAME HERE BECAUSE OF A FRIEND OF YOURS... RYU.
RYU?!
HE MAY BE INVOLVED WITH A GLOBAL CRIME SYNDICATE AND I NEED TO KNOW WHAT YOU WERE DOING WITH HIM THAT NIGHT IN SAN FRANCISCO.
IF YOU OR YOUR FRIENDS ARE SOMEHOW MIXED UP WITH SHADALOO, YOU'D BETTER TELL ME NOW.
SHADALOO?! OH MY GOD, WHAT DO YOU KNOW ABOUT THEM? PEOPLE FROM SHADALOO ALMOST KILLED ME AND MY FIANCE LAST NIGHT JUST TO TRY TO GET TO RYU!
SO RYU ISN'T WORKING WITH THEM?
GOD NO! WE'RE COMPLETELY IN THE DARK ABOUT THIS!
DAMN IT, THEN WHAT COULD SHADALOO WANT WITH HIM...? WE HAVE TO WARN HIM.
KEN ALREADY LEFT TO DO THAT A FEW HOURS AGO. HE SHOULD BE THERE BY NOW...

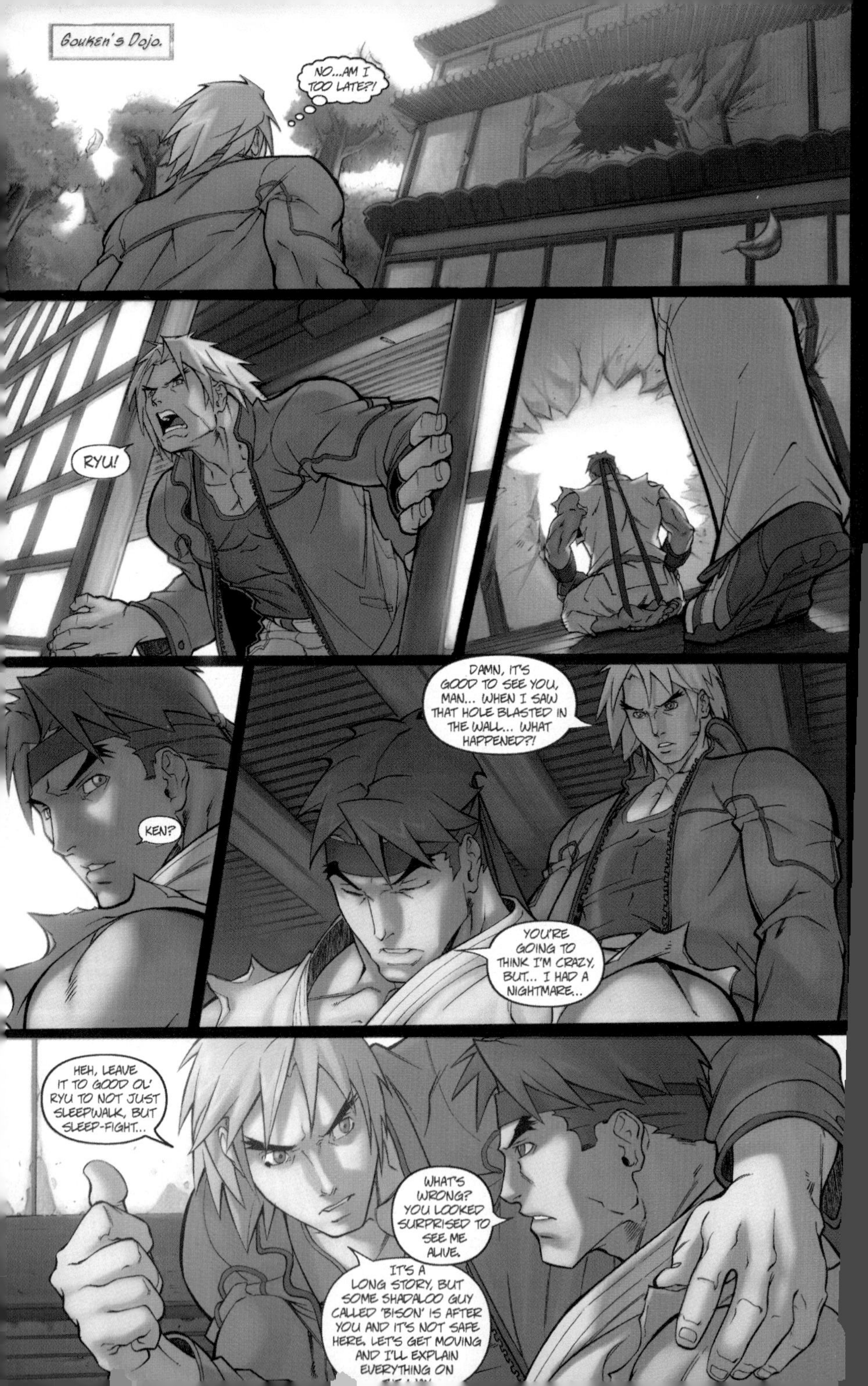
Gouken's Dojo.
NO...AM I TOO LATE?!
RYU!
KEN?
DAMN, IT'S GOOD TO SEE YOU, MAN... WHEN I SAW THAT HOLE BLASTED IN THE WALL... WHAT HAPPENED?!
YOU'RE GOING TO THINK I'M CRAZY, BUT... I HAD A NIGHTMARE...
HEH, LEAVE IT TO GOOD OL' RYU TO NOT JUST SLEEPWALK, BUT SLEEP-FIGHT...
WHAT'S WRONG? YOU LOOKED SURPRISED TO SEE ME ALIVE.
IT'S A LONG STORY, BUT SOME SHADALOO GUY CALLED 'BISON' IS AFTER YOU AND IT'S NOT SAFE HERE. LET'S GET MOVING AND I'LL EXPLAIN EVERYTHING ON

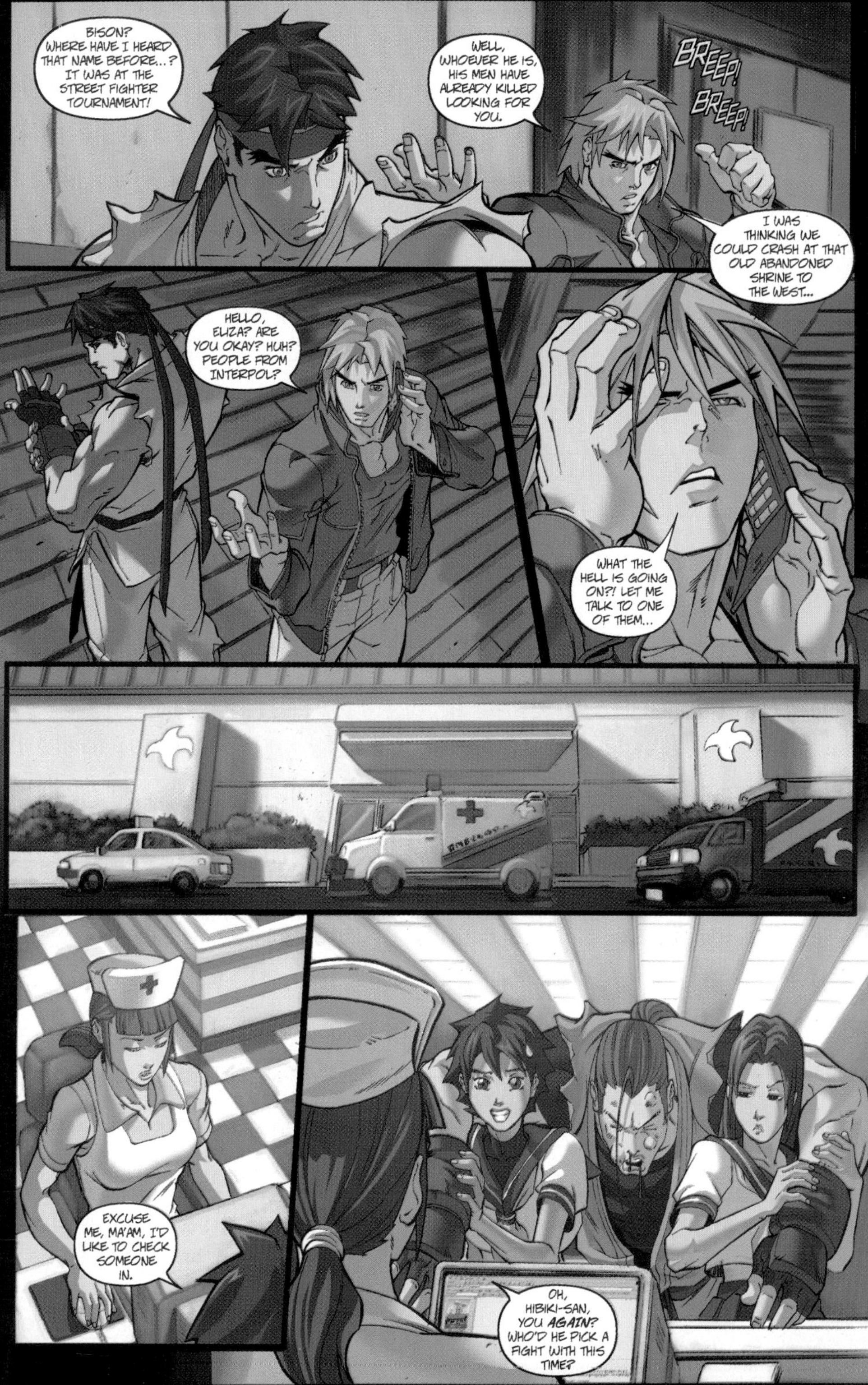

BISON? WHERE HAVE I HEARD THAT NAME BEFORE...? IT WAS AT THE STREET FIGHTER TOURNAMENT!
WELL, WHOEVER HE IS, HIS MEN HAVE ALREADY KILLED LOOKING FOR YOU.
BREEP! BREEP!
I WAS THINKING WE COULD CRASH AT THAT OLD ABANDONED SHRINE TO THE WEST...
HELLO, ELIZA? ARE YOU OKAY? HUH? PEOPLE FROM INTERPOL?
WHAT THE HELL IS GOING ON?! LET ME TALK TO ONE OF THEM...
EXCUSE ME, MA'AM, I'D LIKE TO CHECK SOMEONE IN.
OH, HIBIKI-SAN, YOU AGAIN? WHO'D HE PICK A FIGHT WITH THIS TIME?

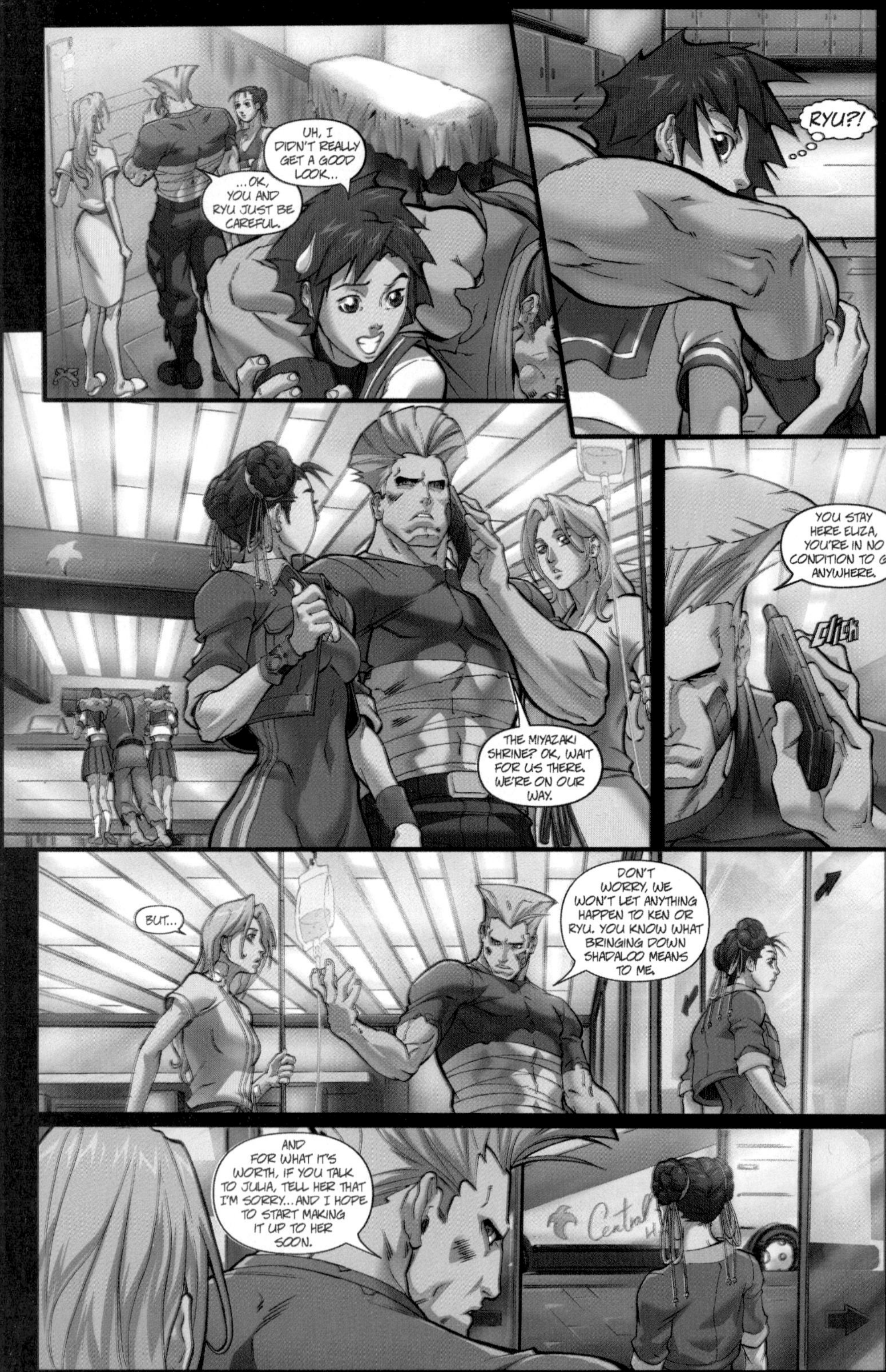
UH, I DIDN'T REALLY GET A GOOD LOOK...
...OK, YOU AND RYU JUST BE CAREFUL.
RYU?!
THE MIYAZAKI SHRINE? OK, WAIT FOR US THERE. WE'RE ON OUR WAY.
YOU STAY HERE ELIZA, YOU'RE IN NO CONDITION TO G ANYWHERE.
CLICK
BUT...
DON'T WORRY, WE WON'T LET ANYTHING HAPPEN TO KEN OR RYU. YOU KNOW WHAT BRINGING DOWN SHADALOO MEANS TO ME.
AND FOR WHAT IT'S WORTH, IF YOU TALK TO JULIA, TELL HER THAT I'M SORRY...AND I HOPE TO START MAKING IT UP TO HER SOON.

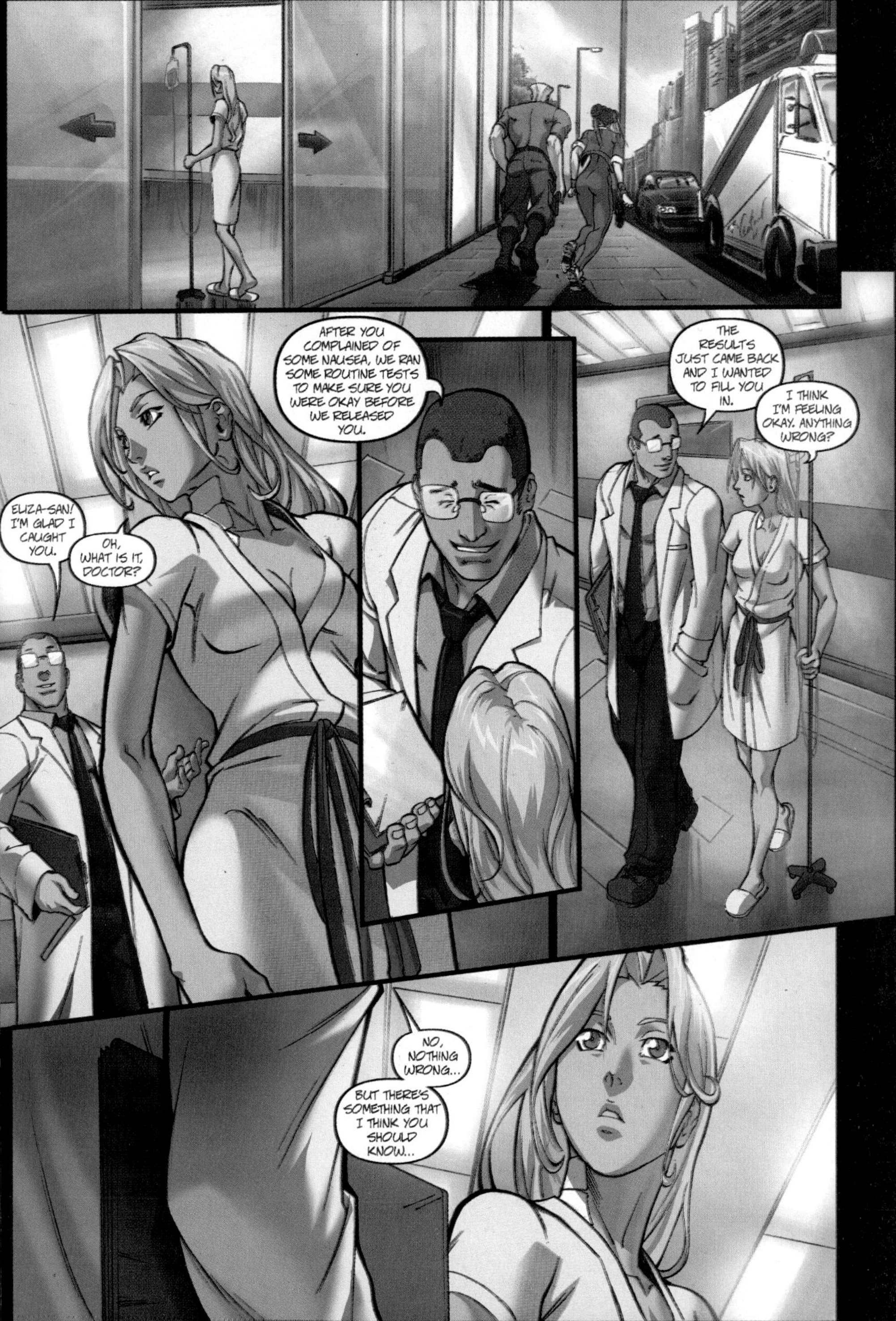
ELIZA-SAN! I'M GLAD I CAUGHT YOU.
OH, WHAT IS IT, DOCTOR?
AFTER YOU COMPLAINED OF SOME NAUSEA, WE RAN SOME ROUTINE TESTS TO MAKE SURE YOU WERE OKAY BEFORE WE RELEASED YOU.
THE RESULTS JUST CAME BACK AND I WANTED TO FILL YOU IN.
I THINK I'M FEELING OKAY. ANYTHING WRONG?
NO, NOTHING WRONG...
BUT THERE'S SOMETHING THAT I THINK YOU SHOULD KNOW...

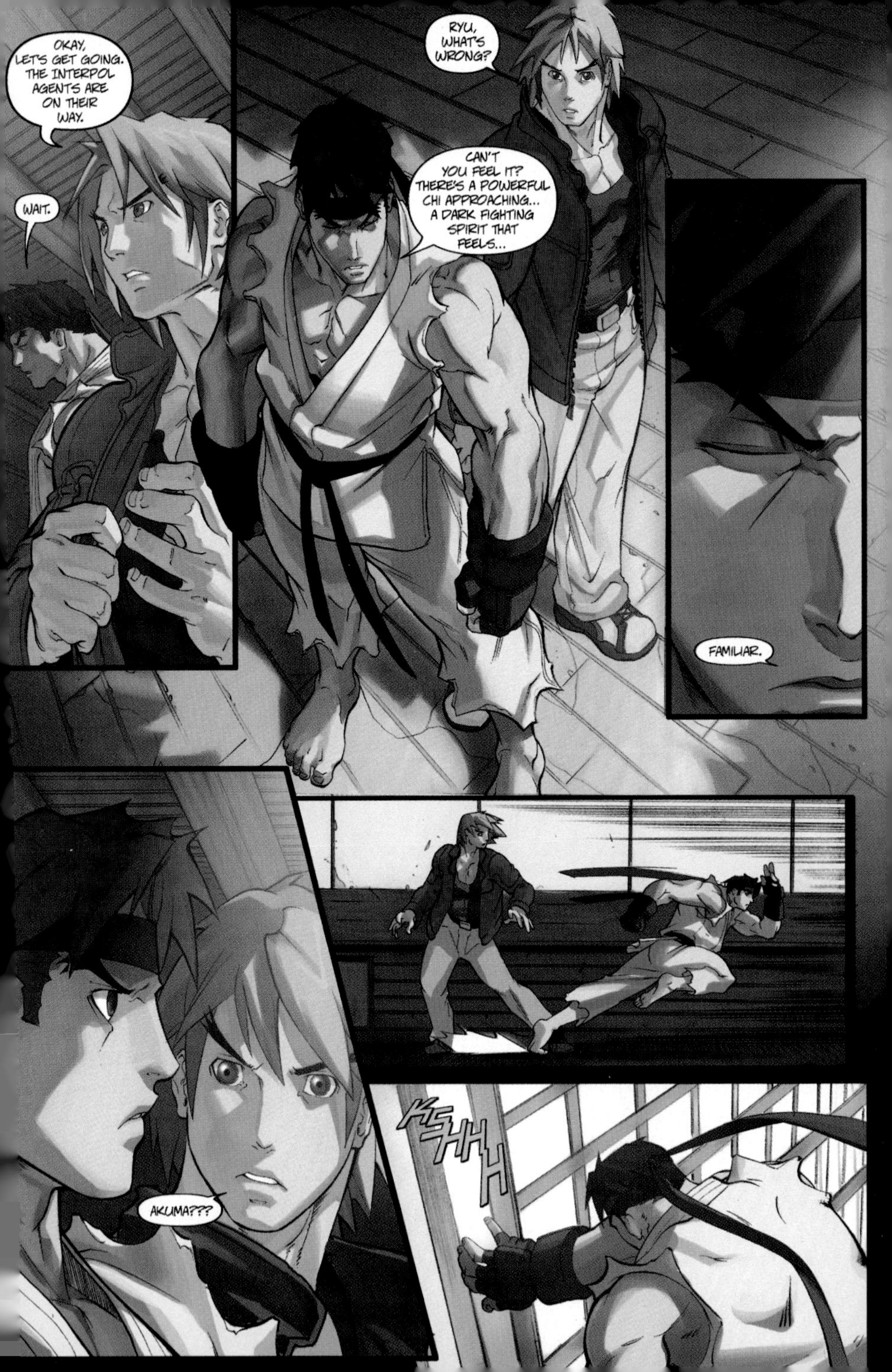

OKAY, LET'S GET GOING. THE INTERPOL AGENTS ARE ON THEIR WAY.
WAIT.
RYU, WHAT'S WRONG?
CAN'T YOU FEEL IT? THERE'S A POWERFUL CHI APPROACHING... A DARK FIGHTING SPIRIT THAT FEELS...
FAMILIAR.
AKUMA???
KSHHH

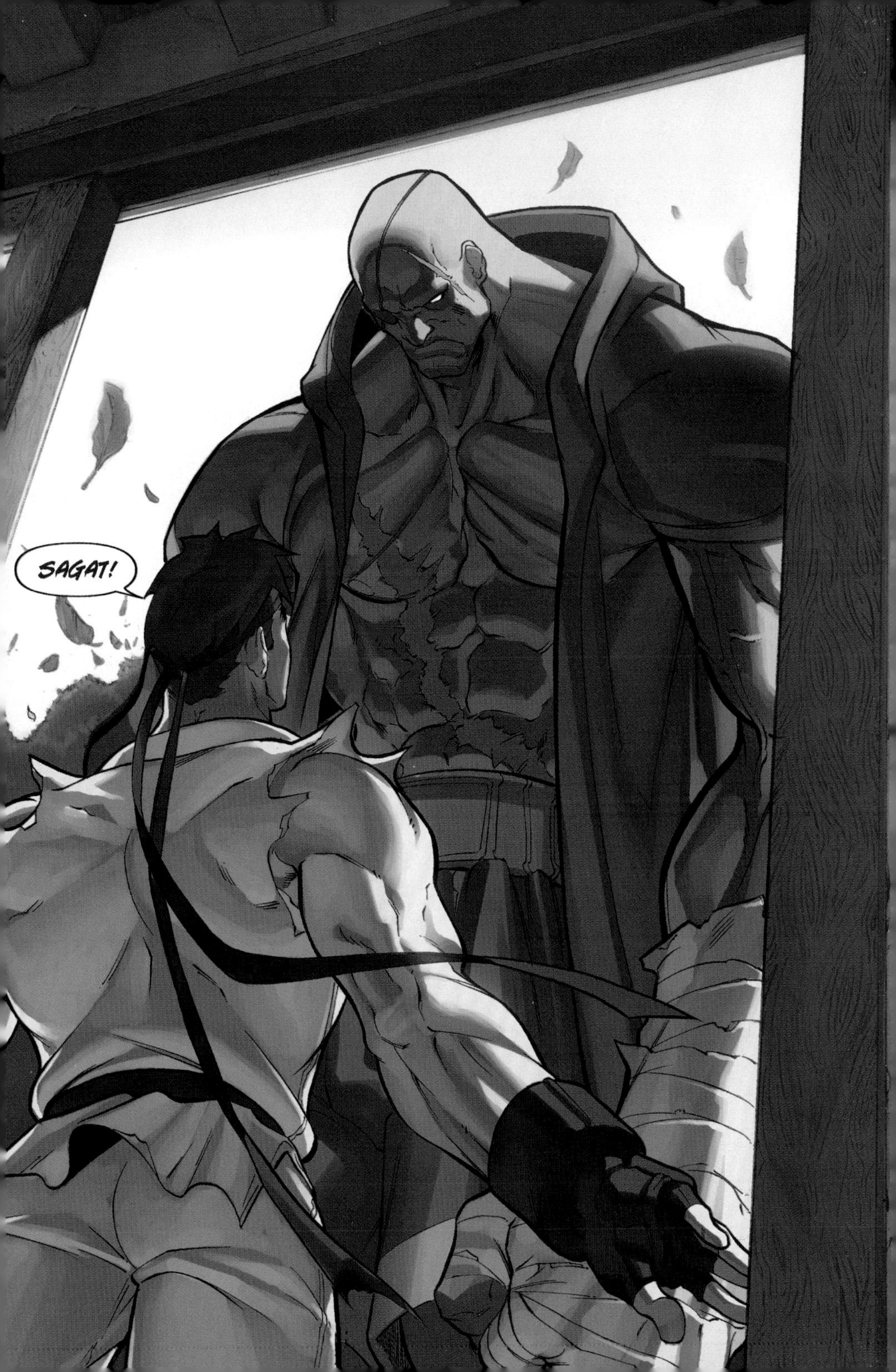
SAGAT!

Chapter 05: PSYCHO POWER

Cover Art by: Alvin Lee and Arnold Tsang

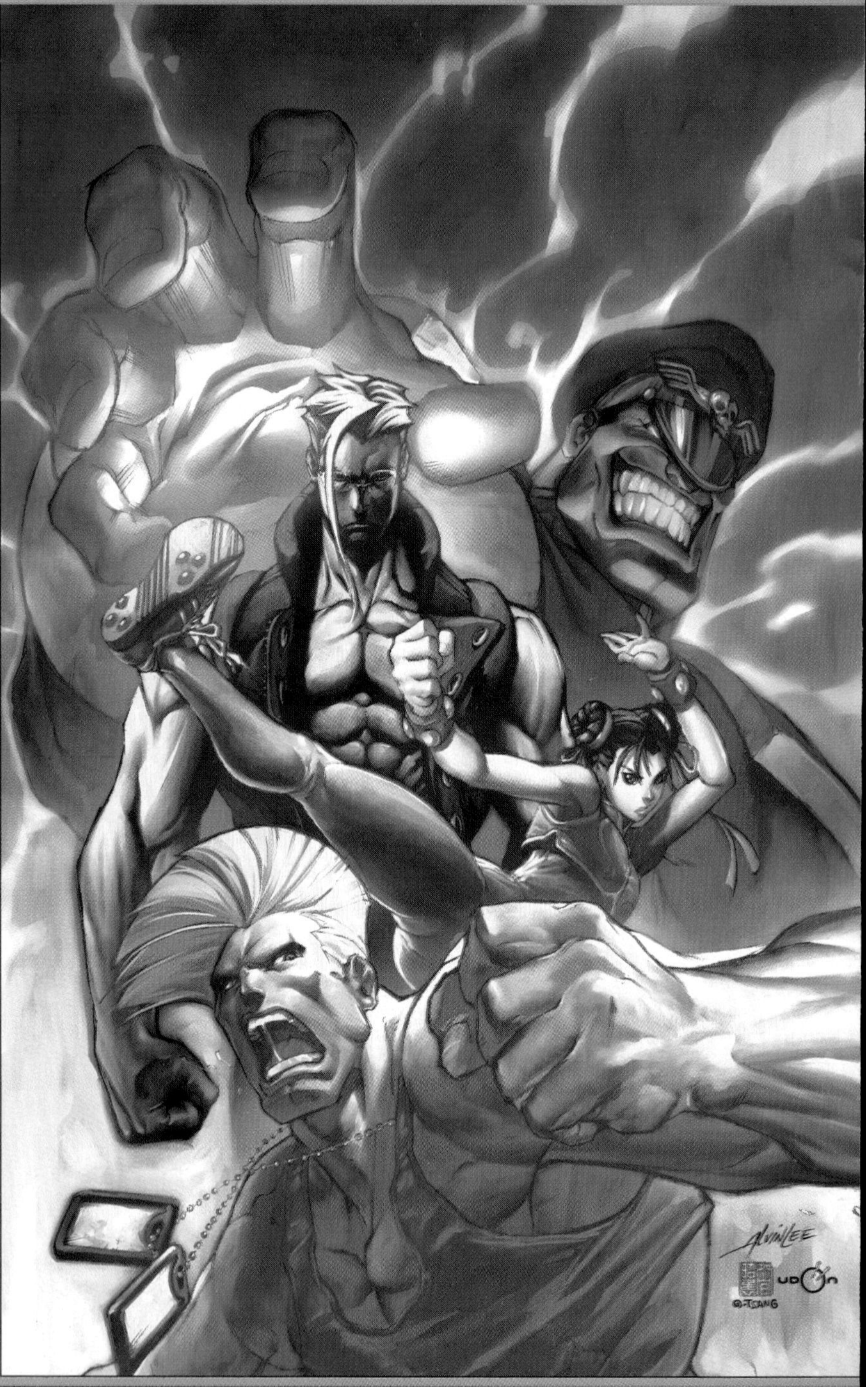

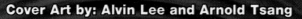

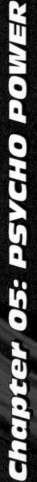

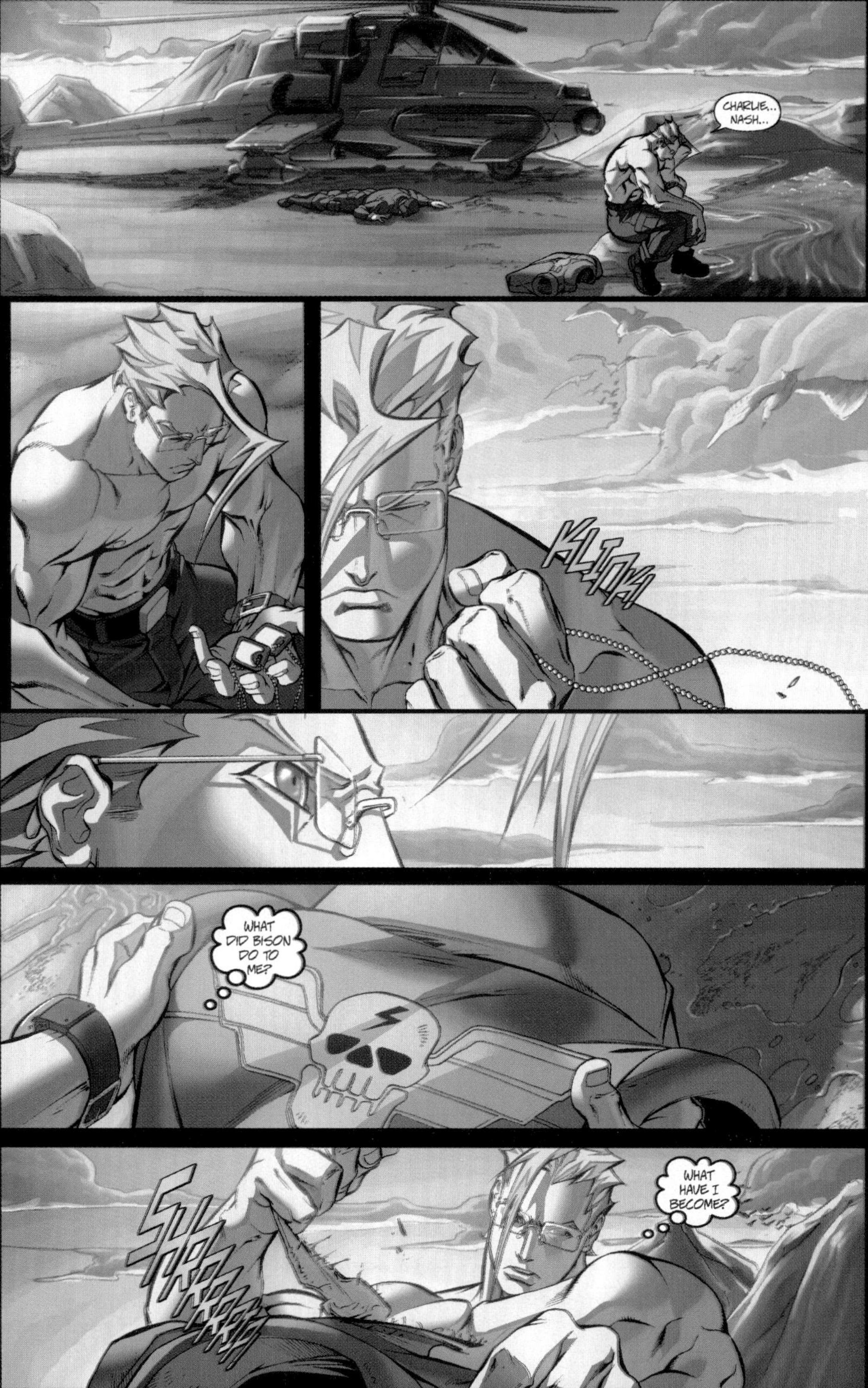
CHARLIE... NASH...
KLICK
WHAT DID BISON DO TO ME?
WHAT HAVE I BECOME?
SKRRRIP

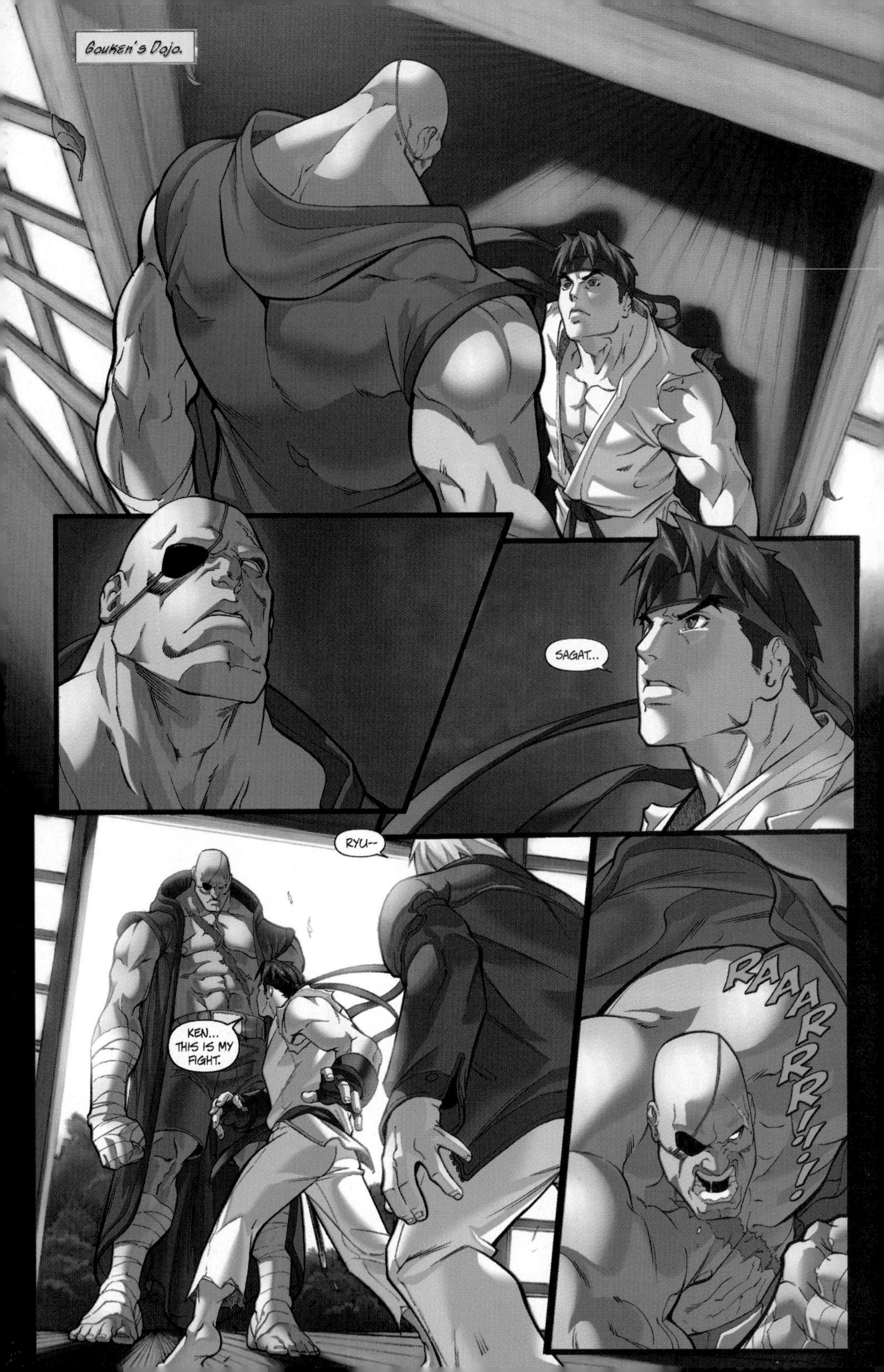
Gouken's Dojo.
SAGAT...
RYU--
KEN... THIS IS MY FIGHT.
RAAARRRR!!!

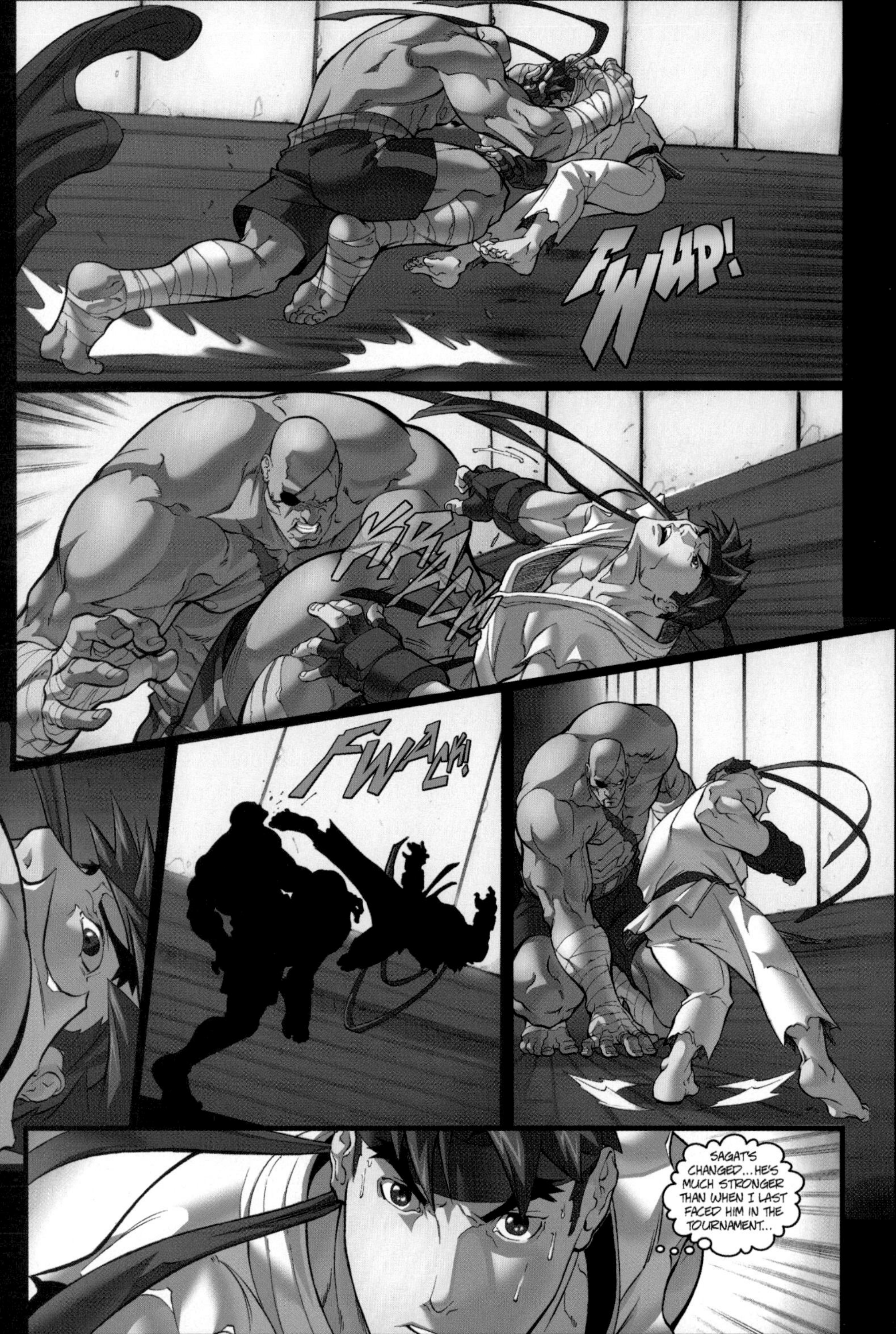
FWUP!
KRAACK!
FWACK!
SAGAT'S CHANGED...HE'S MUCH STRONGER THAN WHEN I LAST FACED HIM IN THE TOURNAMENT...

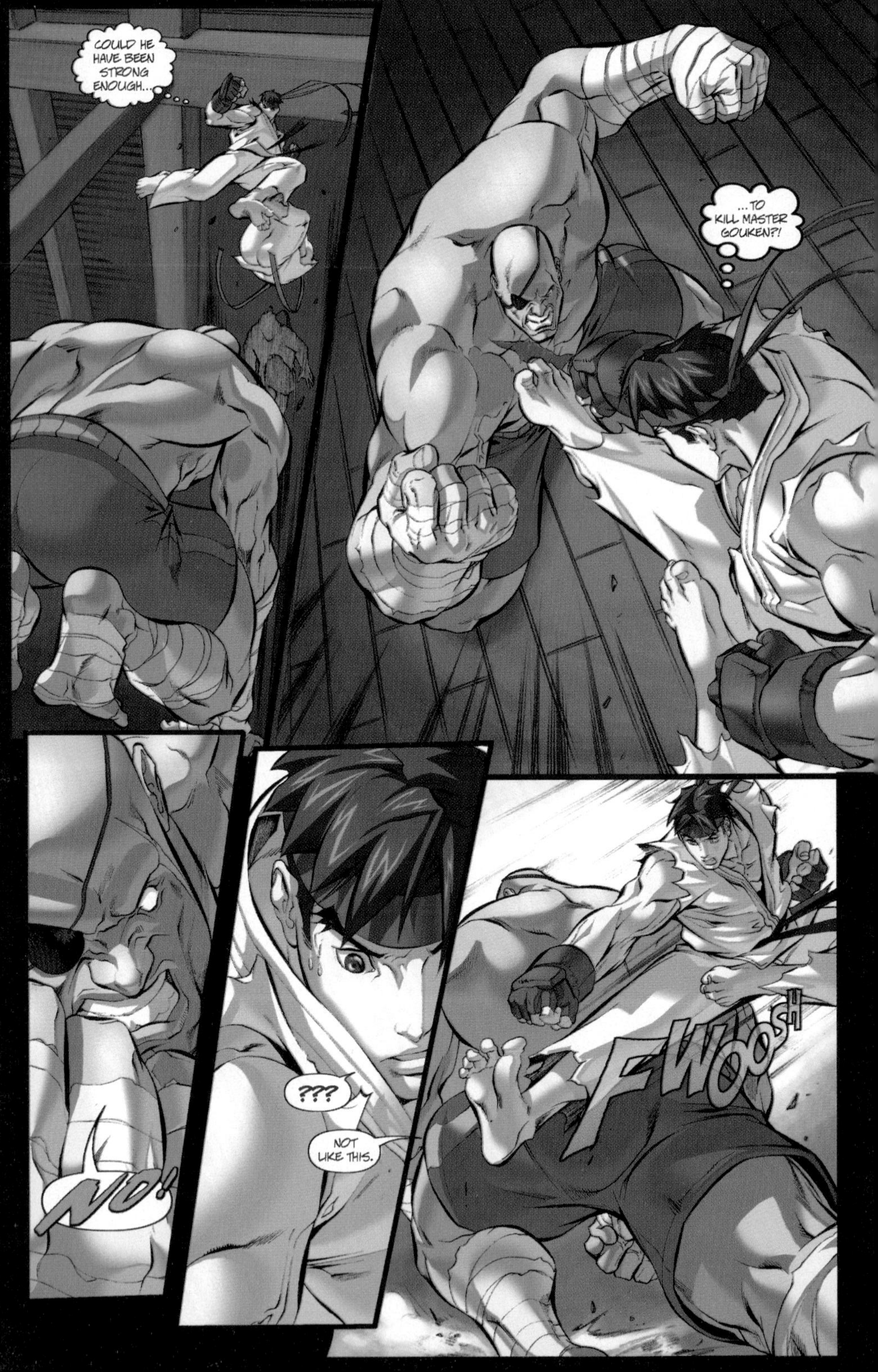
COULD HE HAVE BEEN STRONG ENOUGH...
...TO KILL MASTER GOUKEN?!
NO!
???
NOT LIKE THIS.
FWOOSH

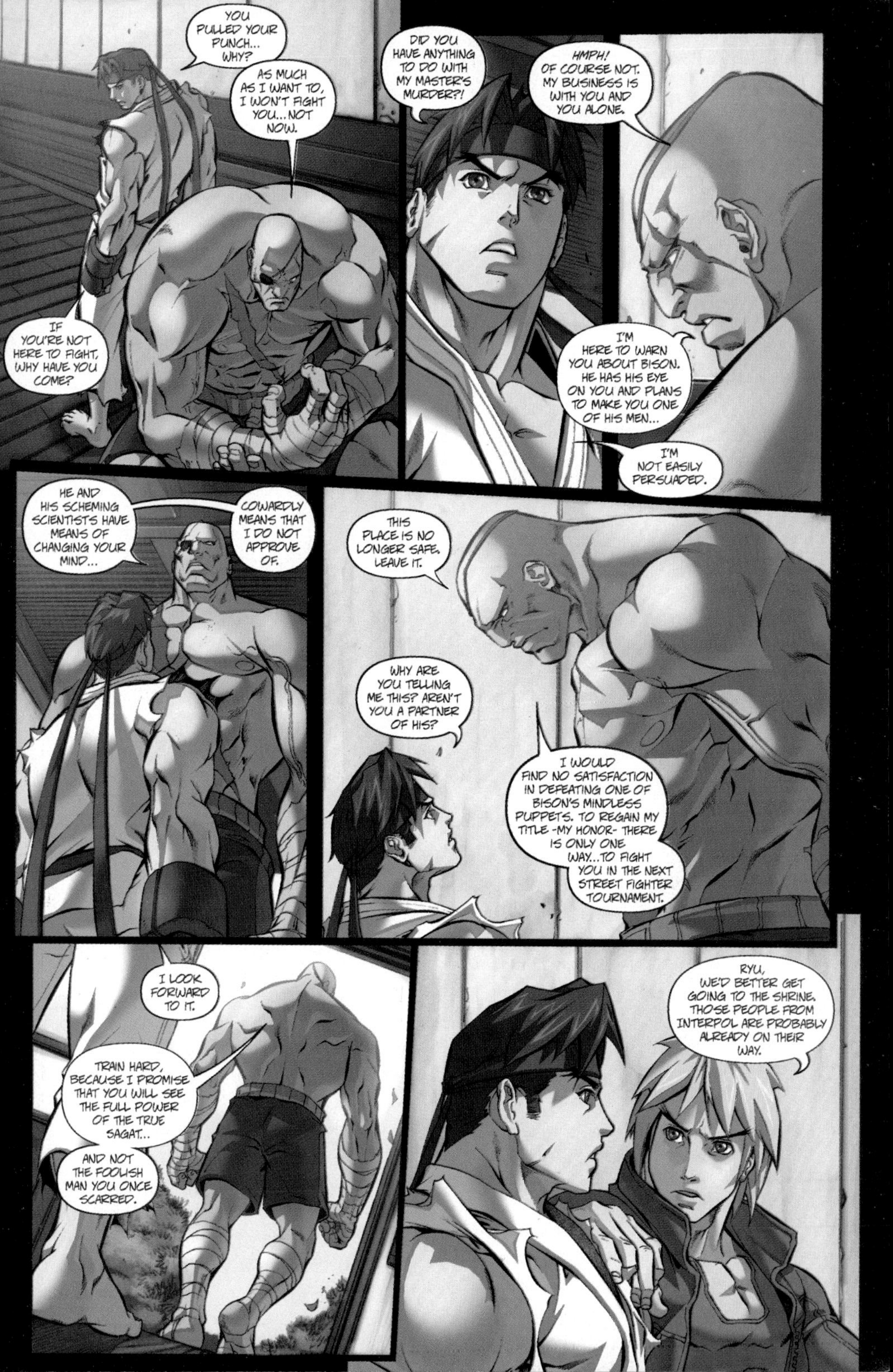
YOU PULLED YOUR PUNCH... WHY?
AS MUCH AS I WANT TO, I WON'T FIGHT YOU...NOT NOW.
IF YOU'RE NOT HERE TO FIGHT, WHY HAVE YOU COME?
DID YOU HAVE ANYTHING TO DO WITH MY MASTER'S MURDER?!
HMPH! OF COURSE NOT. MY BUSINESS IS WITH YOU AND YOU ALONE.
I'M HERE TO WARN YOU ABOUT BISON. HE HAS HIS EYE ON YOU AND PLANS TO MAKE YOU ONE OF HIS MEN...
I'M NOT EASILY PERSUADED.
HE AND HIS SCHEMING SCIENTISTS HAVE MEANS OF CHANGING YOUR MIND...
COWARDLY MEANS THAT I DO NOT APPROVE OF.
THIS PLACE IS NO LONGER SAFE. LEAVE IT.
WHY ARE YOU TELLING ME THIS? AREN'T YOU A PARTNER OF HIS?
I WOULD FIND NO SATISFACTION IN DEFEATING ONE OF BISON'S MINDLESS PUPPETS. TO REGAIN MY TITLE -MY HONOR- THERE IS ONLY ONE WAY...TO FIGHT YOU IN THE NEXT STREET FIGHTER TOURNAMENT.
I LOOK FORWARD TO IT.
TRAIN HARD, BECAUSE I PROMISE THAT YOU WILL SEE THE FULL POWER OF THE TRUE SAGAT...
AND NOT THE FOOLISH MAN YOU ONCE SCARRED.
RYU, WE'D BETTER GET GOING TO THE SHRINE. THOSE PEOPLE FROM INTERPOL ARE PROBABLY ALREADY ON THEIR WAY.

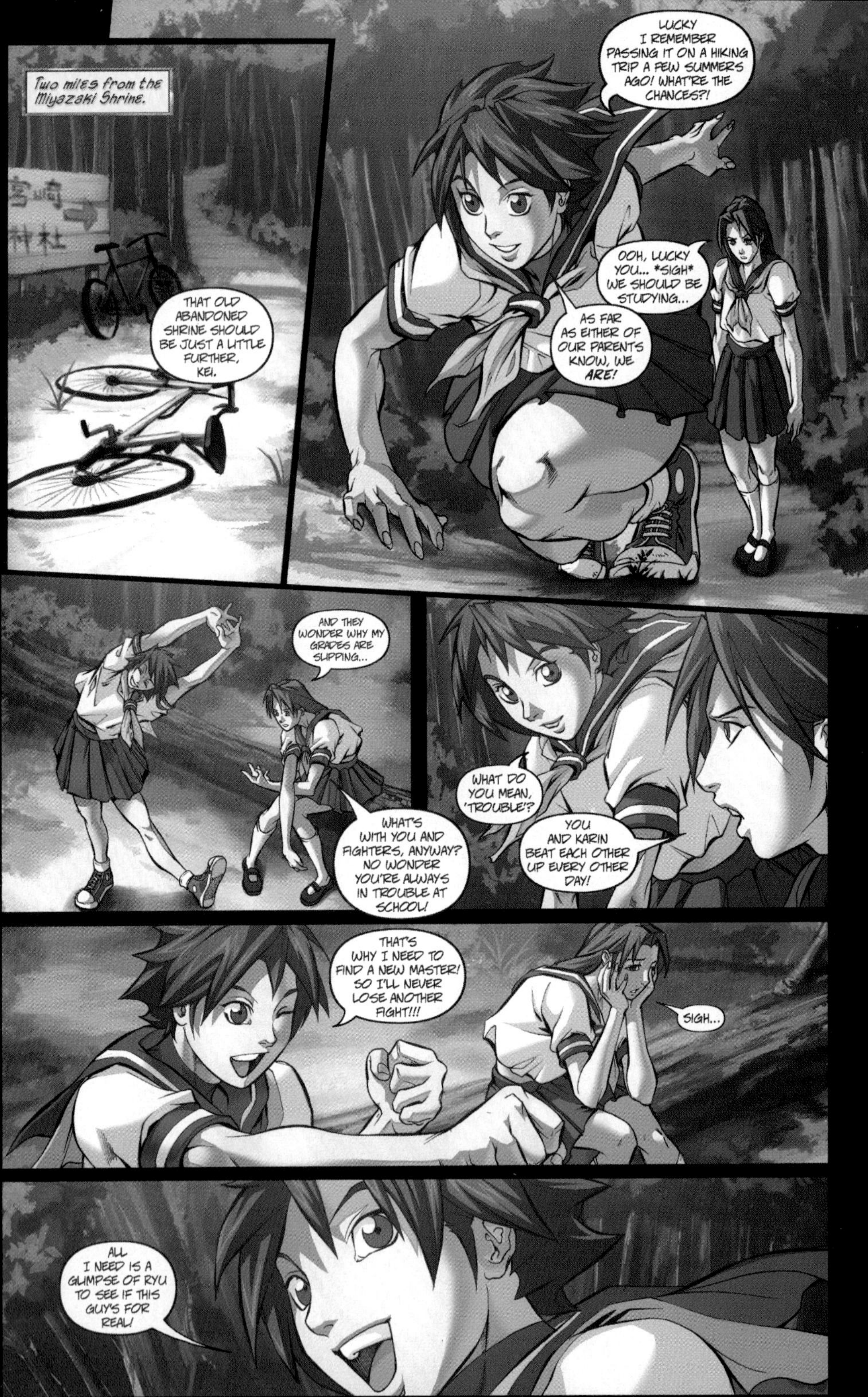
Two miles from the Miyazaki Shrine.
宮崎神社
THAT OLD ABANDONED SHRINE SHOULD BE JUST A LITTLE FURTHER, KEI.
LUCKY I REMEMBER PASSING IT ON A HIKING TRIP A FEW SUMMERS AGO! WHAT'RE THE CHANCES?!
OOH, LUCKY YOU... *SIGH* WE SHOULD BE STUDYING...
AS FAR AS EITHER OF OUR PARENTS KNOW, WE ARE!
AND THEY WONDER WHY MY GRADES ARE SLIPPING...
WHAT'S WITH YOU AND FIGHTERS, ANYWAY? NO WONDER YOU'RE ALWAYS IN TROUBLE AT SCHOOL!
WHAT DO YOU MEAN, 'TROUBLE'?
YOU AND KARIN BEAT EACH OTHER UP EVERY OTHER DAY!
THAT'S WHY I NEED TO FIND A NEW MASTER! SO I'LL NEVER LOSE ANOTHER FIGHT!!!
SIGH...
ALL I NEED IS A GLIMPSE OF RYU TO SEE IF THIS GUY'S FOR REAL!

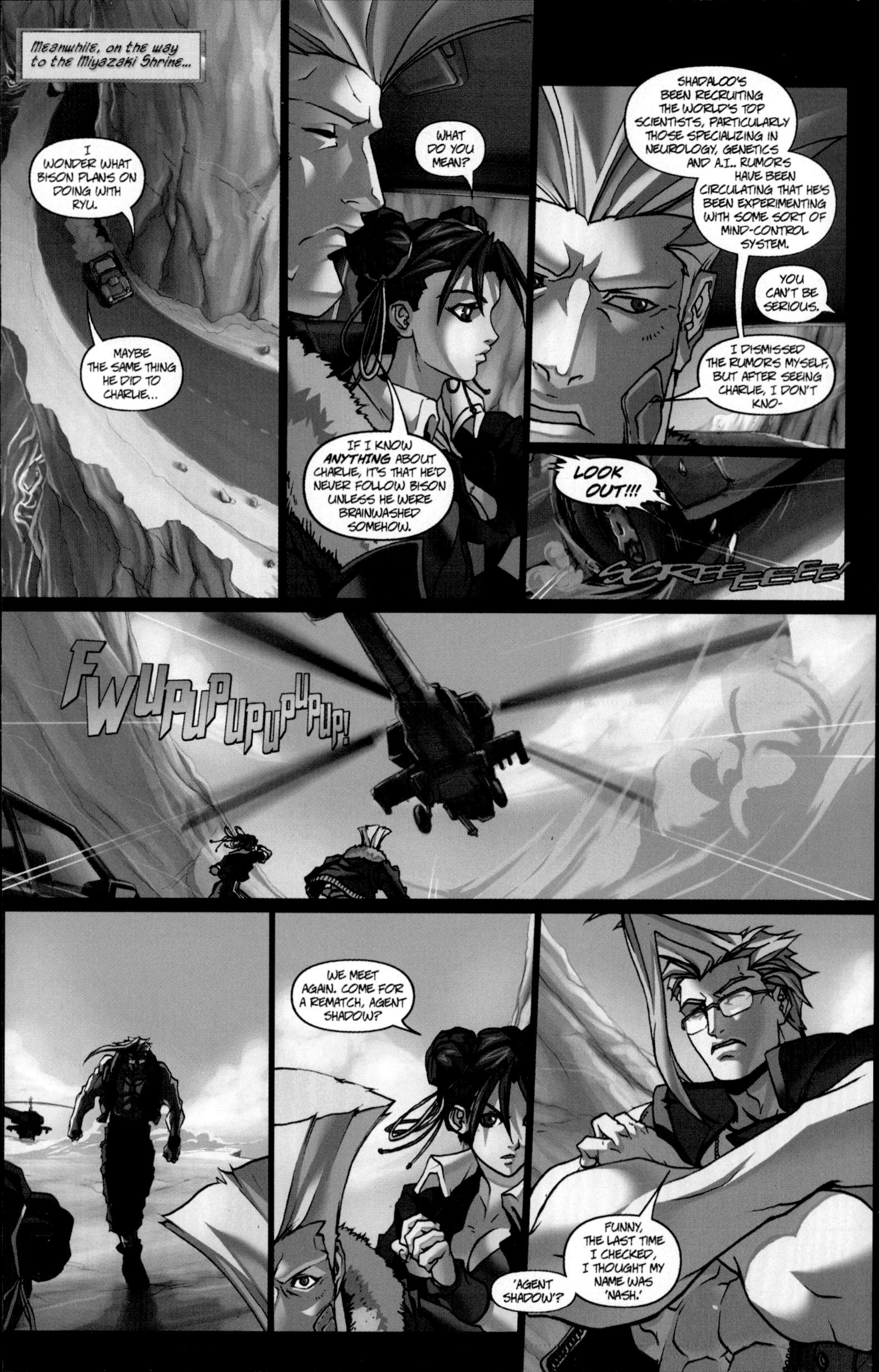
Meanwhile, on the way to the Miyazaki Shrine...
I WONDER WHAT BISON PLANS ON DOING WITH RYU.
MAYBE THE SAME THING HE DID TO CHARLIE...
WHAT DO YOU MEAN?
IF I KNOW ANYTHING ABOUT CHARLIE, IT'S THAT HE'D NEVER FOLLOW BISON UNLESS HE WERE BRAINWASHED SOMEHOW.
SHADALOO'S BEEN RECRUITING THE WORLD'S TOP SCIENTISTS, PARTICULARLY THOSE SPECIALIZING IN NEUROLOGY, GENETICS AND A.I.. RUMORS HAVE BEEN CIRCULATING THAT HE'S BEEN EXPERIMENTING WITH SOME SORT OF MIND-CONTROL SYSTEM.
YOU CAN'T BE SERIOUS.
I DISMISSED THE RUMORS MYSELF, BUT AFTER SEEING CHARLIE, I DON'T KNO-
LOOK OUT!!!
SCREEEEEEE!
FWUPUPUPUPUPUP!
WE MEET AGAIN. COME FOR A REMATCH, AGENT SHADOW?
'AGENT SHADOW'?
FUNNY, THE LAST TIME I CHECKED, I THOUGHT MY NAME WAS 'NASH.'

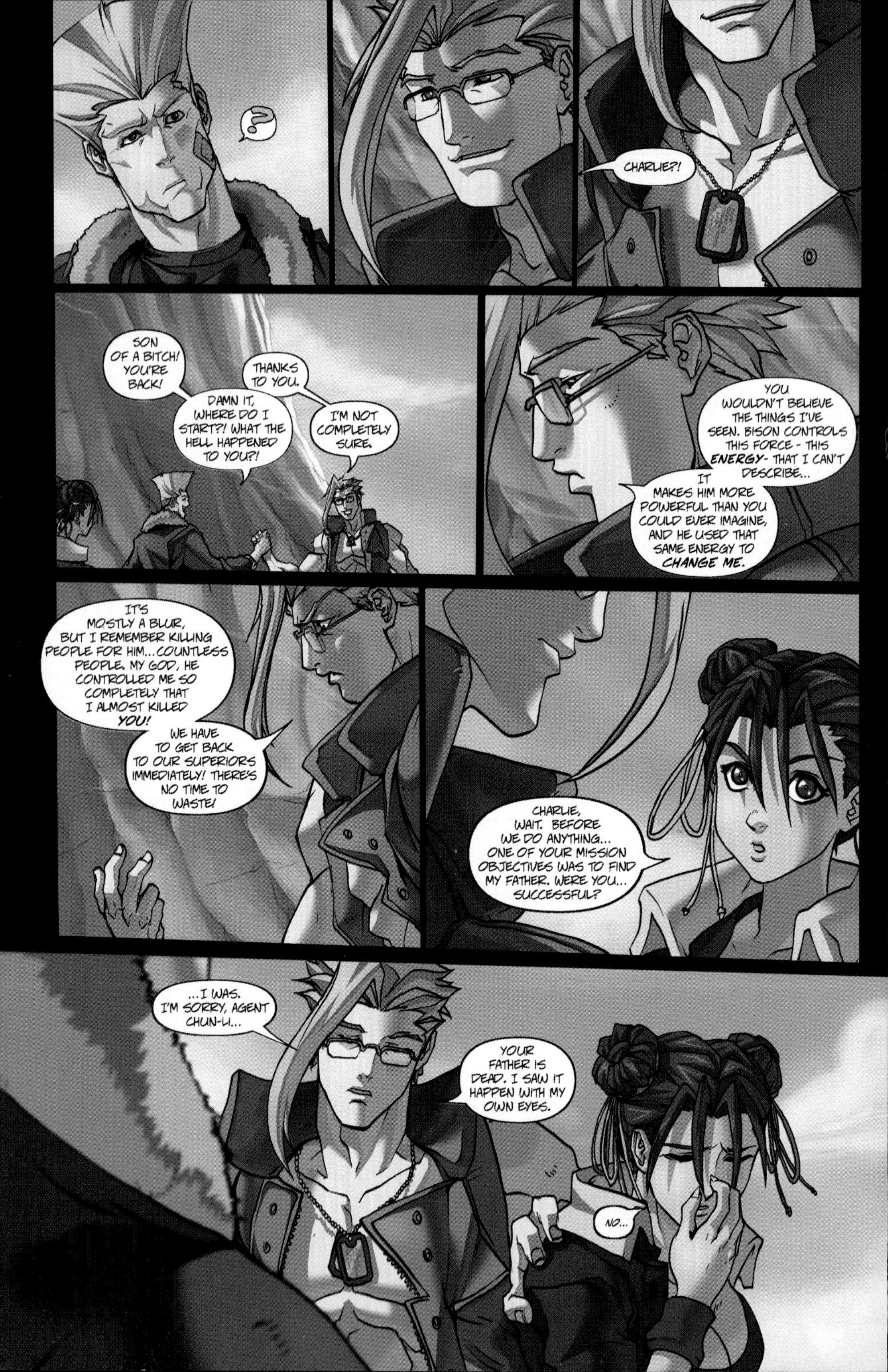
?
CHARLIE?!
SON OF A BITCH! YOU'RE BACK!
DAMN IT, WHERE DO I START?! WHAT THE HELL HAPPENED TO YOU?!
THANKS TO YOU.
I'M NOT COMPLETELY SURE.
YOU WOULDN'T BELIEVE THE THINGS I'VE SEEN. BISON CONTROLS THIS FORCE - THIS ENERGY- THAT I CAN'T DESCRIBE...
IT MAKES HIM MORE POWERFUL THAN YOU COULD EVER IMAGINE, AND HE USED THAT SAME ENERGY TO CHANGE ME.
IT'S MOSTLY A BLUR, BUT I REMEMBER KILLING PEOPLE FOR HIM...COUNTLESS PEOPLE. MY GOD, HE CONTROLLED ME SO COMPLETELY THAT I ALMOST KILLED YOU!
WE HAVE TO GET BACK TO OUR SUPERIORS IMMEDIATELY! THERE'S NO TIME TO WASTE!
CHARLIE, WAIT. BEFORE WE DO ANYTHING... ONE OF YOUR MISSION OBJECTIVES WAS TO FIND MY FATHER. WERE YOU... SUCCESSFUL?
...I WAS. I'M SORRY, AGENT CHUN-LI...
YOUR FATHER IS DEAD. I SAW IT HAPPEN WITH MY OWN EYES.
NO...

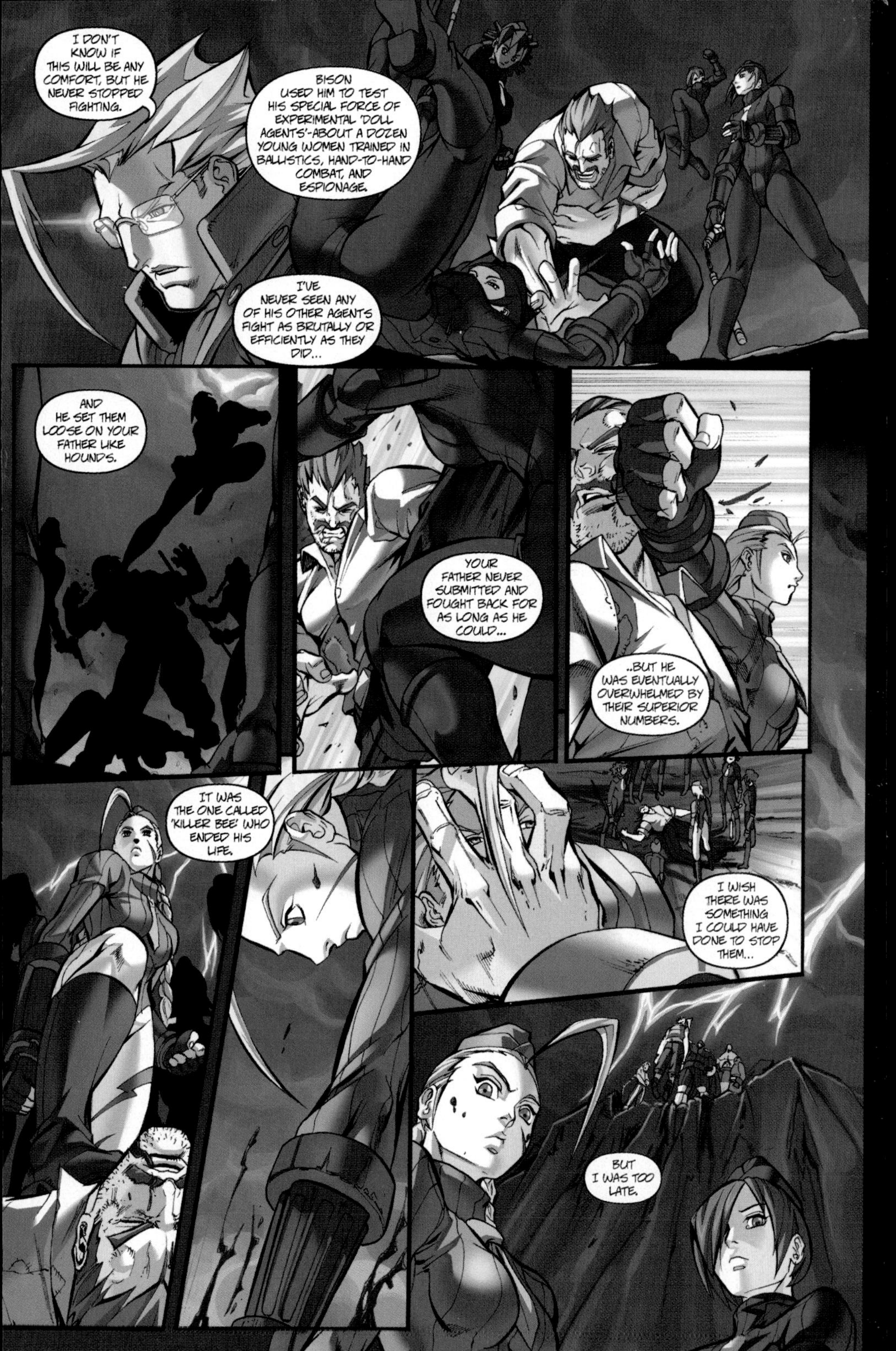
I DON'T KNOW IF THIS WILL BE ANY COMFORT, BUT HE NEVER STOPPED FIGHTING.
BISON USED HIM TO TEST HIS SPECIAL FORCE OF EXPERIMENTAL 'DOLL AGENTS'-ABOUT A DOZEN YOUNG WOMEN TRAINED IN BALLISTICS, HAND-TO-HAND COMBAT, AND ESPIONAGE.
I'VE NEVER SEEN ANY OF HIS OTHER AGENTS FIGHT AS BRUTALLY OR EFFICIENTLY AS THEY DID...
AND HE SET THEM LOOSE ON YOUR FATHER LIKE HOUNDS.
YOUR FATHER NEVER SUBMITTED AND FOUGHT BACK FOR AS LONG AS HE COULD...
..BUT HE WAS EVENTUALLY OVERWHELMED BY THEIR SUPERIOR NUMBERS.
IT WAS THE ONE CALLED 'KILLER BEE' WHO ENDED HIS LIFE.
I WISH THERE WAS SOMETHING I COULD HAVE DONE TO STOP THEM...
BUT I WAS TOO LATE.

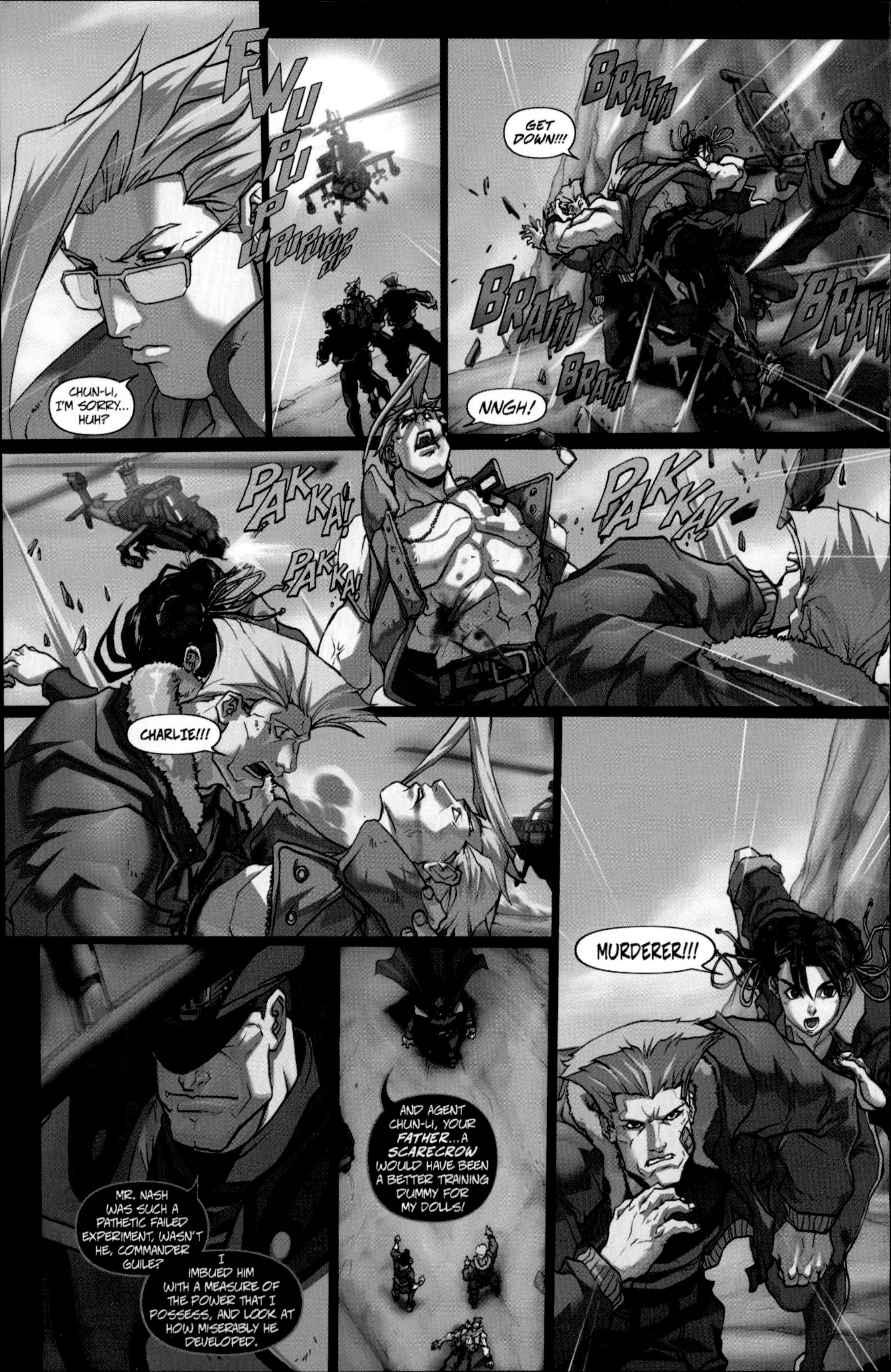

FWUPUPUPUPURURURURURRR
CHUN-LI, I'M SORRY... HUH?
GET DOWN!!!
BRATTA
BRATTA
BRATTA
BRATTA
NNGH!
PAKKA!
PAKKA!
PAKKA!
CHARLIE!!!
MURDERER!!!
MR. NASH WAS SUCH A PATHETIC FAILED EXPERIMENT, WASN'T HE, COMMANDER GUILE?
I IMBUED HIM WITH A MEASURE OF THE POWER THAT I POSSESS, AND LOOK AT HOW MISERABLY HE DEVELOPED.
AND AGENT CHUN-LI, YOUR FATHER...A SCARECROW WOULD HAVE BEEN A BETTER TRAINING DUMMY FOR MY DOLLS!

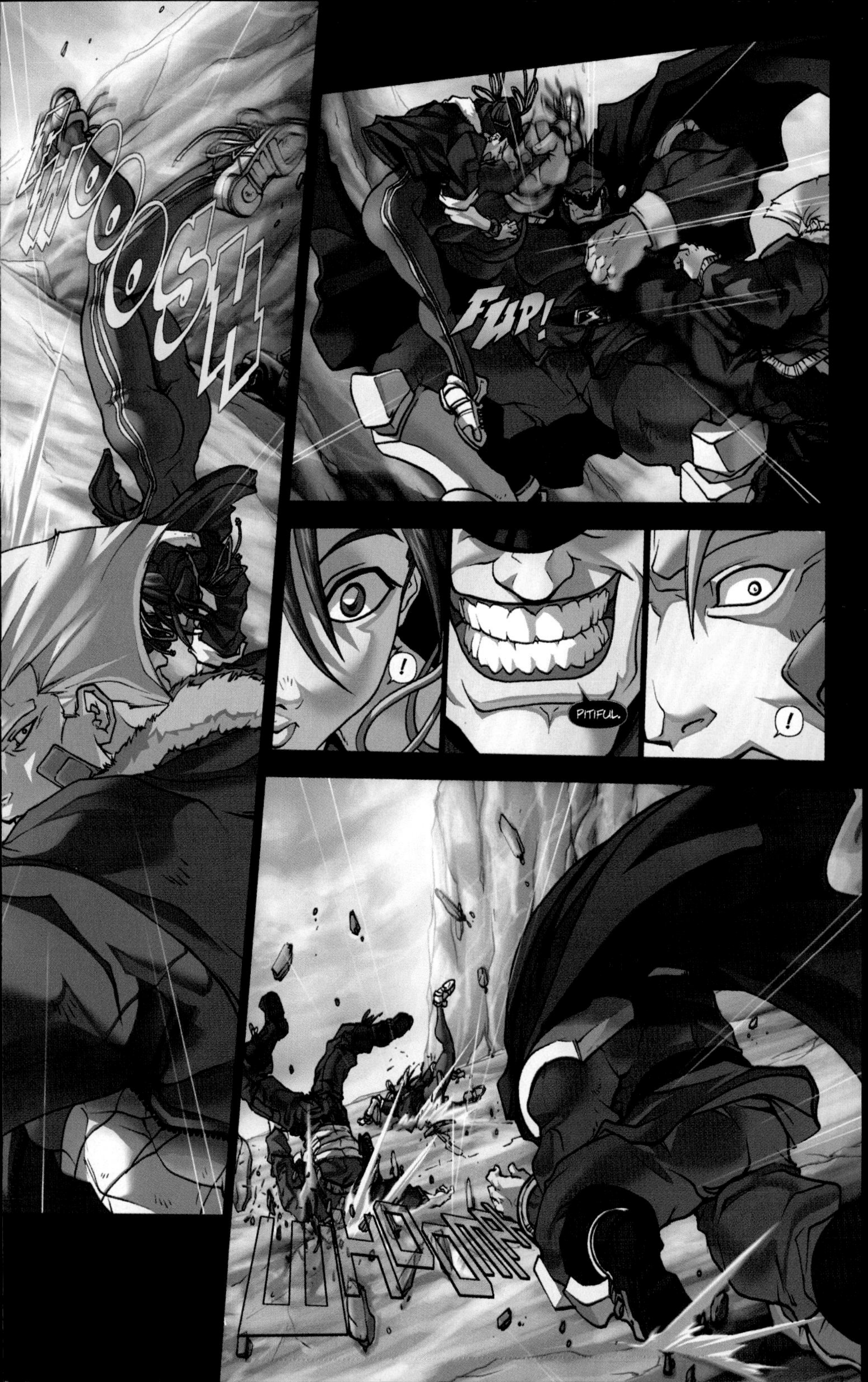
WHOOSH
FWP!
!
PITIFUL.
!

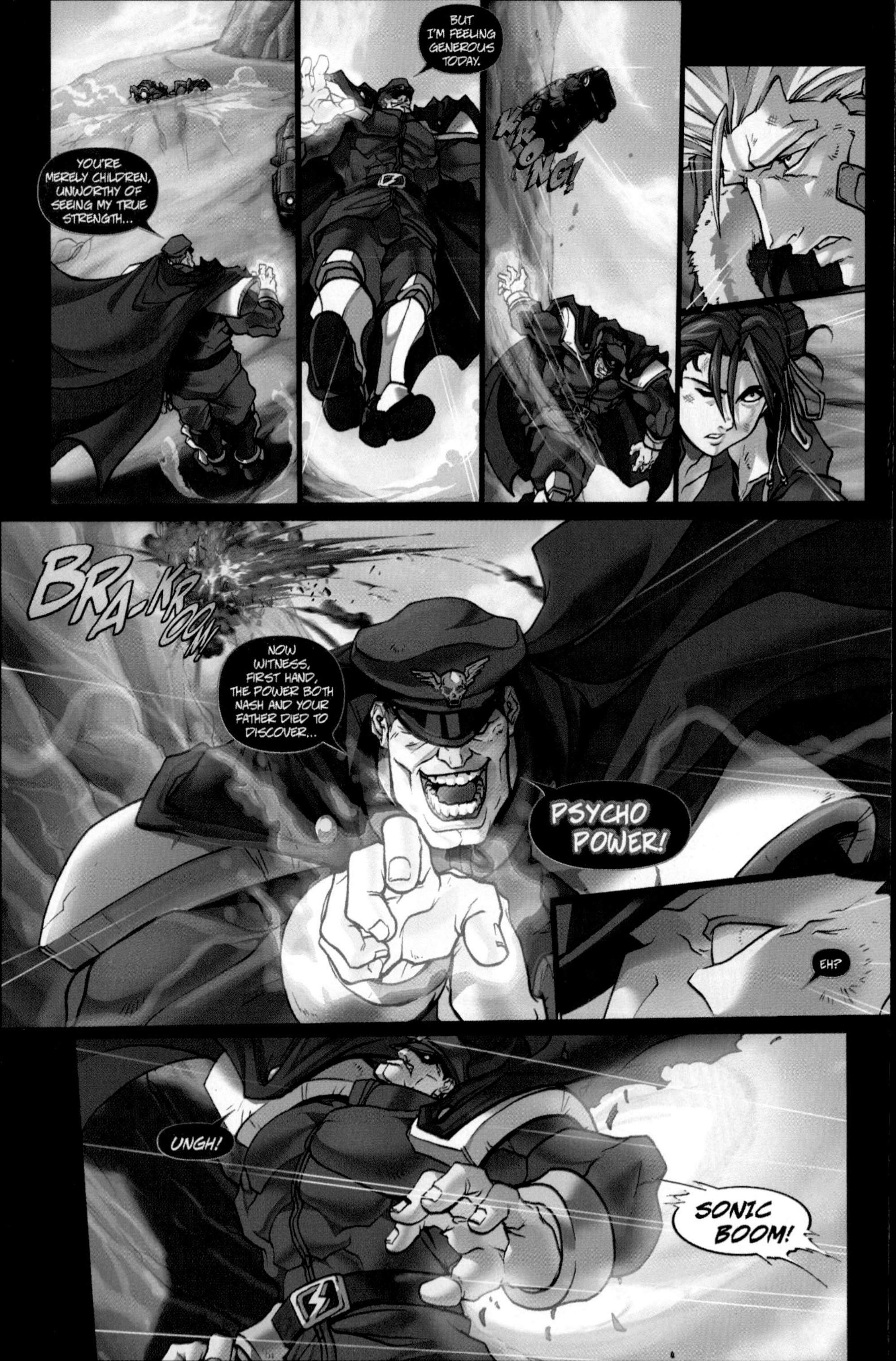
YOU'RE MERELY CHILDREN, UNWORTHY OF SEEING MY TRUE STRENGTH...
BUT I'M FEELING GENEROUS TODAY.
KRONG!
BRA-KROOM
NOW WITNESS, FIRST HAND, THE POWER BOTH NASH AND YOUR FATHER DIED TO DISCOVER...
PSYCHO POWER!
EH?
UNGH!
SONIC BOOM!

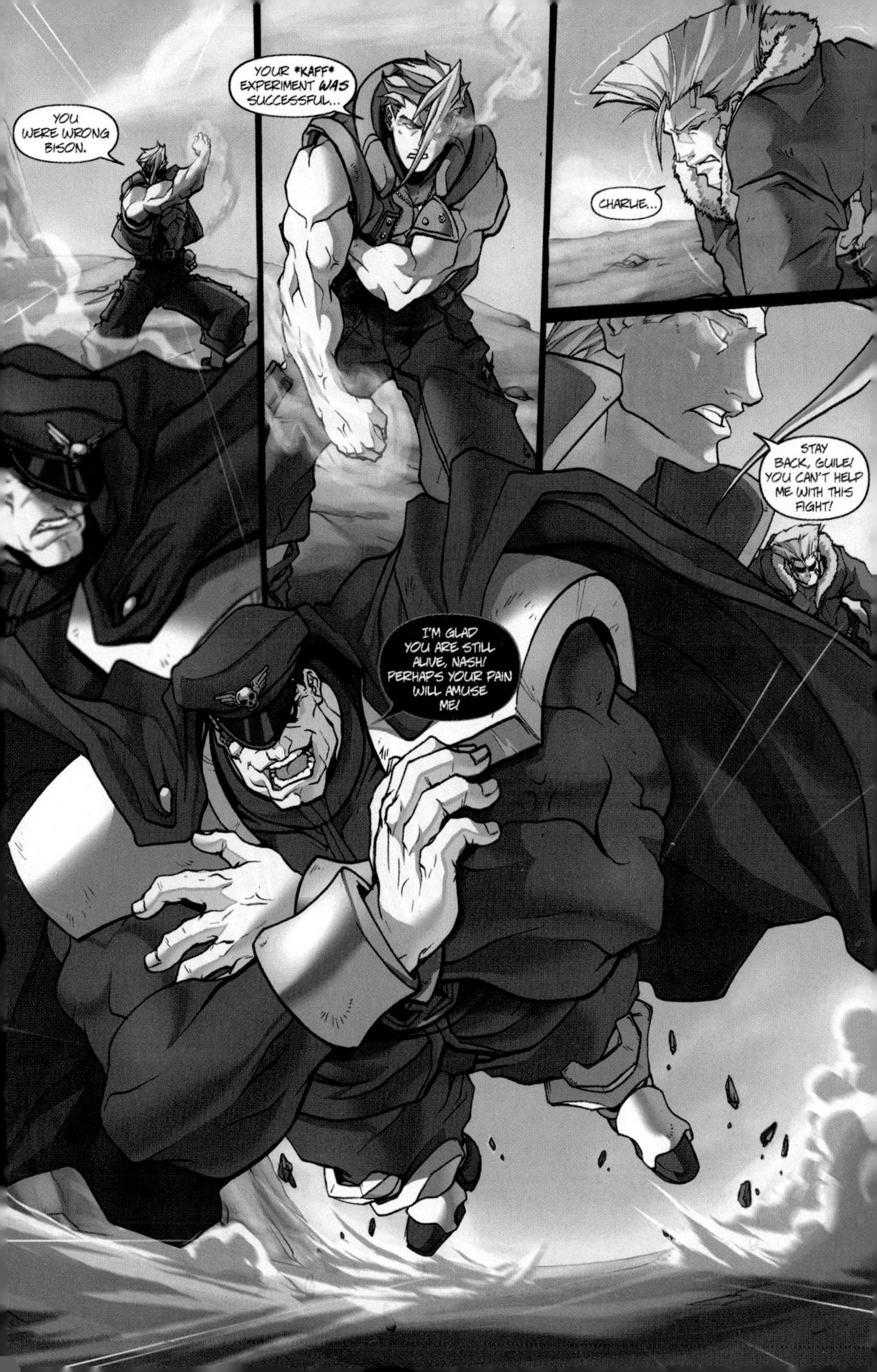
YOU WERE WRONG BISON.
YOUR *KAFF* EXPERIMENT WAS SUCCESSFUL...
CHARLIE...
STAY BACK, GUILE! YOU CAN'T HELP ME WITH THIS FIGHT!
I'M GLAD YOU ARE STILL ALIVE, NASH! PERHAPS YOUR PAIN WILL AMUSE ME!

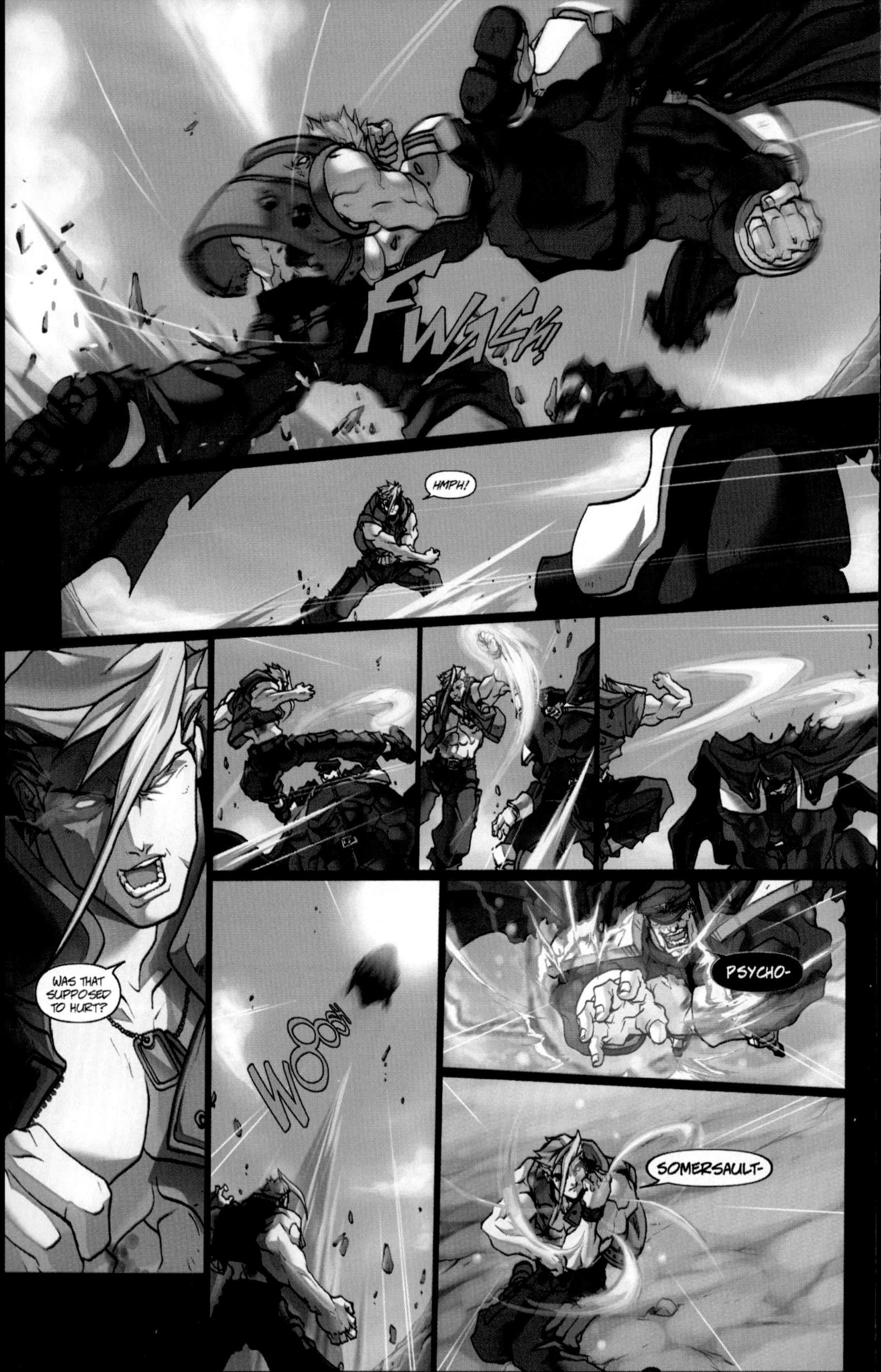
FWACK!
HMPH!
WAS THAT SUPPOSED TO HURT?
WOOOSH
PSYCHO-
SOMERSAULT-

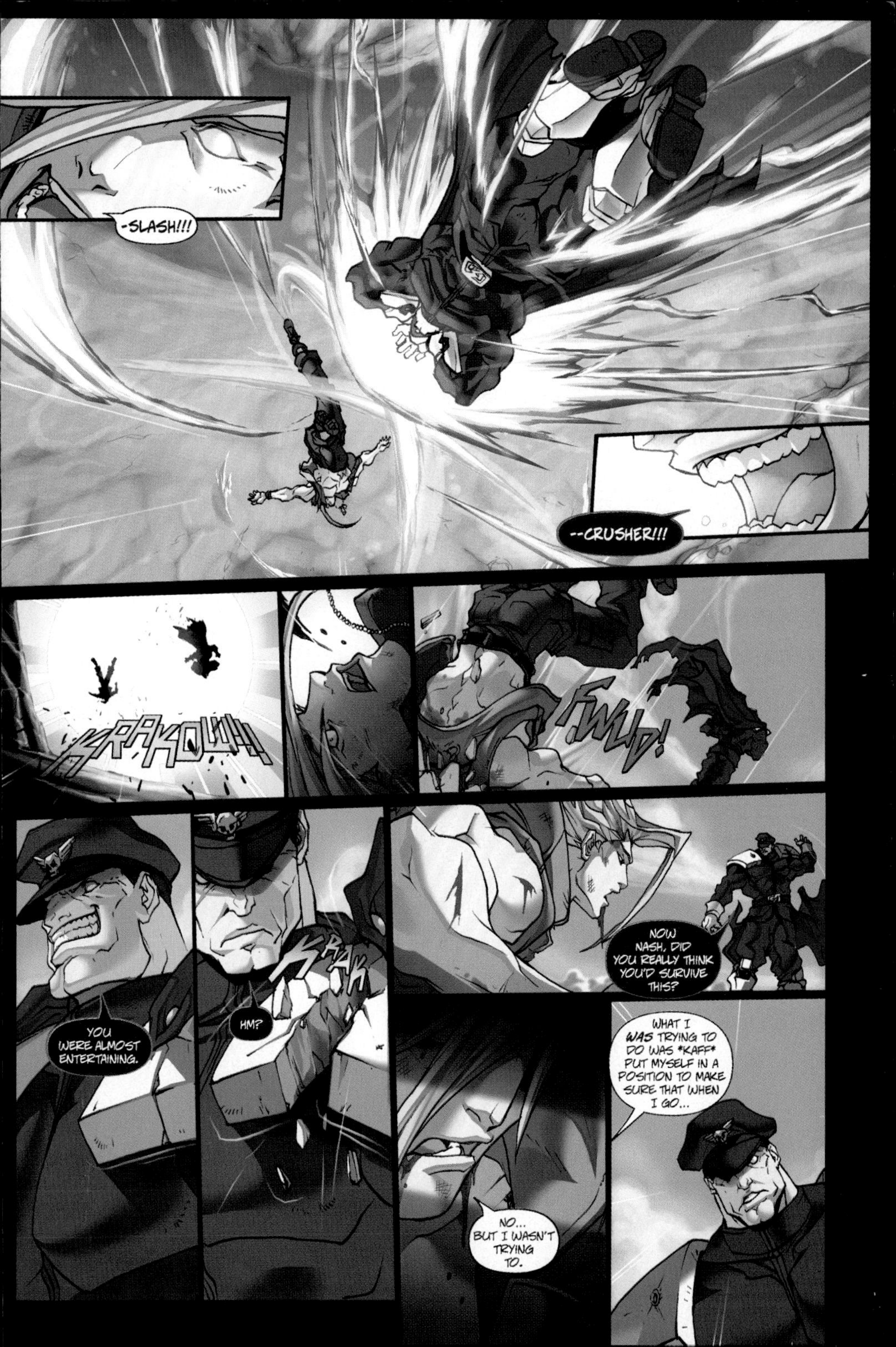
-SLASH!!!
--CRUSHER!!!
KRAKOW!!!
FWUD!
YOU WERE ALMOST ENTERTAINING.
HM?
KRAK
NOW NASH, DID YOU REALLY THINK YOU'D SURVIVE THIS?
NO... BUT I WASN'T TRYING TO.
WHAT I WAS TRYING TO DO WAS *KAFF* PUT MYSELF IN A POSITION TO MAKE SURE THAT WHEN I GO...

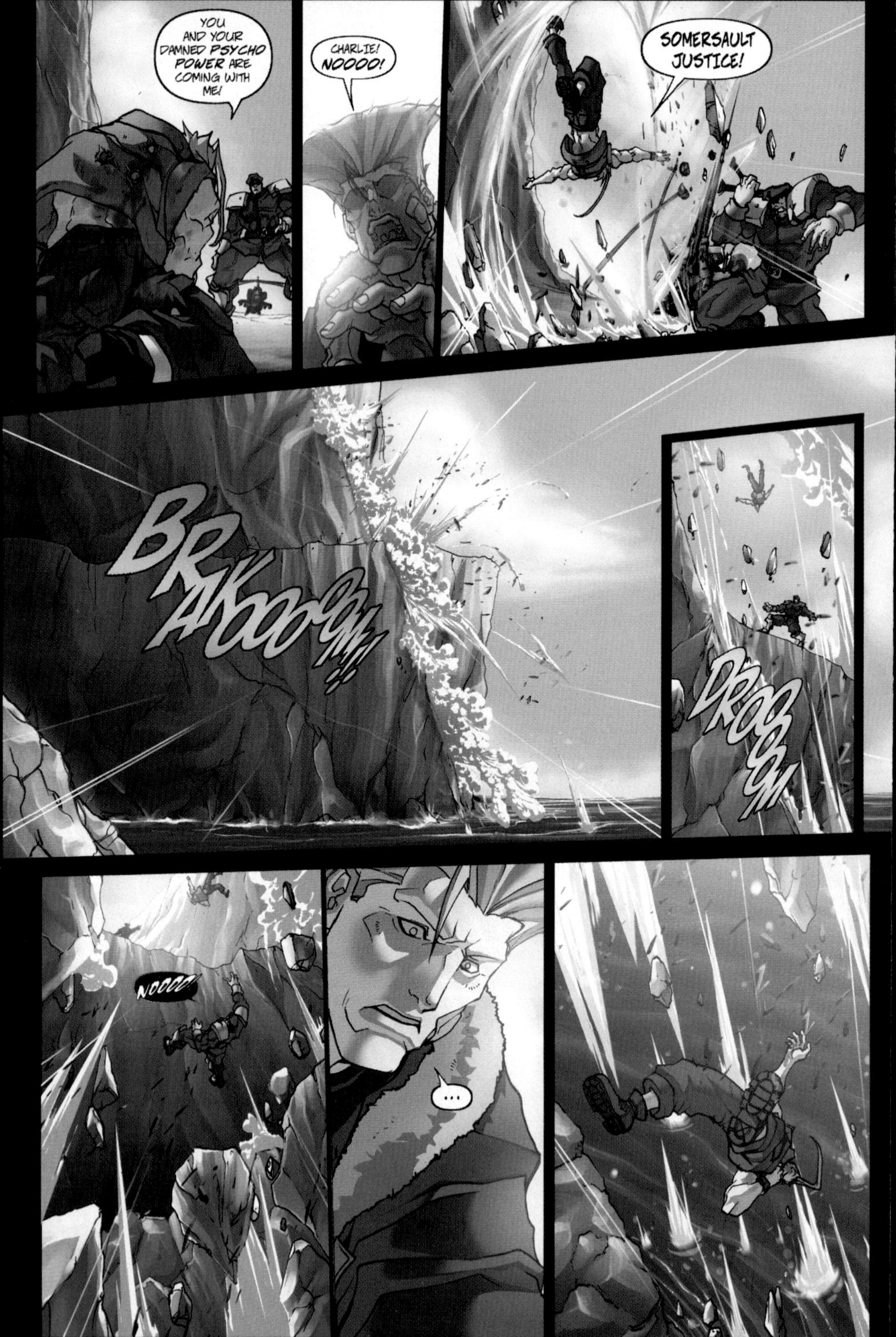
YOU AND YOUR DAMNED PSYCHO POWER ARE COMING WITH ME!
CHARLIE! NOOOO!
SOMERSAULT JUSTICE!
BRAKOOOOM!!
DROOOOM
NOOOO!
...

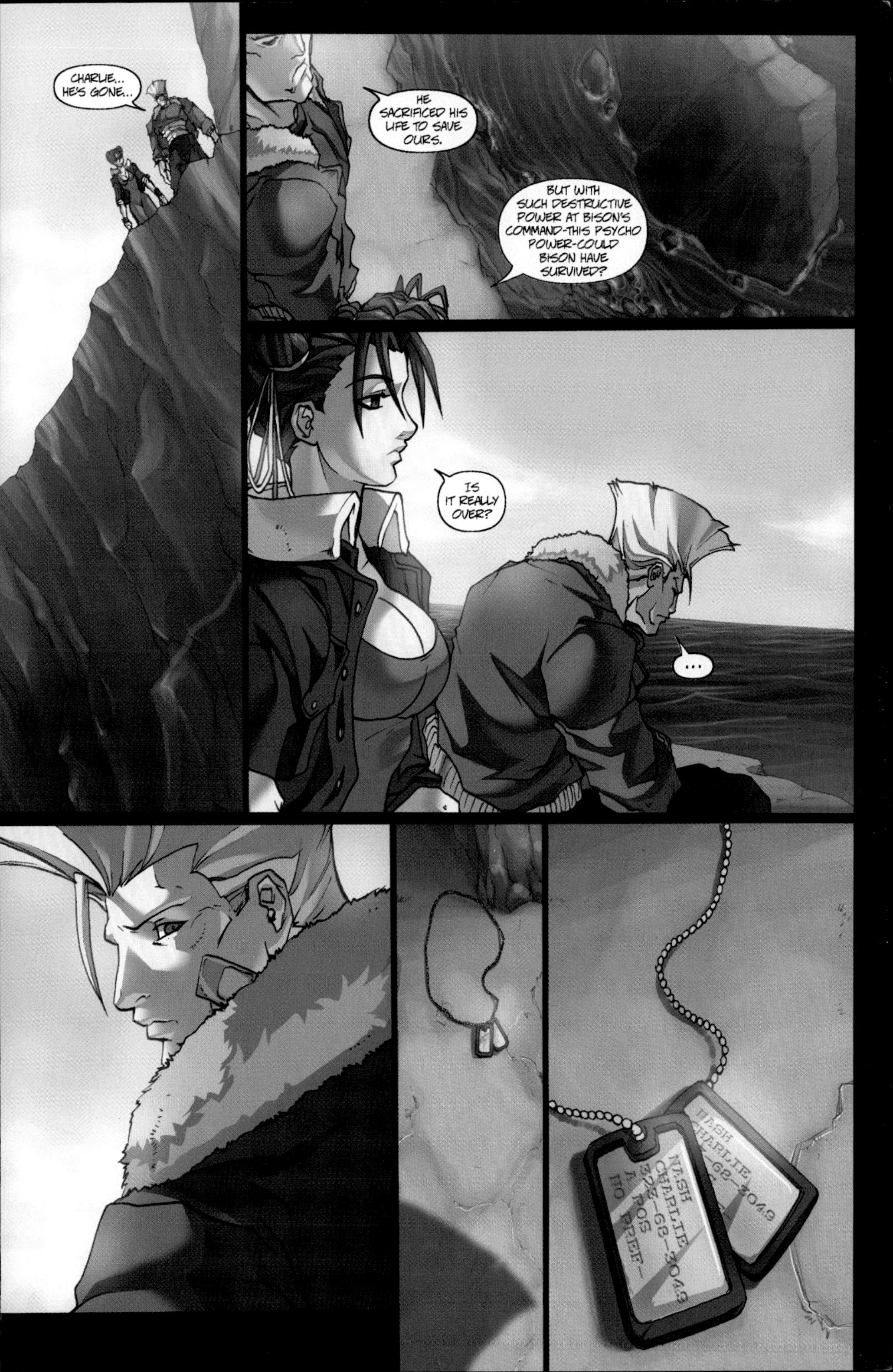
CHARLIE... HE'S GONE...
HE SACRIFICED HIS LIFE TO SAVE OURS.
BUT WITH SUCH DESTRUCTIVE POWER AT BISON'S COMMAND-THIS PSYCHO POWER-COULD BISON HAVE SURVIVED?
IS IT REALLY OVER?
...
NASH
CHARLIE
322-68-3049
A POS
NO PREF-

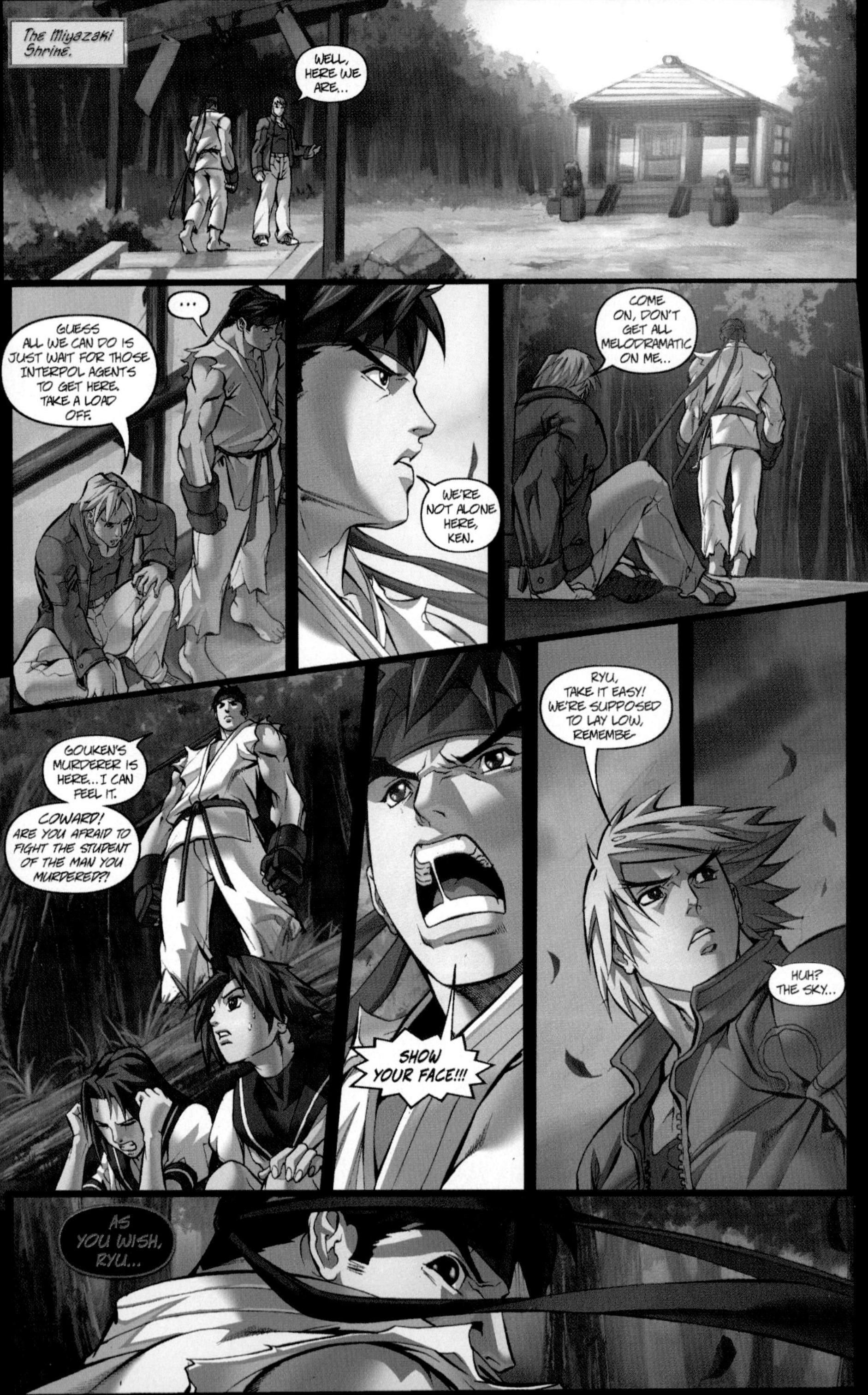
The Miyazaki Shrine.
WELL, HERE WE ARE...
...
GUESS ALL WE CAN DO IS JUST WAIT FOR THOSE INTERPOL AGENTS TO GET HERE. TAKE A LOAD OFF.
WE'RE NOT ALONE HERE, KEN.
COME ON, DON'T GET ALL MELODRAMATIC ON ME...
GOUKEN'S MURDERER IS HERE... I CAN FEEL IT.
COWARD! ARE YOU AFRAID TO FIGHT THE STUDENT OF THE MAN YOU MURDERED?!
SHOW YOUR FACE!!!
RYU, TAKE IT EASY! WE'RE SUPPOSED TO LAY LOW, REMEMBE-
HUH? THE SKY...
AS YOU WISH, RYU...

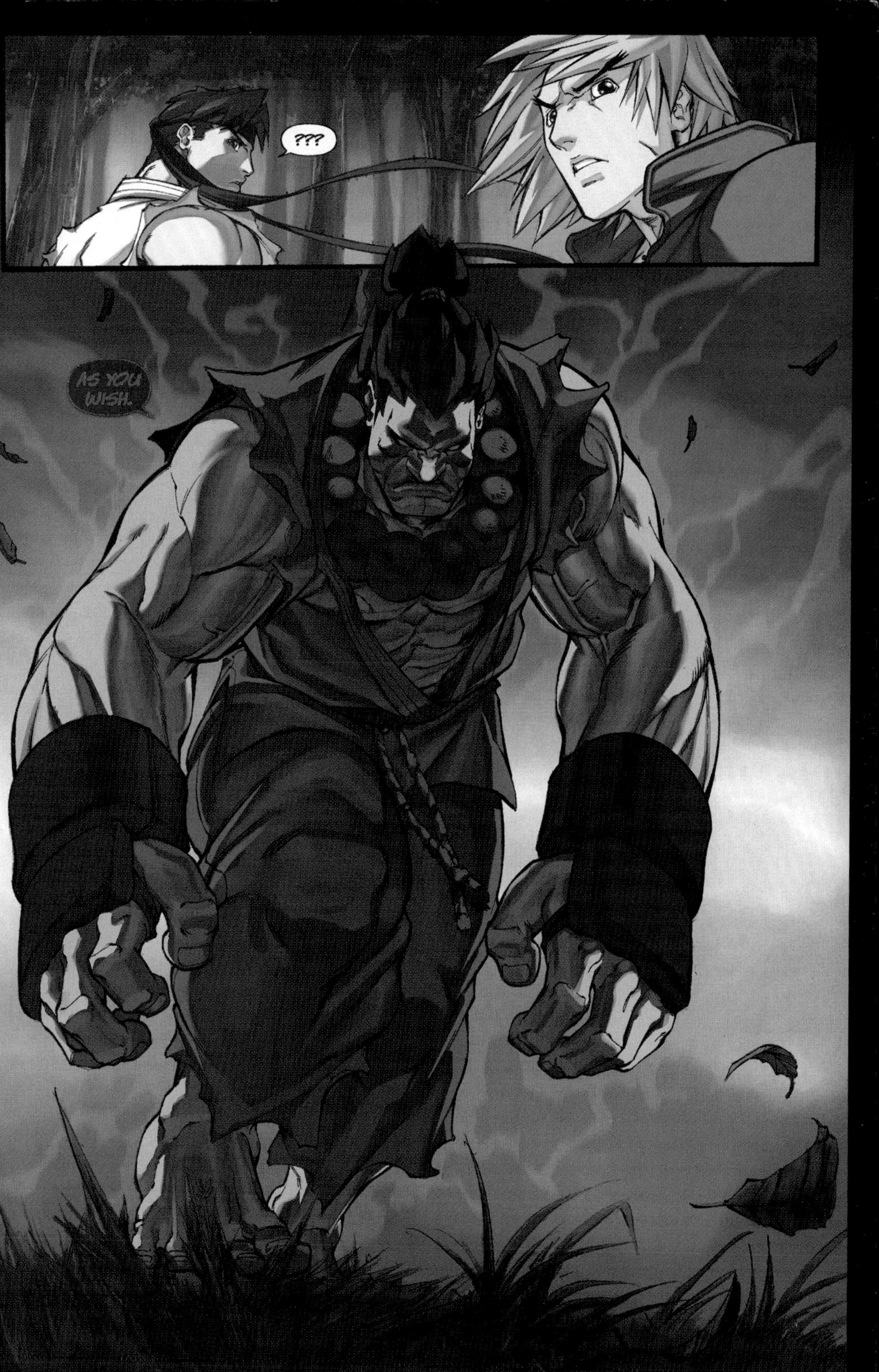
???
AS YOU WISH.

Cover Art by: Alvin Lee and Arnold Tsang

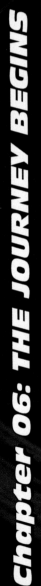

Chapter 06: THE JOURNEY BEGINS

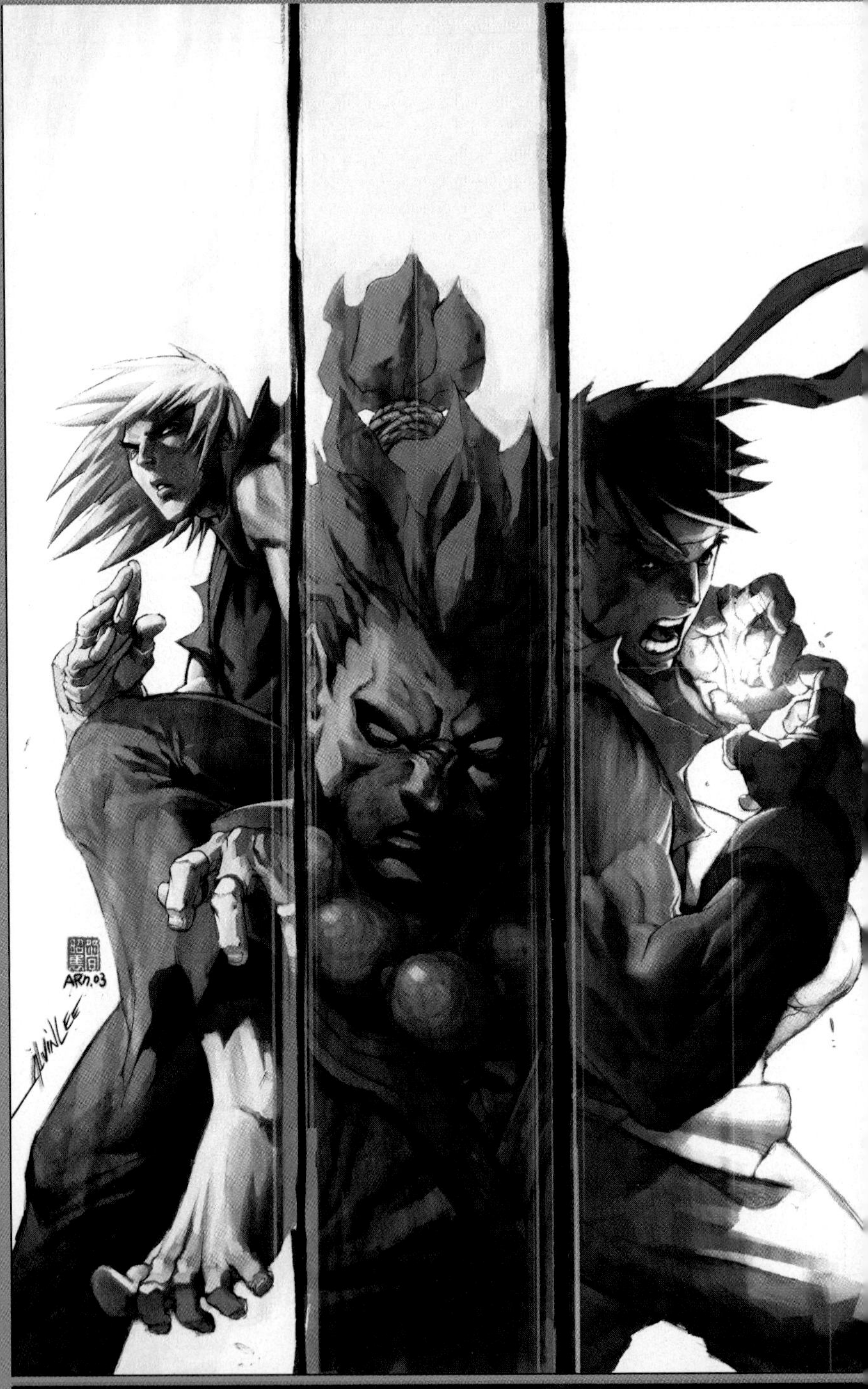

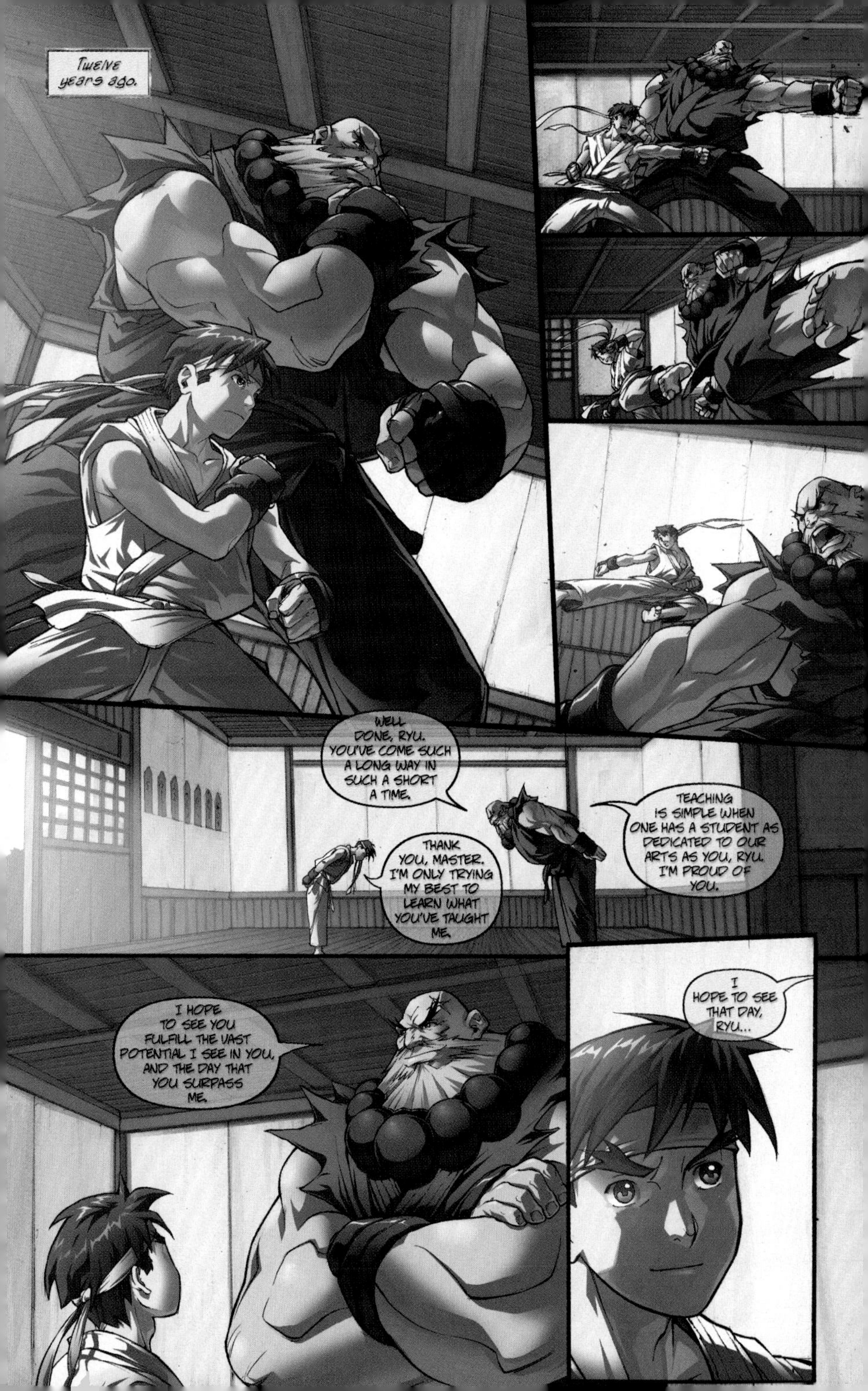
Twelve years ago.
WELL DONE, RYU. YOU'VE COME SUCH A LONG WAY IN SUCH A SHORT A TIME.
THANK YOU, MASTER. I'M ONLY TRYING MY BEST TO LEARN WHAT YOU'VE TAUGHT ME.
TEACHING IS SIMPLE WHEN ONE HAS A STUDENT AS DEDICATED TO OUR ARTS AS YOU, RYU. I'M PROUD OF YOU.
I HOPE TO SEE YOU FULFILL THE VAST POTENTIAL I SEE IN YOU, AND THE DAY THAT YOU SURPASS ME.
I HOPE TO SEE THAT DAY, RYU...

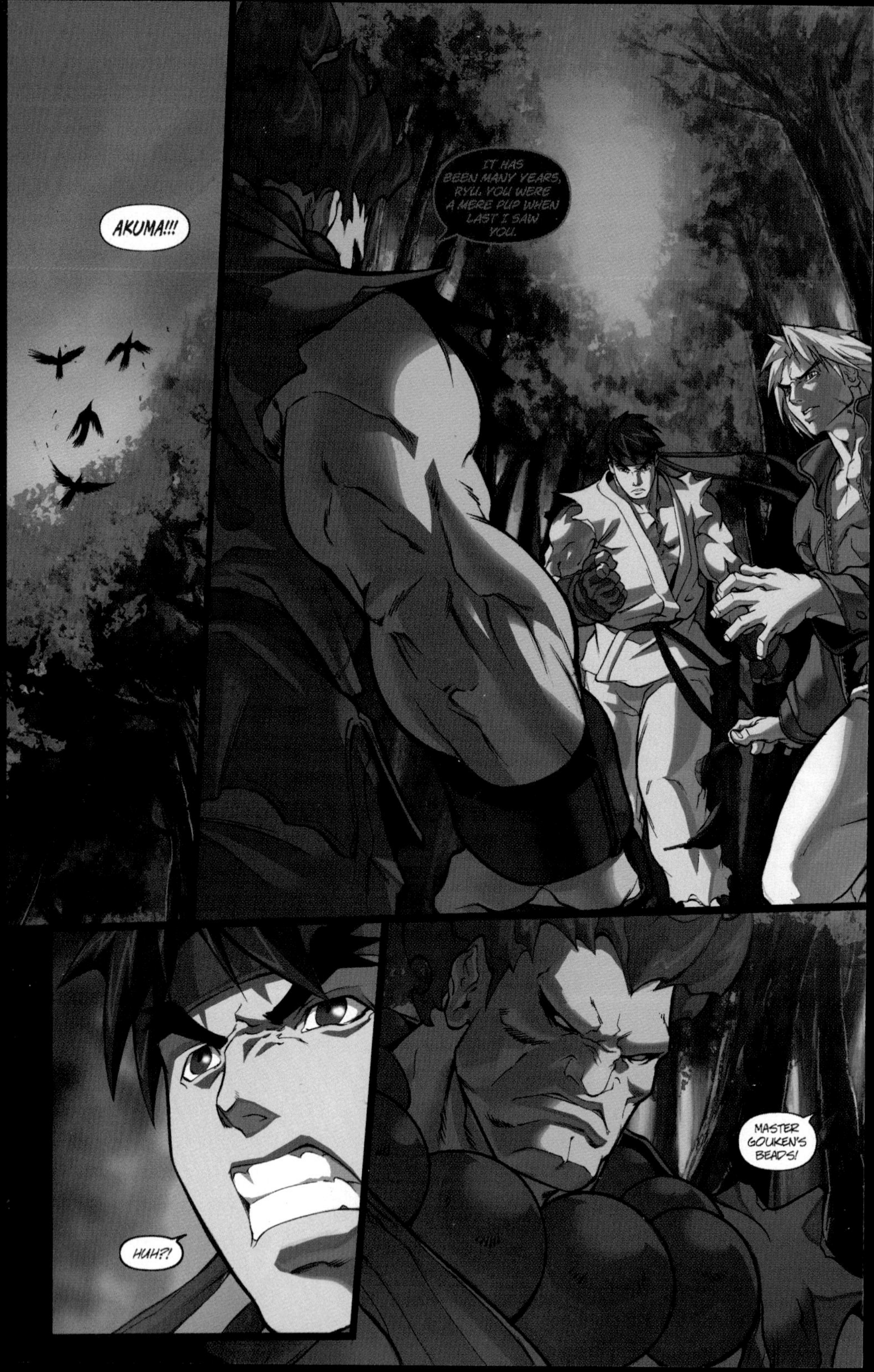
AKUMA!!!
IT HAS BEEN MANY YEARS, RYU. YOU WERE A MERE PUP WHEN LAST I SAW YOU.
HUH?!
MASTER GOUKEN'S BEADS!

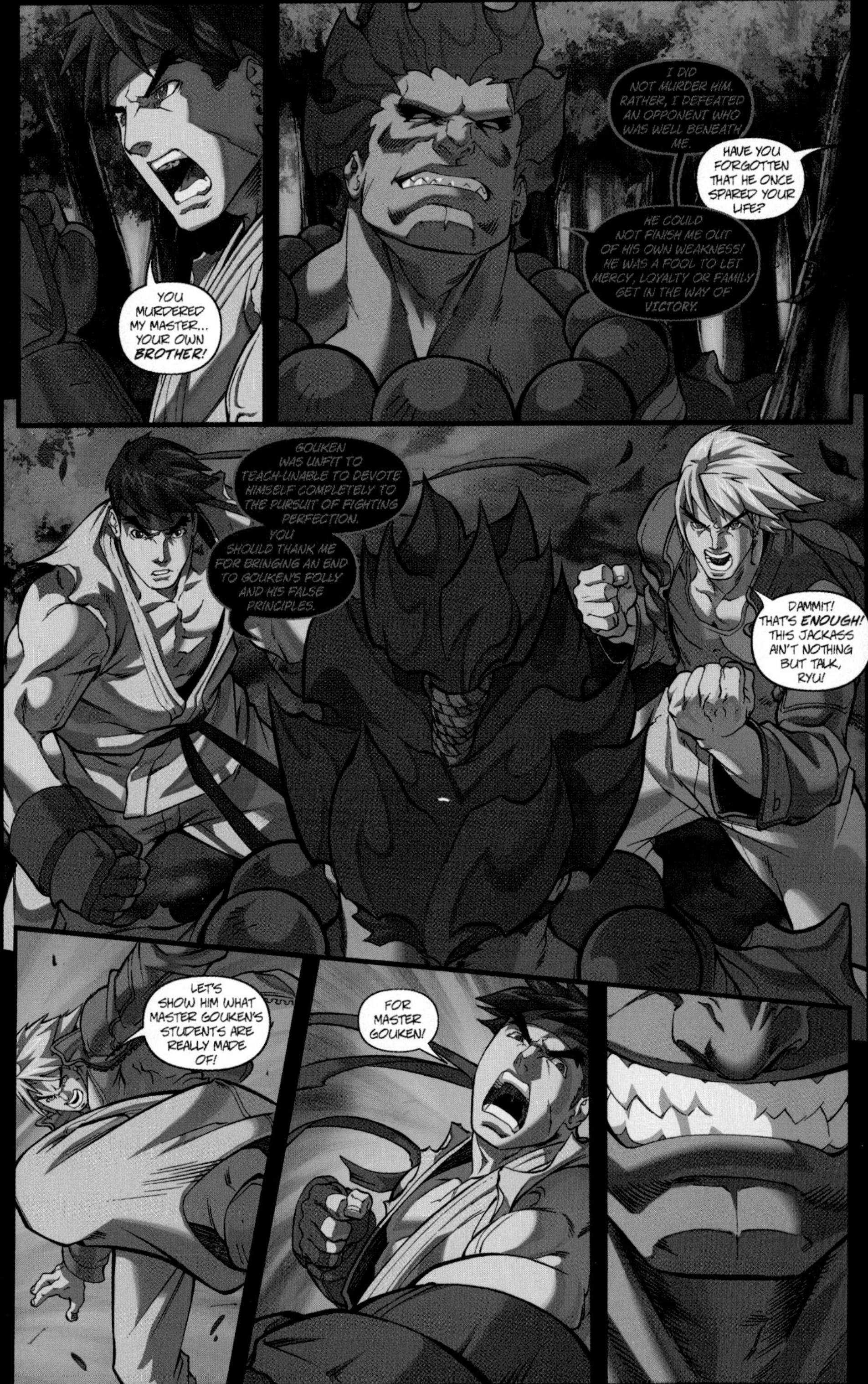
YOU MURDERED MY MASTER... YOUR OWN BROTHER!
I DID NOT MURDER HIM. RATHER, I DEFEATED AN OPPONENT WHO WAS WELL BENEATH ME.
HAVE YOU FORGOTTEN THAT HE ONCE SPARED YOUR LIFE?
HE COULD NOT FINISH ME OUT OF HIS OWN WEAKNESS! HE WAS A FOOL TO LET MERCY, LOYALTY OR FAMILY GET IN THE WAY OF VICTORY.
GOUKEN WAS UNFIT TO TEACH-UNABLE TO DEVOTE HIMSELF COMPLETELY TO THE PURSUIT OF FIGHTING PERFECTION.
YOU SHOULD THANK ME FOR BRINGING AN END TO GOUKEN'S FOLLY AND HIS FALSE PRINCIPLES.
DAMMIT! THAT'S ENOUGH! THIS JACKASS AIN'T NOTHING BUT TALK, RYU!
LET'S SHOW HIM WHAT MASTER GOUKEN'S STUDENTS ARE REALLY MADE OF!
FOR MASTER GOUKEN!

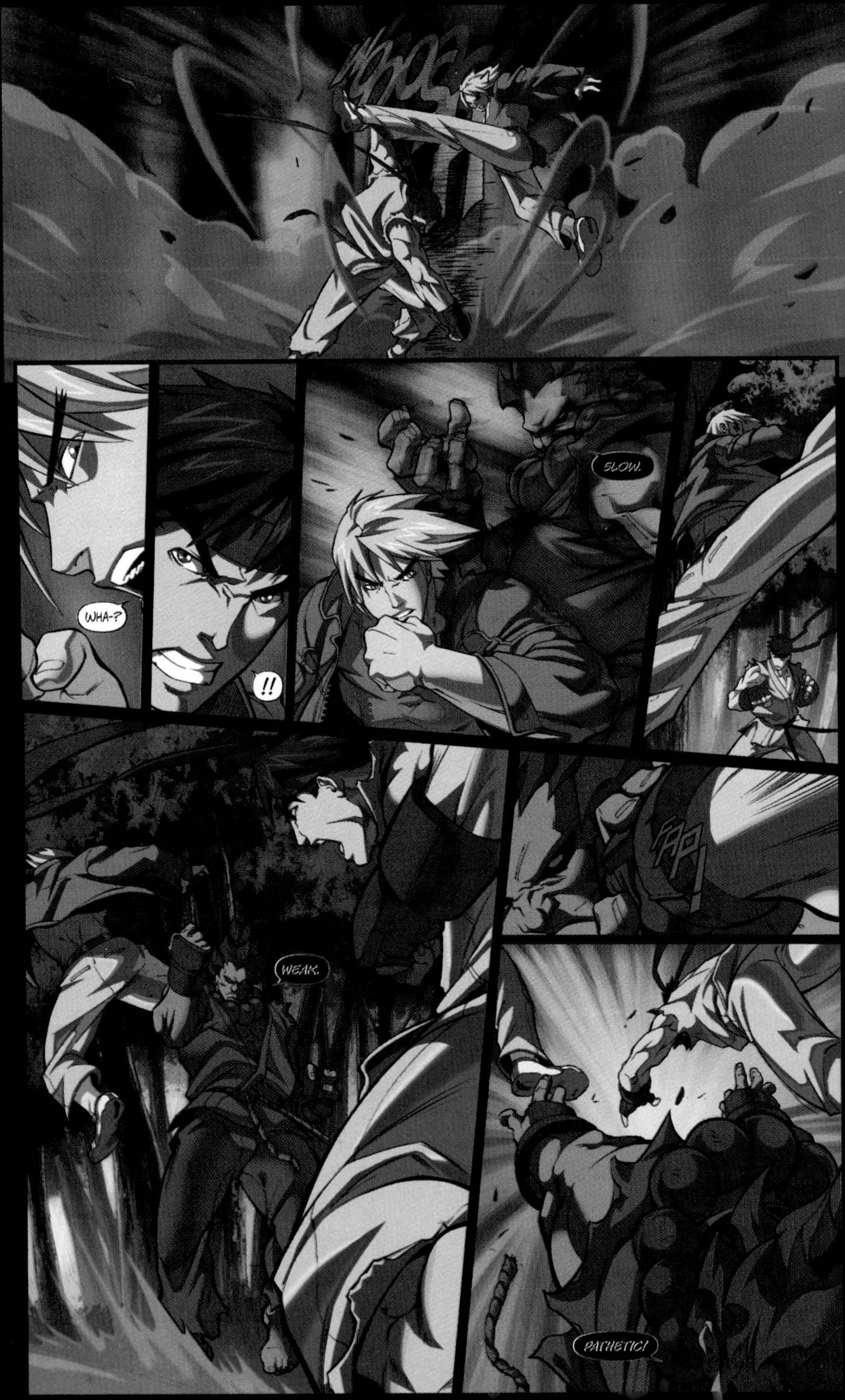
WHA-?
!!
SLOW.
FAP!
WEAK.
PATHETIC!

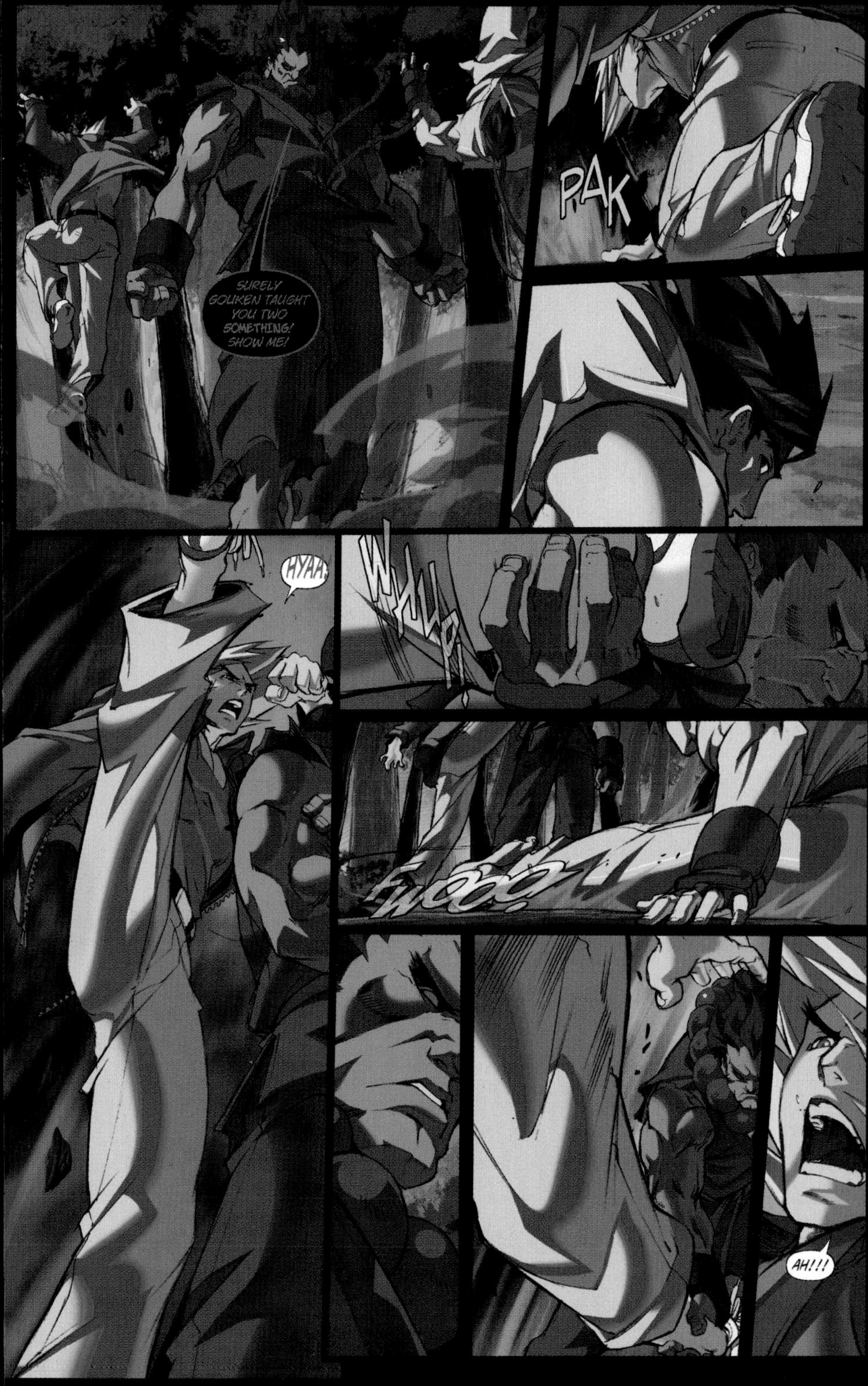
SURELY GOUKEN TAUGHT YOU TWO SOMETHING! SHOW ME!
PAK
HYAA!
WHUP!
FWOOO!
AH!!!

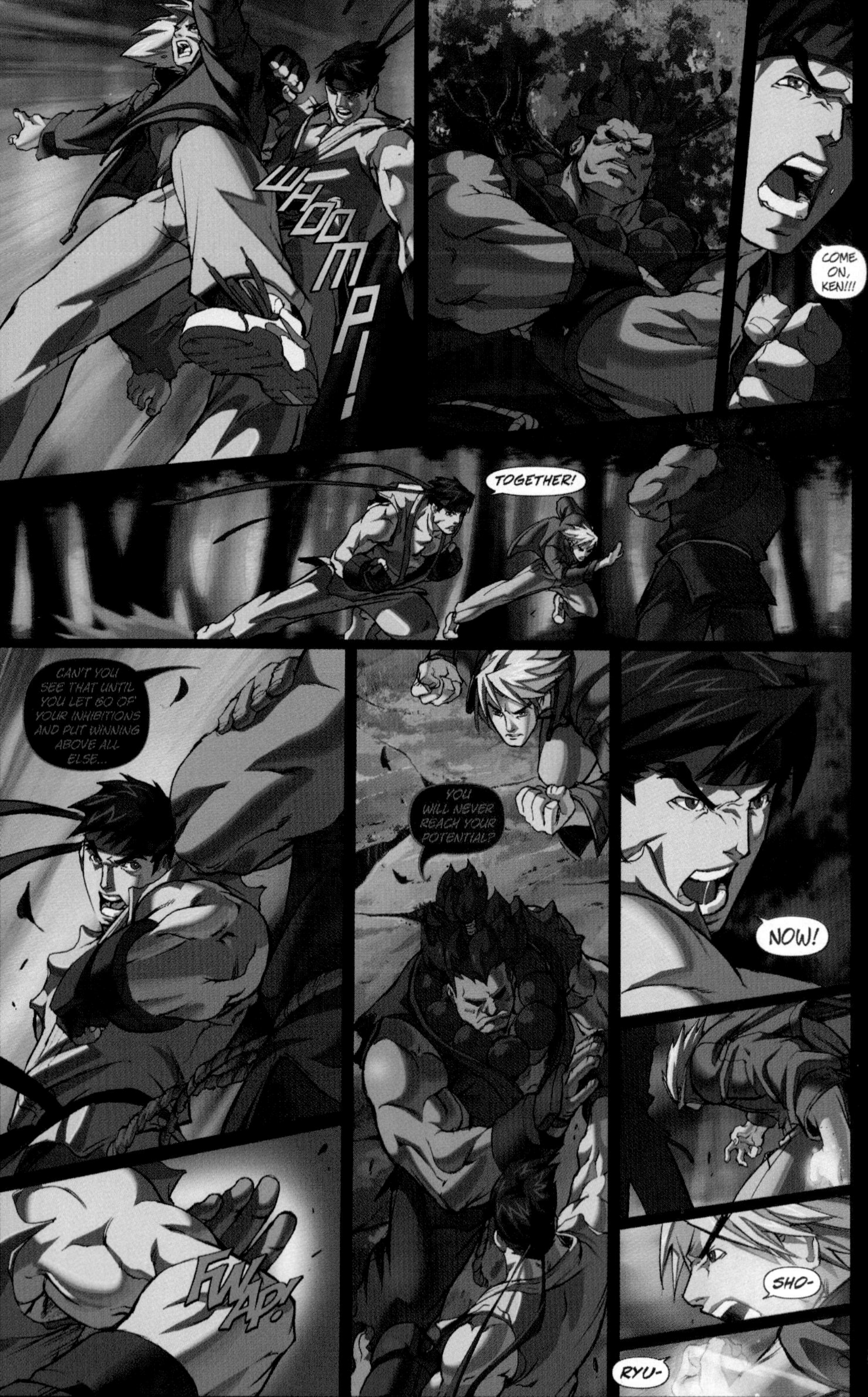
WHOOMP!!
COME ON, KEN!!!
TOGETHER!
CAN'T YOU SEE THAT UNTIL YOU LET GO OF YOUR INHIBITIONS AND PUT WINNING ABOVE ALL ELSE...
YOU WILL NEVER REACH YOUR POTENTIAL?
NOW!
FWAP!
SHO-
RYU-

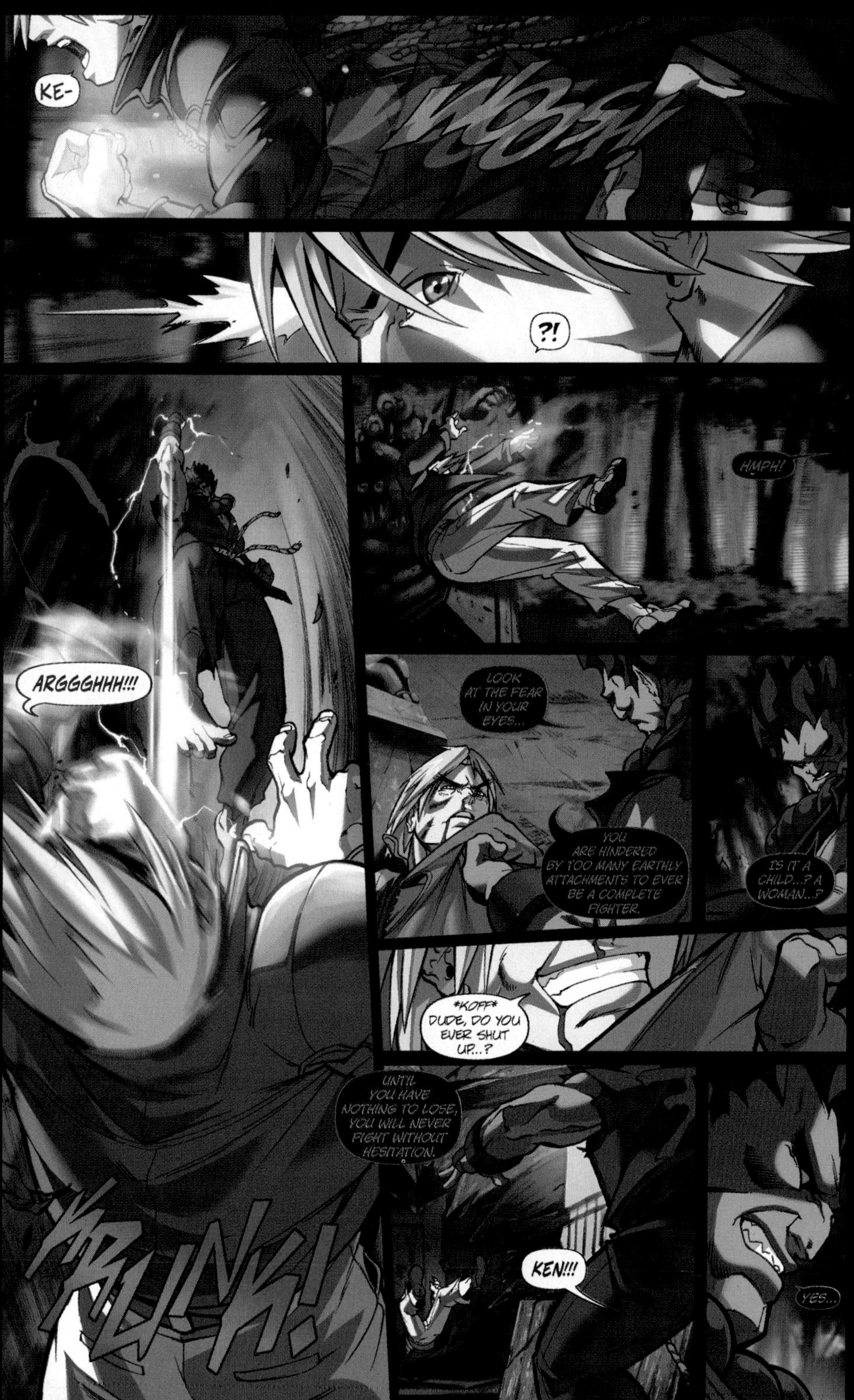
KE-
WHOOSH
?!
HMPH!
ARGGGHHH!!!
LOOK AT THE FEAR IN YOUR EYES...
YOU ARE HINDERED BY TOO MANY EARTHLY ATTACHMENTS TO EVER BE A COMPLETE FIGHTER.
IS IT A CHILD...? A WOMAN...?
KOFF DUDE, DO YOU EVER SHUT UP...?
UNTIL YOU HAVE NOTHING TO LOSE, YOU WILL NEVER FIGHT WITHOUT HESITATION.
KRUNK!
KEN!!!
YES...

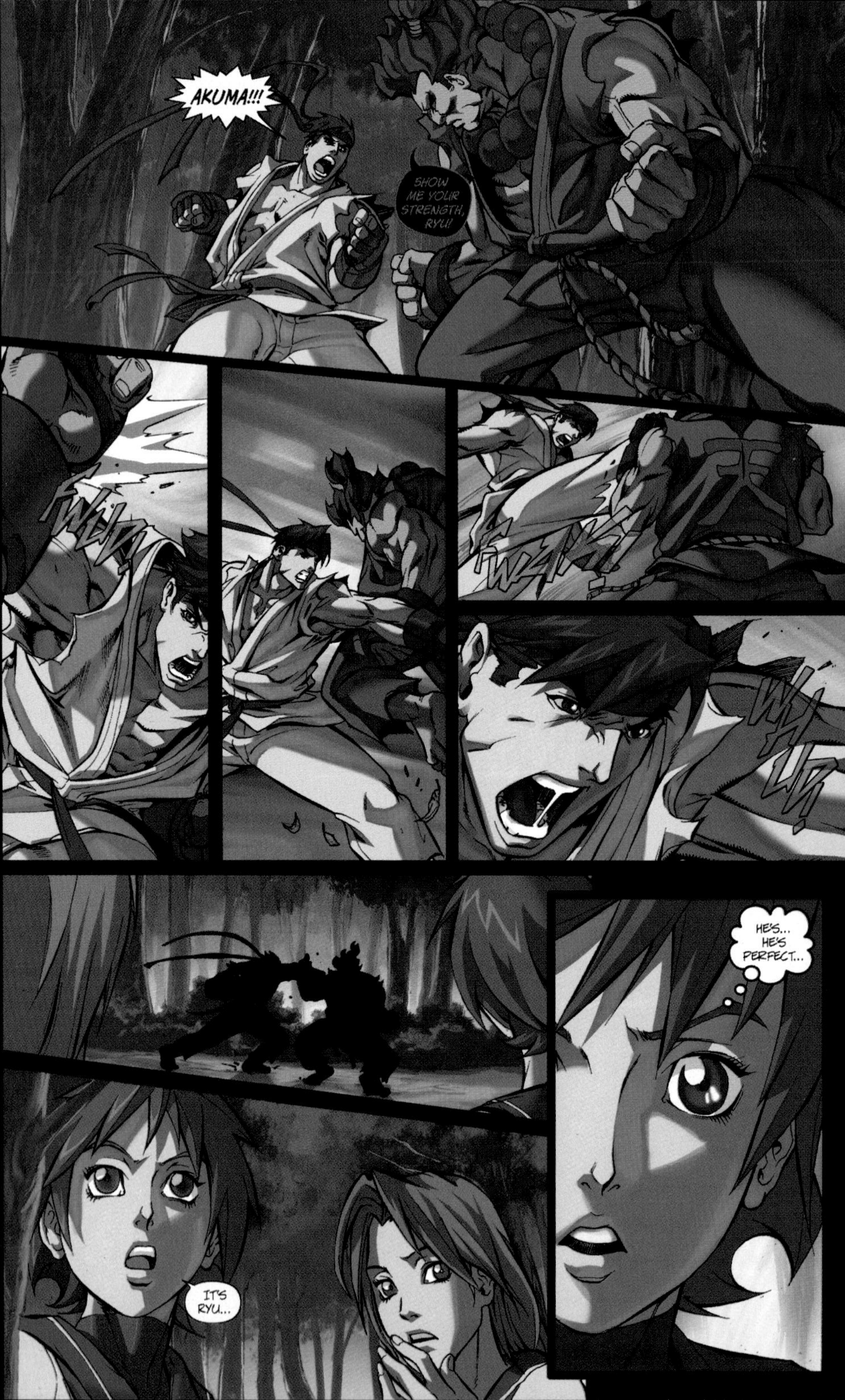
AKUMA!!!
SHOW ME YOUR STRENGTH, RYU!!
IT'S RYU...
HE'S... HE'S PERFECT...

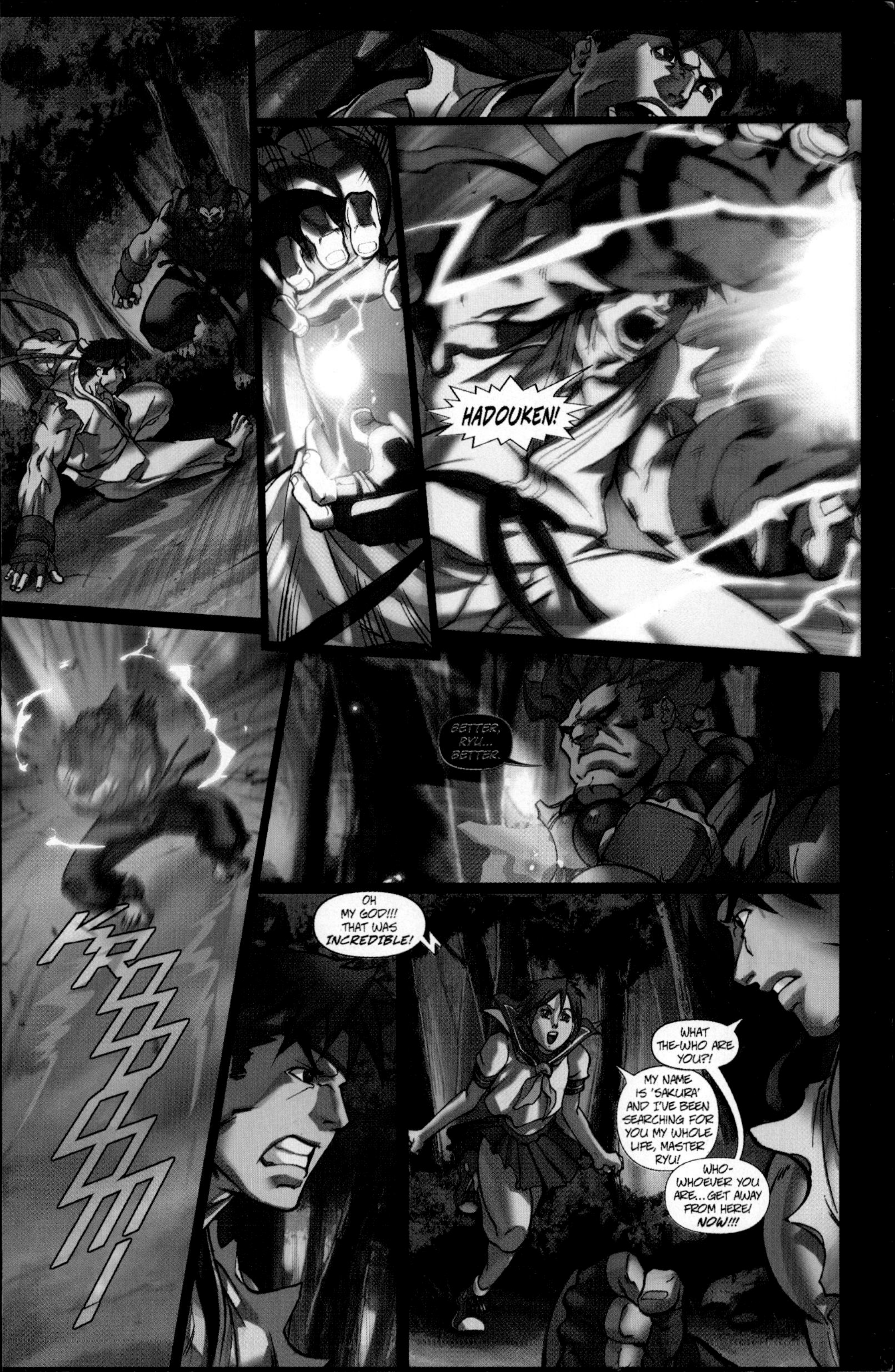
HADOUKEN!
BETTER, RYU... BETTER.
KRAKOOM!
OH MY GOD!!! THAT WAS INCREDIBLE!
WHAT THE-WHO ARE YOU?!
MY NAME IS 'SAKURA' AND I'VE BEEN SEARCHING FOR YOU MY WHOLE LIFE, MASTER RYU!
WHO- WHOEVER YOU ARE... GET AWAY FROM HERE! NOW!!!

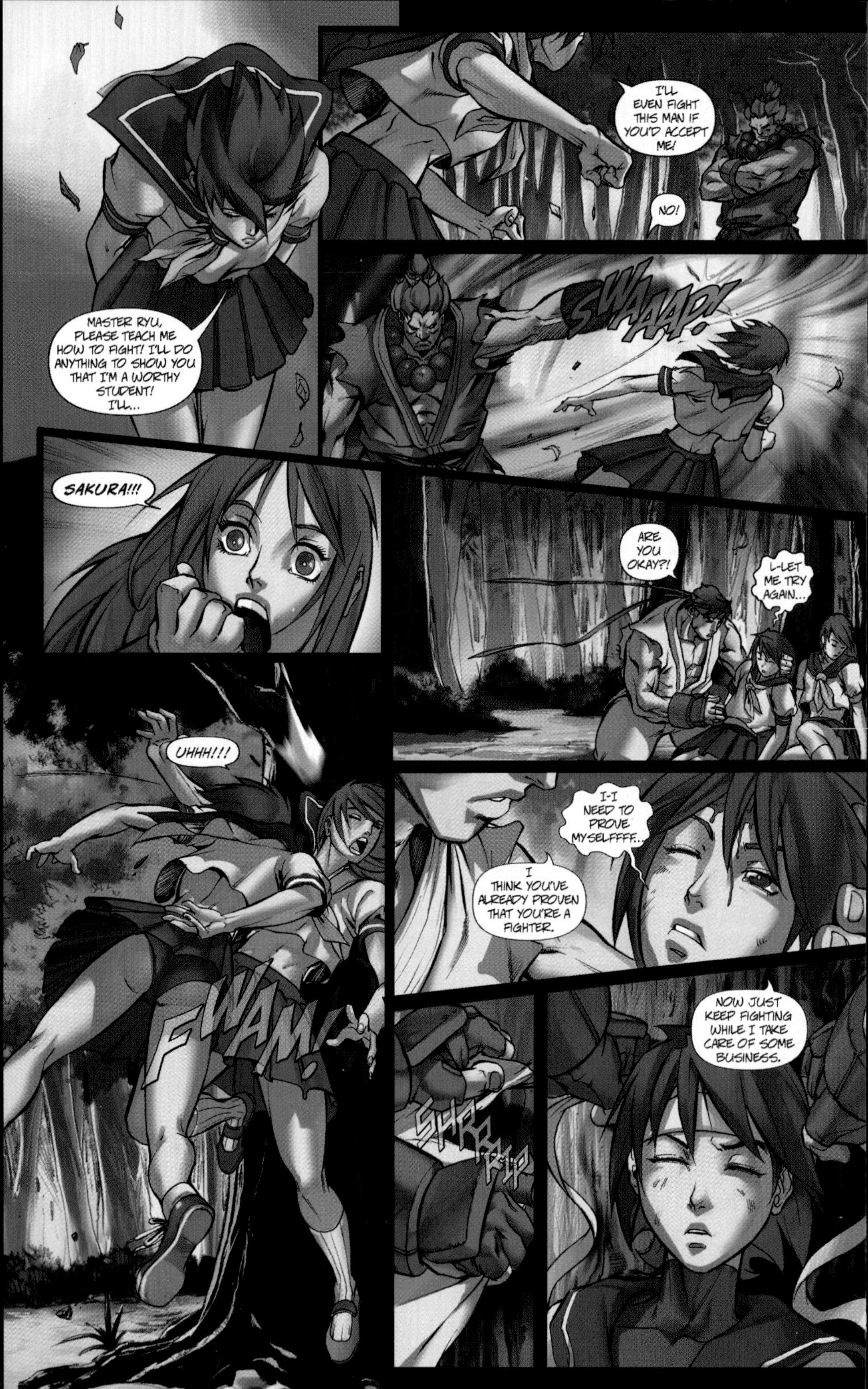

MASTER RYU, PLEASE TEACH ME HOW TO FIGHT! I'LL DO ANYTHING TO SHOW YOU THAT I'M A WORTHY STUDENT! I'LL...
I'LL EVEN FIGHT THIS MAN IF YOU'D ACCEPT ME!
NO!
SWAAAP!
SAKURA!!!
ARE YOU OKAY?!
L-LET ME TRY AGAIN...
UHHH!!!
FWAM!
I-I NEED TO PROVE MYSELFFFF...
I THINK YOU'VE ALREADY PROVEN THAT YOU'RE A FIGHTER.
NOW JUST KEEP FIGHTING WHILE I TAKE CARE OF SOME BUSINESS.
SHRRRIP

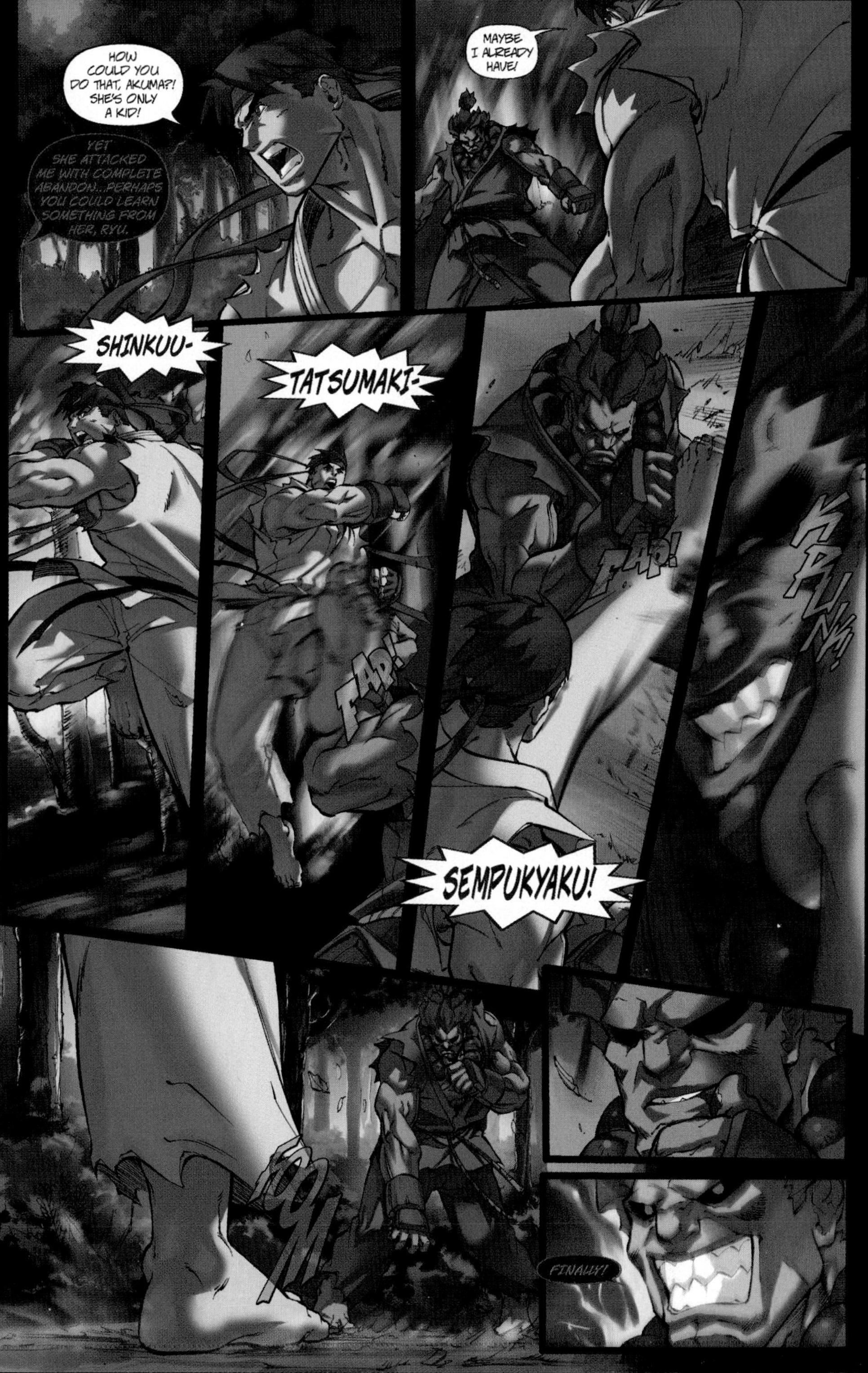
HOW COULD YOU DO THAT, AKUMA?! SHE'S ONLY A KID!
YET SHE ATTACKED ME WITH COMPLETE ABANDON...PERHAPS YOU COULD LEARN SOMETHING FROM HER, RYU.
MAYBE I ALREADY HAVE!
SHINKUU-
TATSUMAKI-
FAP!
FAP!
SEMPUKYAKU!
FINALLY!

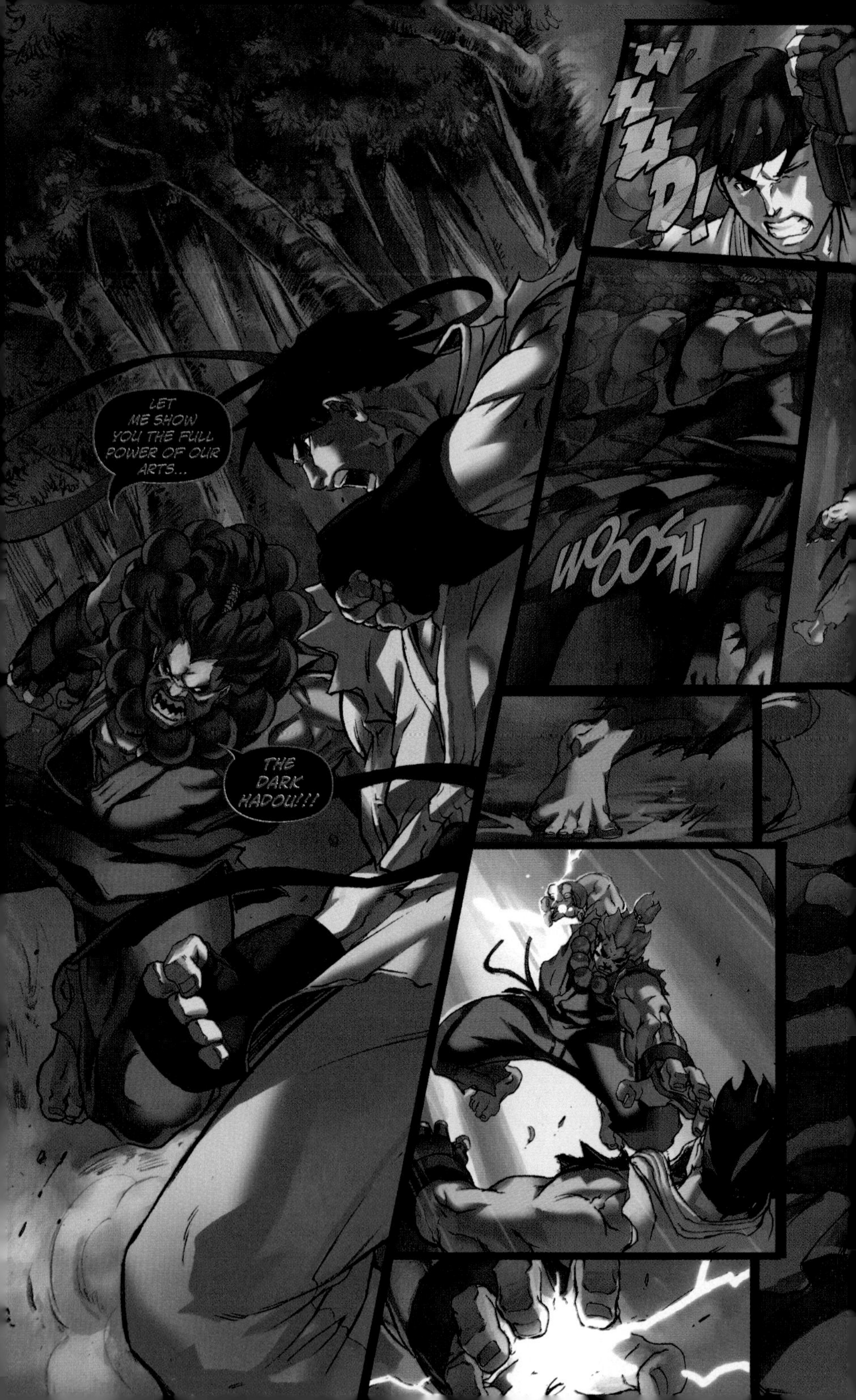

WHUD!
LET ME SHOW YOU THE FULL POWER OF OUR ARTS...
WOOOSH
THE DARK HADOU!!!

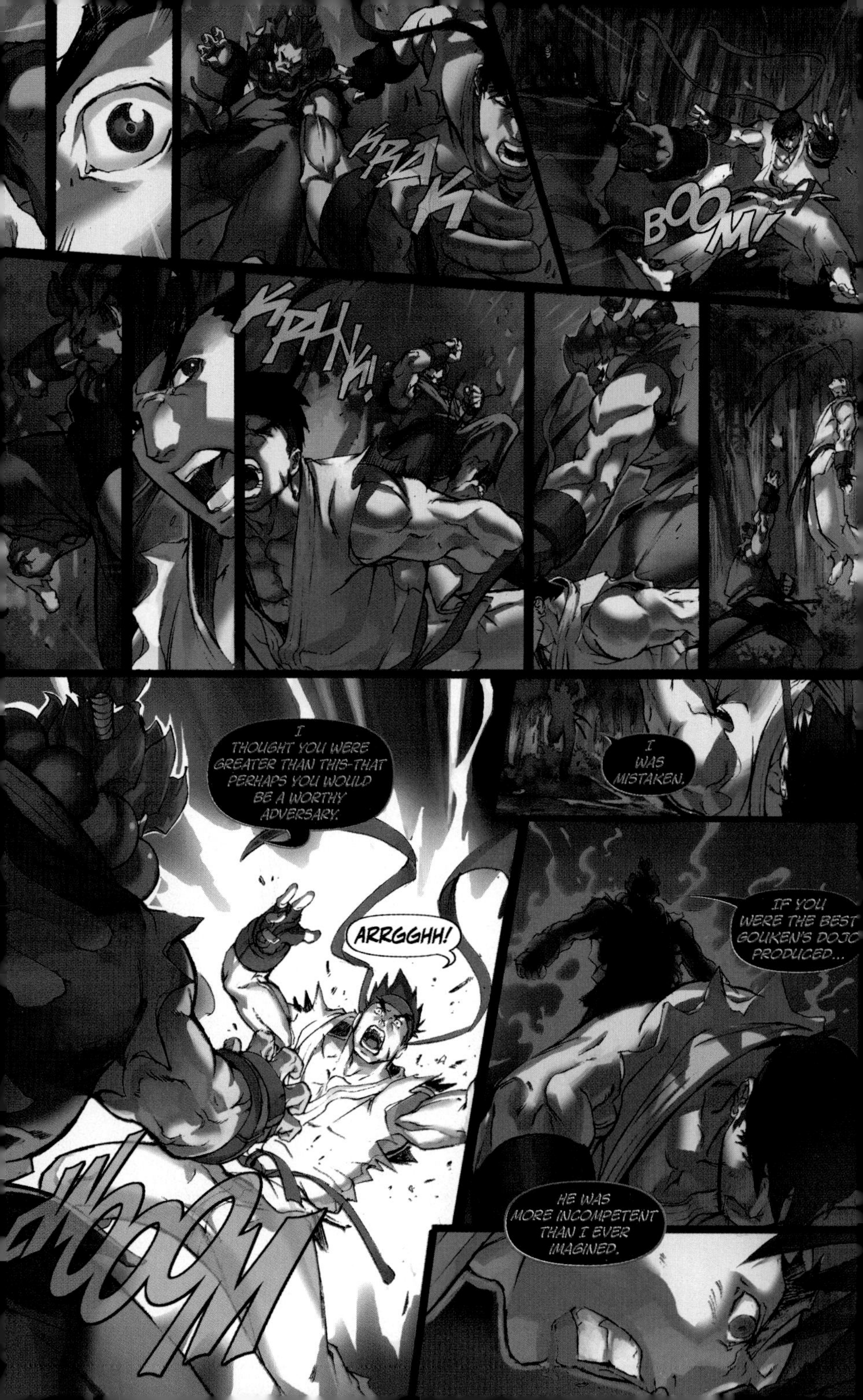
KRAK
BOOM!
KRAKK!
I THOUGHT YOU WERE GREATER THAN THIS-THAT PERHAPS YOU WOULD BE A WORTHY ADVERSARY.
I WAS MISTAKEN.
ARRGGHH!
IF YOU WERE THE BEST GOUKEN'S DOJO PRODUCED...
HE WAS MORE INCOMPETENT THAN I EVER IMAGINED.

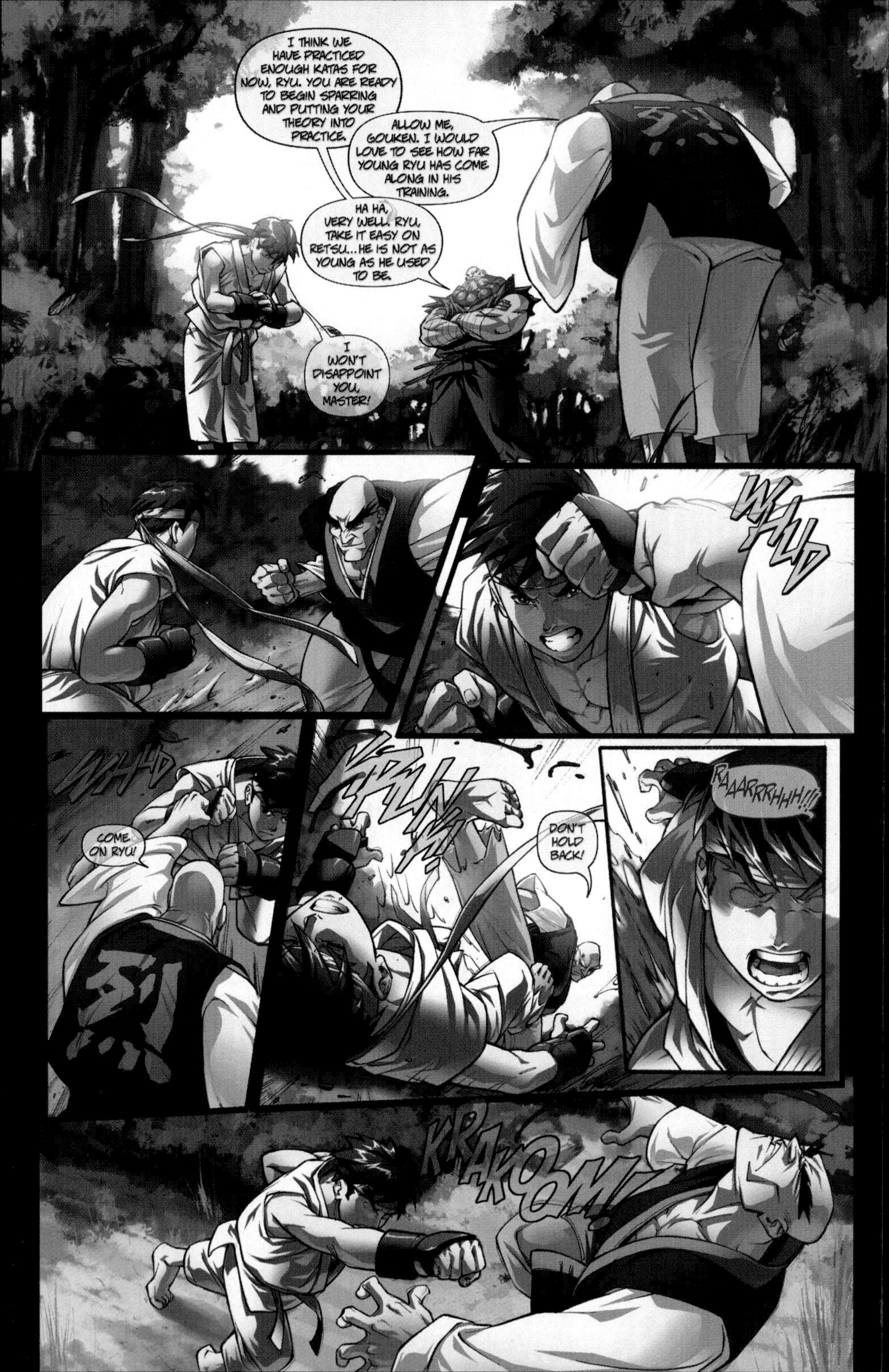
I THINK WE HAVE PRACTICED ENOUGH KATAS FOR NOW, RYU. YOU ARE READY TO BEGIN SPARRING AND PUTTING YOUR THEORY INTO PRACTICE.
ALLOW ME, GOUKEN. I WOULD LOVE TO SEE HOW FAR YOUNG RYU HAS COME ALONG IN HIS TRAINING.
HA HA, VERY WELL. RYU, TAKE IT EASY ON RETSU...HE IS NOT AS YOUNG AS HE USED TO BE.
I WON'T DISAPPOINT YOU, MASTER!
WHUD
WHUD
COME ON RYU!
KRUNCH
DON'T HOLD BACK!
RAAARRRHHH!!!
KRAKOOM!

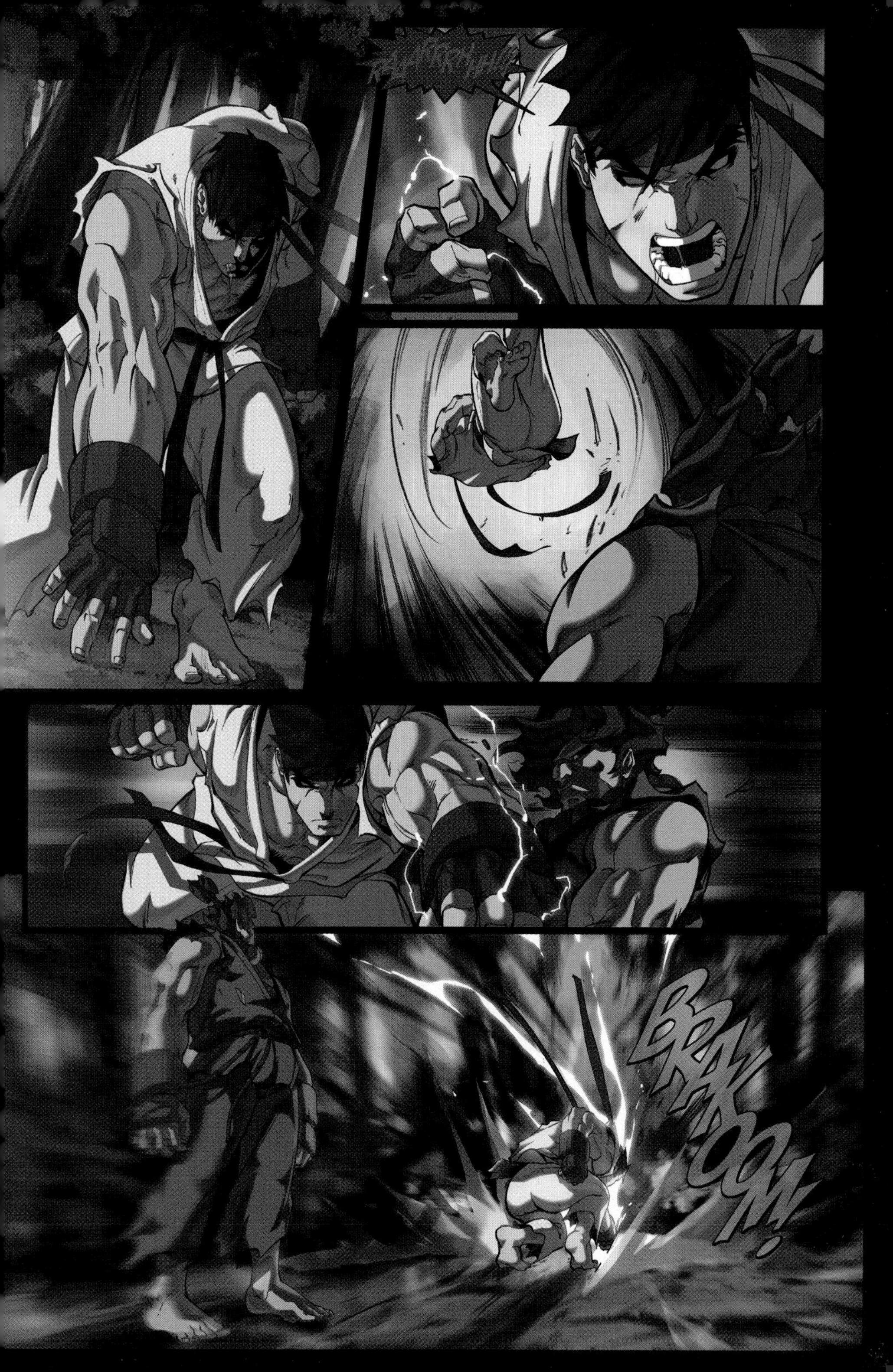
BRAKOOM!

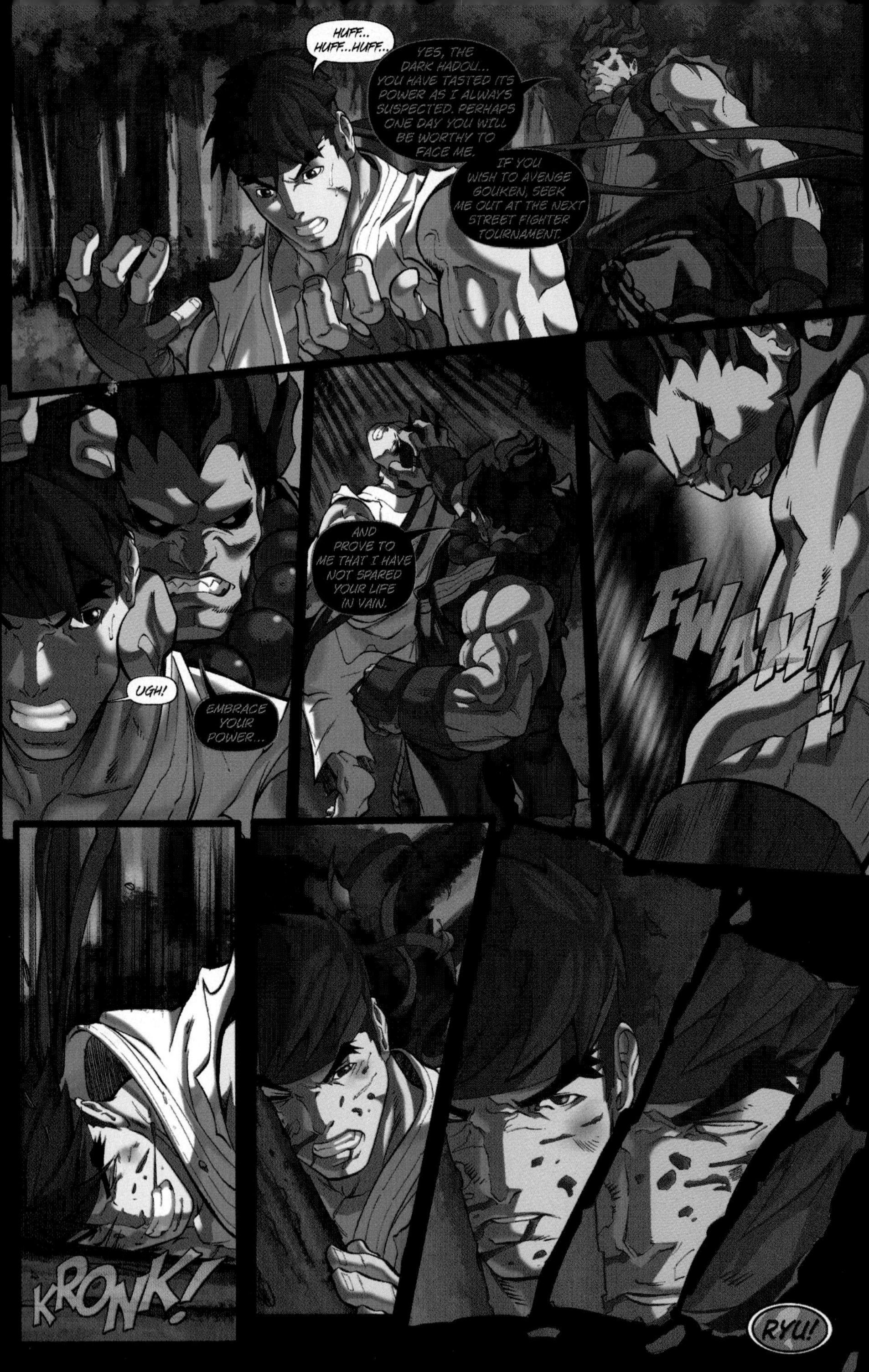
HUFF... HUFF...HUFF...
YES, THE DARK HADOU... YOU HAVE TASTED ITS POWER AS I ALWAYS SUSPECTED. PERHAPS ONE DAY YOU WILL BE WORTHY TO FACE ME.
IF YOU WISH TO AVENGE GOUKEN, SEEK ME OUT AT THE NEXT STREET FIGHTER TOURNAMENT.
UGH!
EMBRACE YOUR POWER...
AND PROVE TO ME THAT I HAVE NOT SPARED YOUR LIFE IN VAIN.
FWAM!!
KRONK!
RYU!

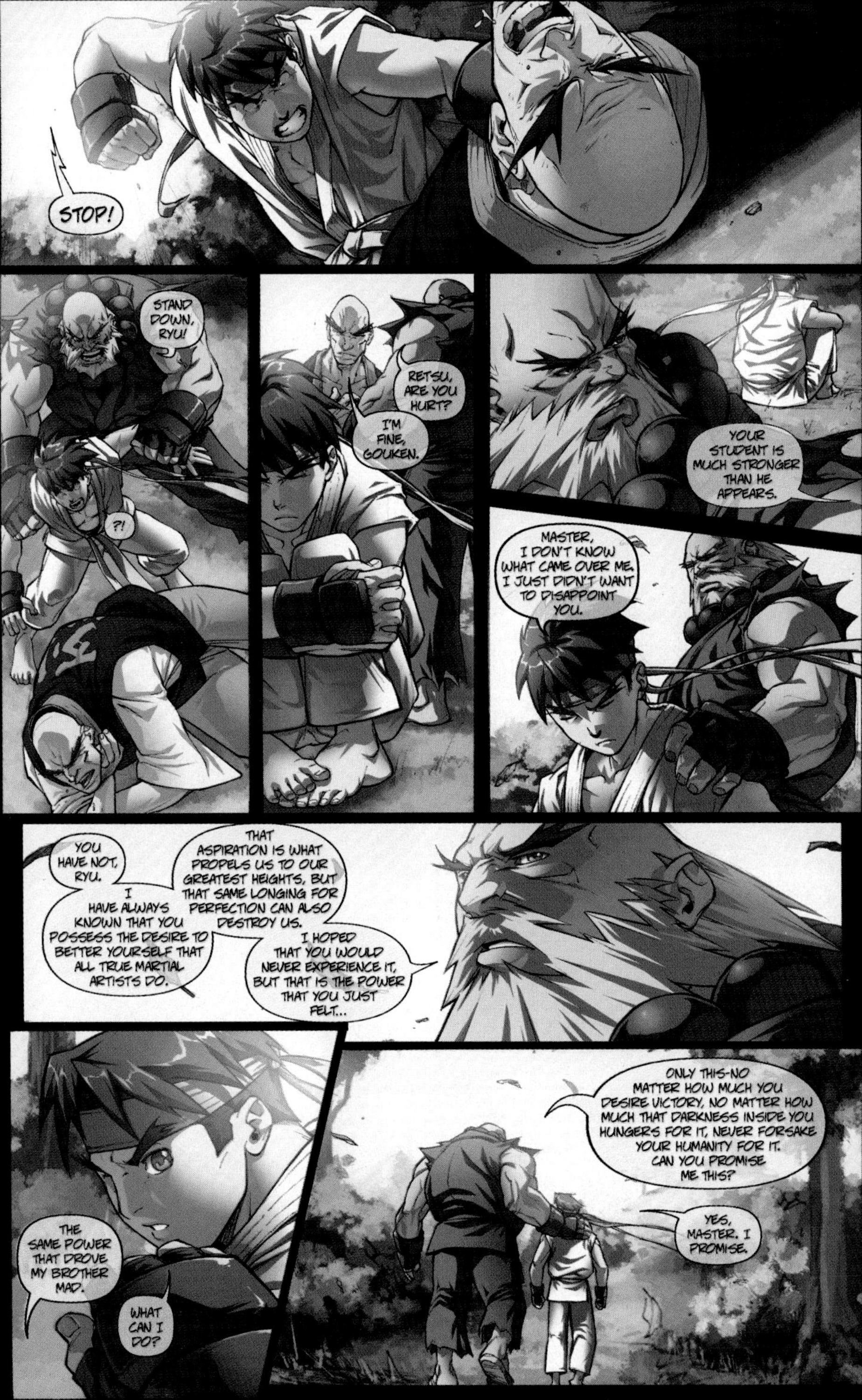
STOP!
STAND DOWN, RYU!
?!
RETSU, ARE YOU HURT?
I'M FINE, GOUKEN.
YOUR STUDENT IS MUCH STRONGER THAN HE APPEARS.
MASTER, I DON'T KNOW WHAT CAME OVER ME. I JUST DIDN'T WANT TO DISAPPOINT YOU.
YOU HAVE NOT, RYU.
I HAVE ALWAYS KNOWN THAT YOU POSSESS THE DESIRE TO BETTER YOURSELF THAT ALL TRUE MARTIAL ARTISTS DO.
THAT ASPIRATION IS WHAT PROPELS US TO OUR GREATEST HEIGHTS, BUT THAT SAME LONGING FOR PERFECTION CAN ALSO DESTROY US.
I HOPED THAT YOU WOULD NEVER EXPERIENCE IT, BUT THAT IS THE POWER THAT YOU JUST FELT...
THE SAME POWER THAT DROVE MY BROTHER MAD.
WHAT CAN I DO?
ONLY THIS-NO MATTER HOW MUCH YOU DESIRE VICTORY, NO MATTER HOW MUCH THAT DARKNESS INSIDE YOU HUNGERS FOR IT, NEVER FORSAKE YOUR HUMANITY FOR IT. CAN YOU PROMISE ME THIS?
YES, MASTER. I PROMISE.

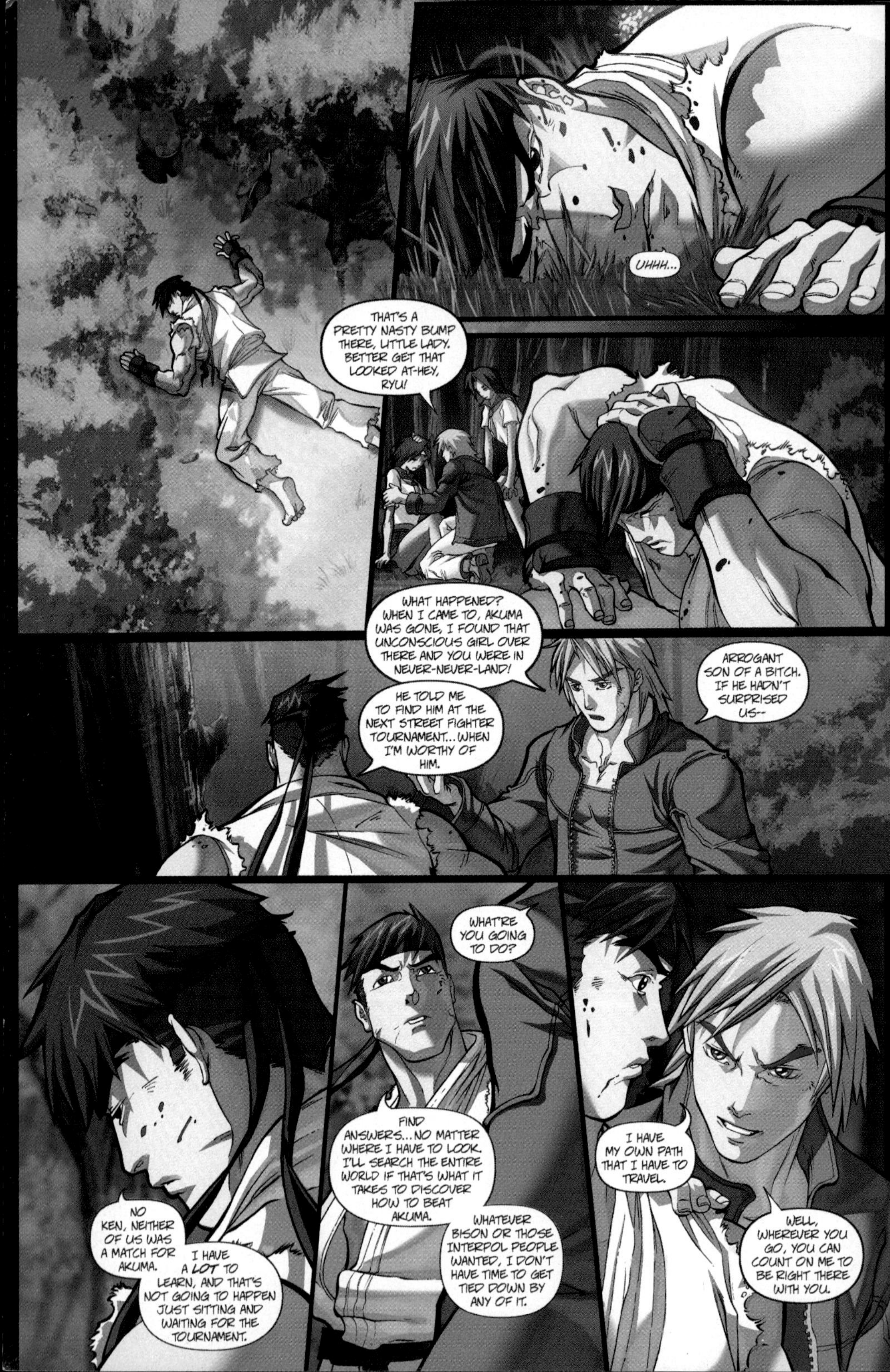
UHHH...
THAT'S A PRETTY NASTY BUMP THERE, LITTLE LADY. BETTER GET THAT LOOKED AT-HEY, RYU!
WHAT HAPPENED? WHEN I CAME TO, AKUMA WAS GONE, I FOUND THAT UNCONSCIOUS GIRL OVER THERE AND YOU WERE IN NEVER-NEVER-LAND!
HE TOLD ME TO FIND HIM AT THE NEXT STREET FIGHTER TOURNAMENT... WHEN I'M WORTHY OF HIM.
ARROGANT SON OF A BITCH. IF HE HADN'T SURPRISED US--
NO KEN, NEITHER OF US WAS A MATCH FOR AKUMA.
I HAVE A LOT TO LEARN, AND THAT'S NOT GOING TO HAPPEN JUST SITTING AND WAITING FOR THE TOURNAMENT.
WHAT'RE YOU GOING TO DO?
FIND ANSWERS... NO MATTER WHERE I HAVE TO LOOK. I'LL SEARCH THE ENTIRE WORLD IF THAT'S WHAT IT TAKES TO DISCOVER HOW TO BEAT AKUMA.
WHATEVER BISON OR THOSE INTERPOL PEOPLE WANTED, I DON'T HAVE TIME TO GET TIED DOWN BY ANY OF IT.
I HAVE MY OWN PATH THAT I HAVE TO TRAVEL.
WELL, WHEREVER YOU GO, YOU CAN COUNT ON ME TO BE RIGHT THERE WITH YOU.

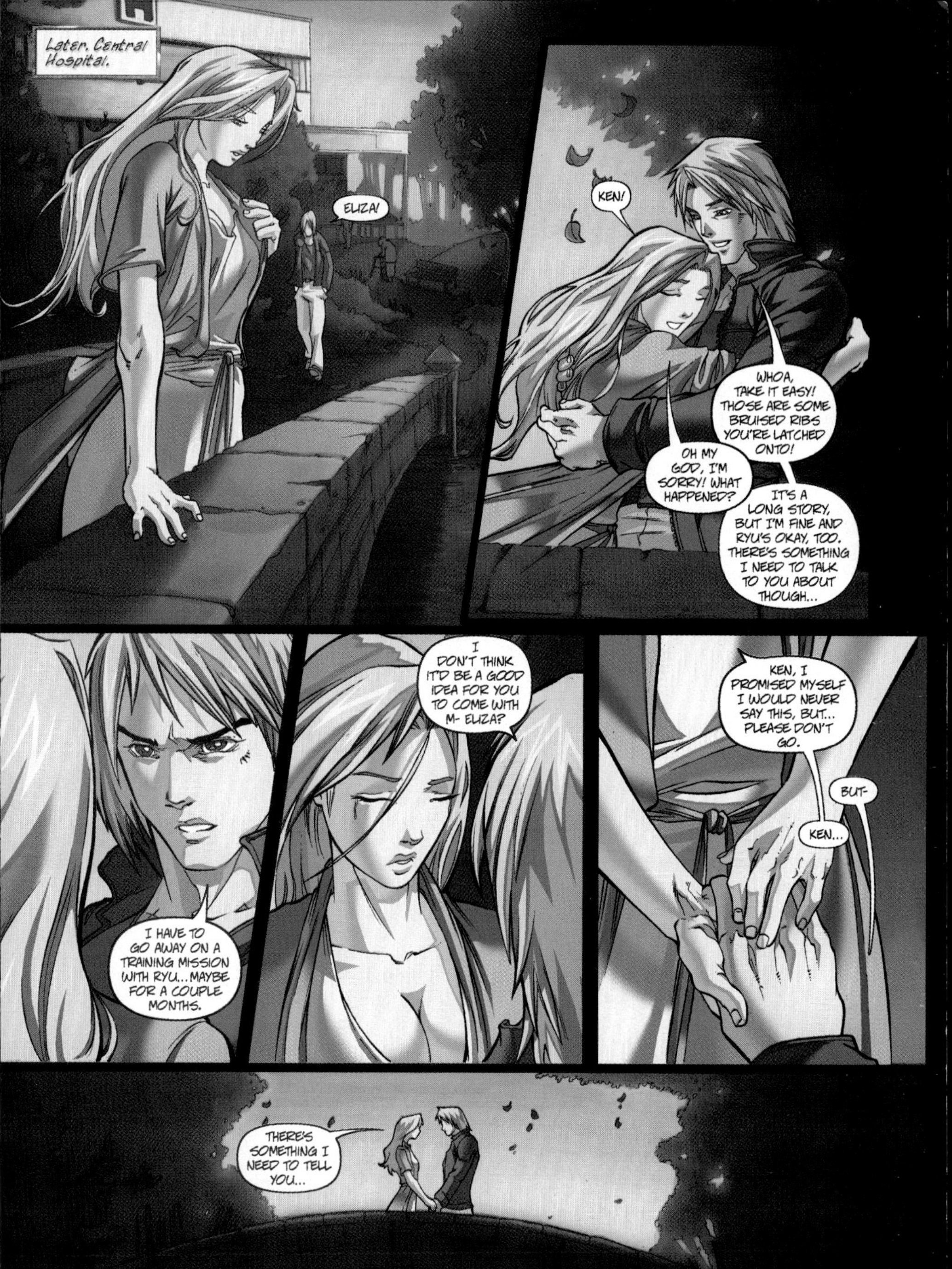
Later. Central Hospital.
ELIZA!
KEN!
WHOA, TAKE IT EASY! THOSE ARE SOME BRUISED RIBS YOU'RE LATCHED ONTO!
OH MY GOD, I'M SORRY! WHAT HAPPENED?
IT'S A LONG STORY, BUT I'M FINE AND RYU'S OKAY, TOO. THERE'S SOMETHING I NEED TO TALK TO YOU ABOUT THOUGH...
I HAVE TO GO AWAY ON A TRAINING MISSION WITH RYU... MAYBE FOR A COUPLE MONTHS.
I DON'T THINK IT'D BE A GOOD IDEA FOR YOU TO COME WITH M- ELIZA?
KEN, I PROMISED MYSELF I WOULD NEVER SAY THIS, BUT... PLEASE DON'T GO.
BUT-
KEN...
THERE'S SOMETHING I NEED TO TELL YOU...

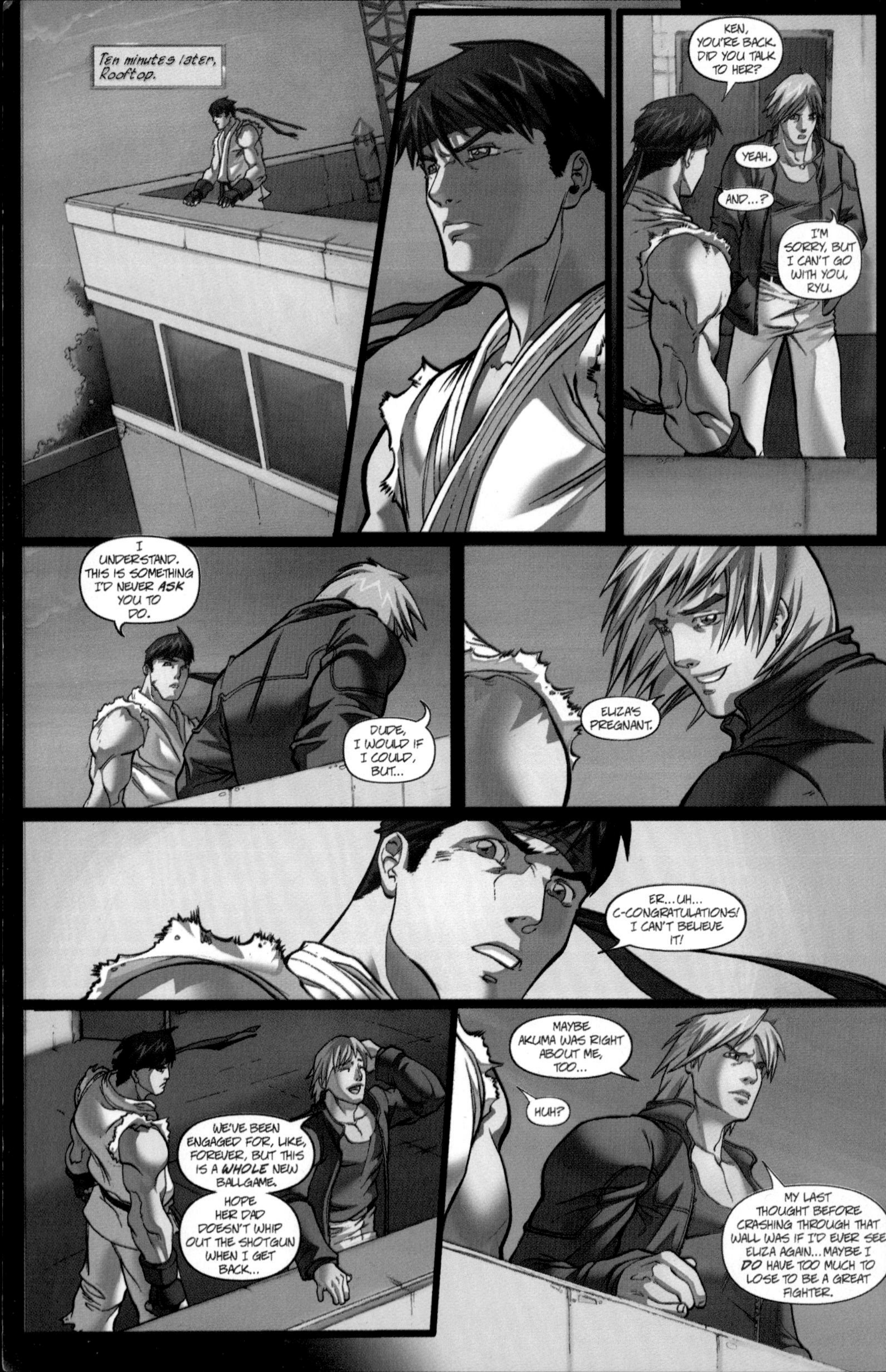
Ten minutes later, Rooftop.
KEN, YOU'RE BACK. DID YOU TALK TO HER?
YEAH.
AND...?
I'M SORRY, BUT I CAN'T GO WITH YOU, RYU.
I UNDERSTAND. THIS IS SOMETHING I'D NEVER ASK YOU TO DO.
DUDE, I WOULD IF I COULD, BUT...
ELIZA'S PREGNANT.
ER...UH... C-CONGRATULATIONS! I CAN'T BELIEVE IT!
WE'VE BEEN ENGAGED FOR, LIKE, FOREVER, BUT THIS IS A WHOLE NEW BALLGAME.
HOPE HER DAD DOESN'T WHIP OUT THE SHOTGUN WHEN I GET BACK...
MAYBE AKUMA WAS RIGHT ABOUT ME, TOO...
HUH?
MY LAST THOUGHT BEFORE CRASHING THROUGH THAT WALL WAS IF I'D EVER SEE ELIZA AGAIN...MAYBE I DO HAVE TOO MUCH TO LOSE TO BE A GREAT FIGHTER.

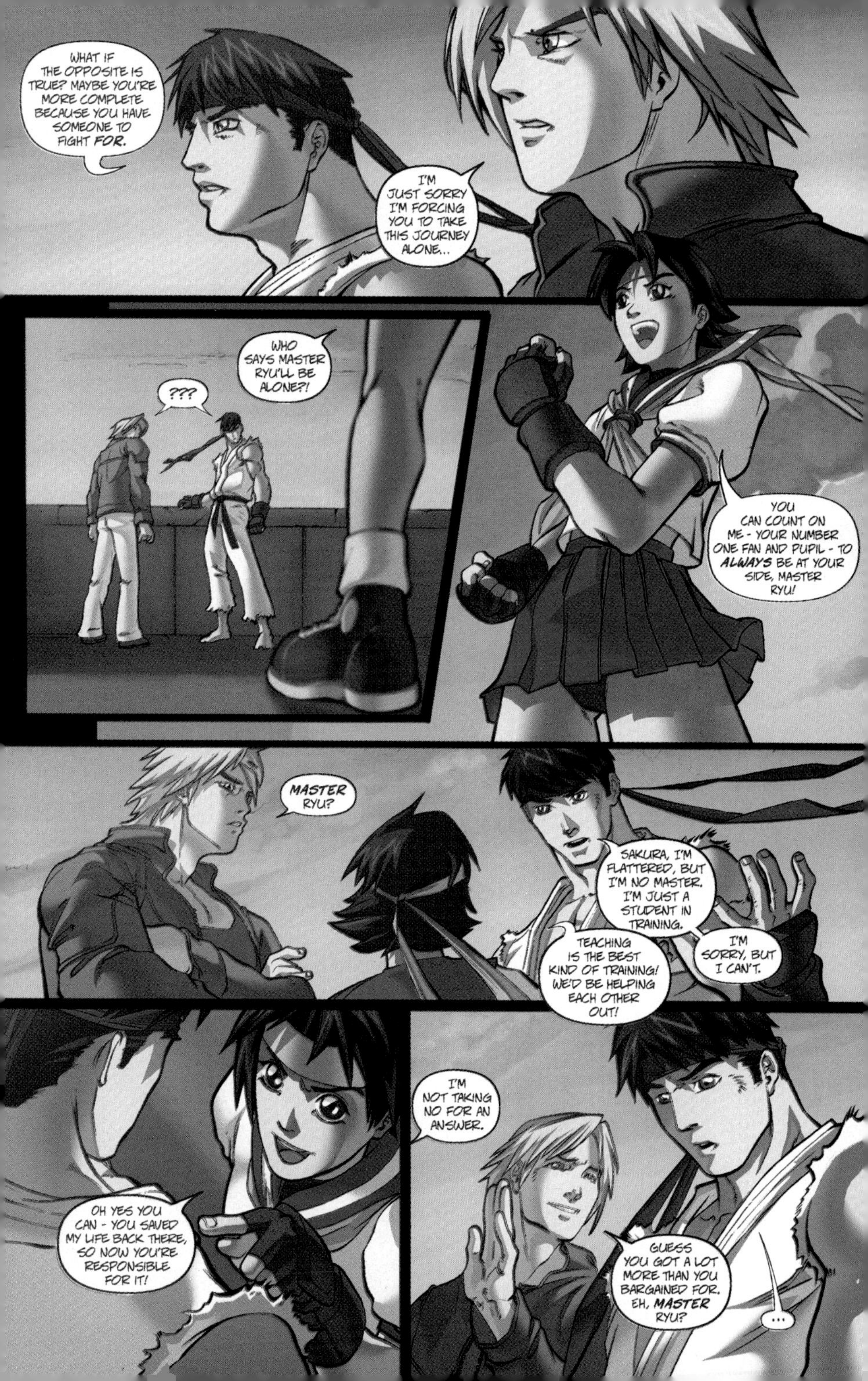
WHAT IF THE OPPOSITE IS TRUE? MAYBE YOU'RE MORE COMPLETE BECAUSE YOU HAVE SOMEONE TO FIGHT FOR.
I'M JUST SORRY I'M FORCING YOU TO TAKE THIS JOURNEY ALONE...
WHO SAYS MASTER RYU'LL BE ALONE?!
???
YOU CAN COUNT ON ME - YOUR NUMBER ONE FAN AND PUPIL - TO ALWAYS BE AT YOUR SIDE, MASTER RYU!
MASTER RYU?
SAKURA, I'M FLATTERED, BUT I'M NO MASTER. I'M JUST A STUDENT IN TRAINING.
TEACHING IS THE BEST KIND OF TRAINING! WE'D BE HELPING EACH OTHER OUT!
I'M SORRY, BUT I CAN'T.
OH YES YOU CAN - YOU SAVED MY LIFE BACK THERE, SO NOW YOU'RE RESPONSIBLE FOR IT!
I'M NOT TAKING NO FOR AN ANSWER.
GUESS YOU GOT A LOT MORE THAN YOU BARGAINED FOR. EH, MASTER RYU?
...

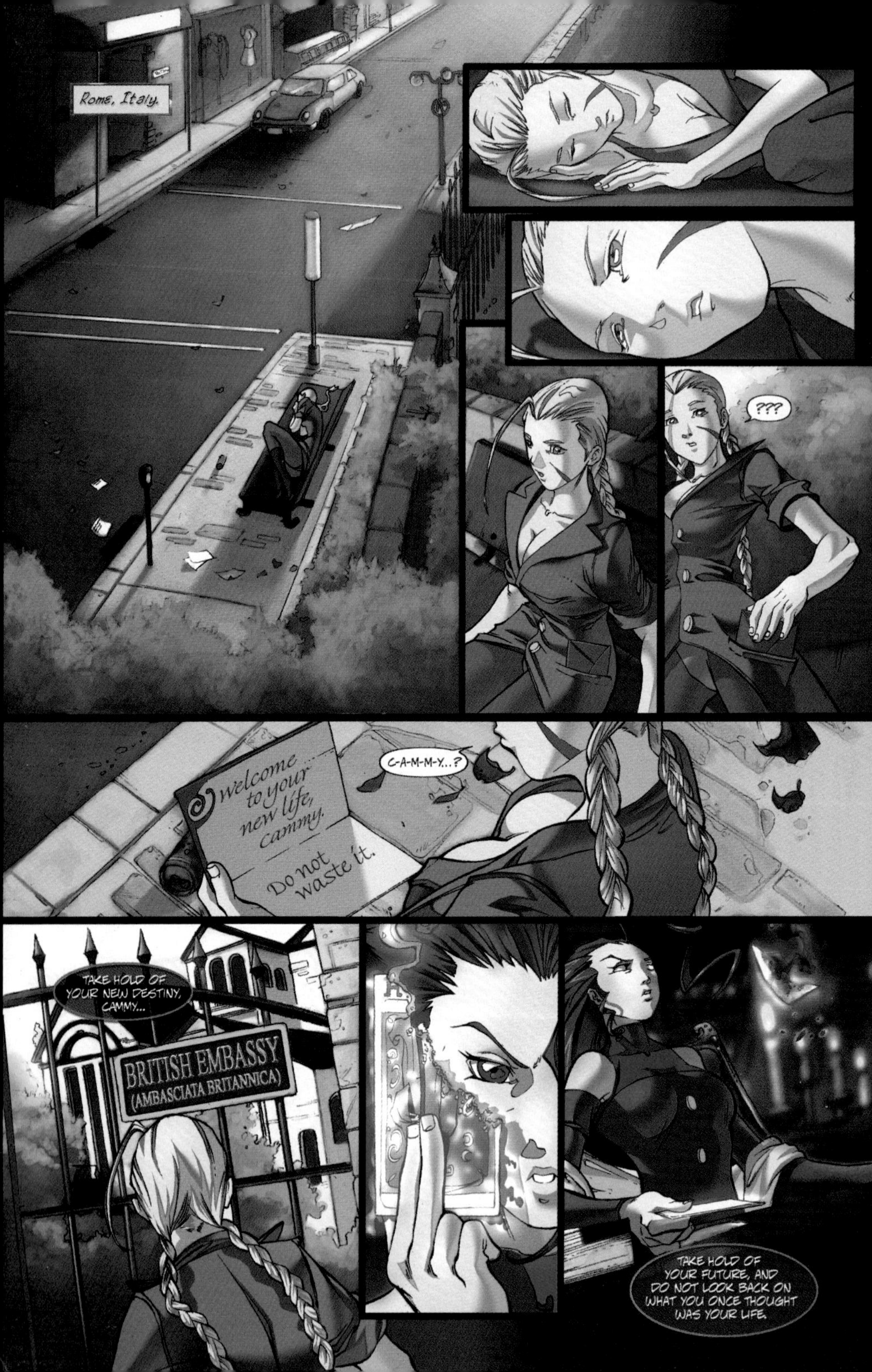
Rome, Italy.
???
C-A-M-M-Y...?
welcome... to your new life, cammy.
Do not waste it.
BRITISH EMBASSY
(AMBASCIATA BRITANNICA)
TAKE HOLD OF YOUR NEW DESTINY, CAMMY...
TAKE HOLD OF YOUR FUTURE, AND DO NOT LOOK BACK ON WHAT YOU ONCE THOUGHT WAS YOUR LIFE.

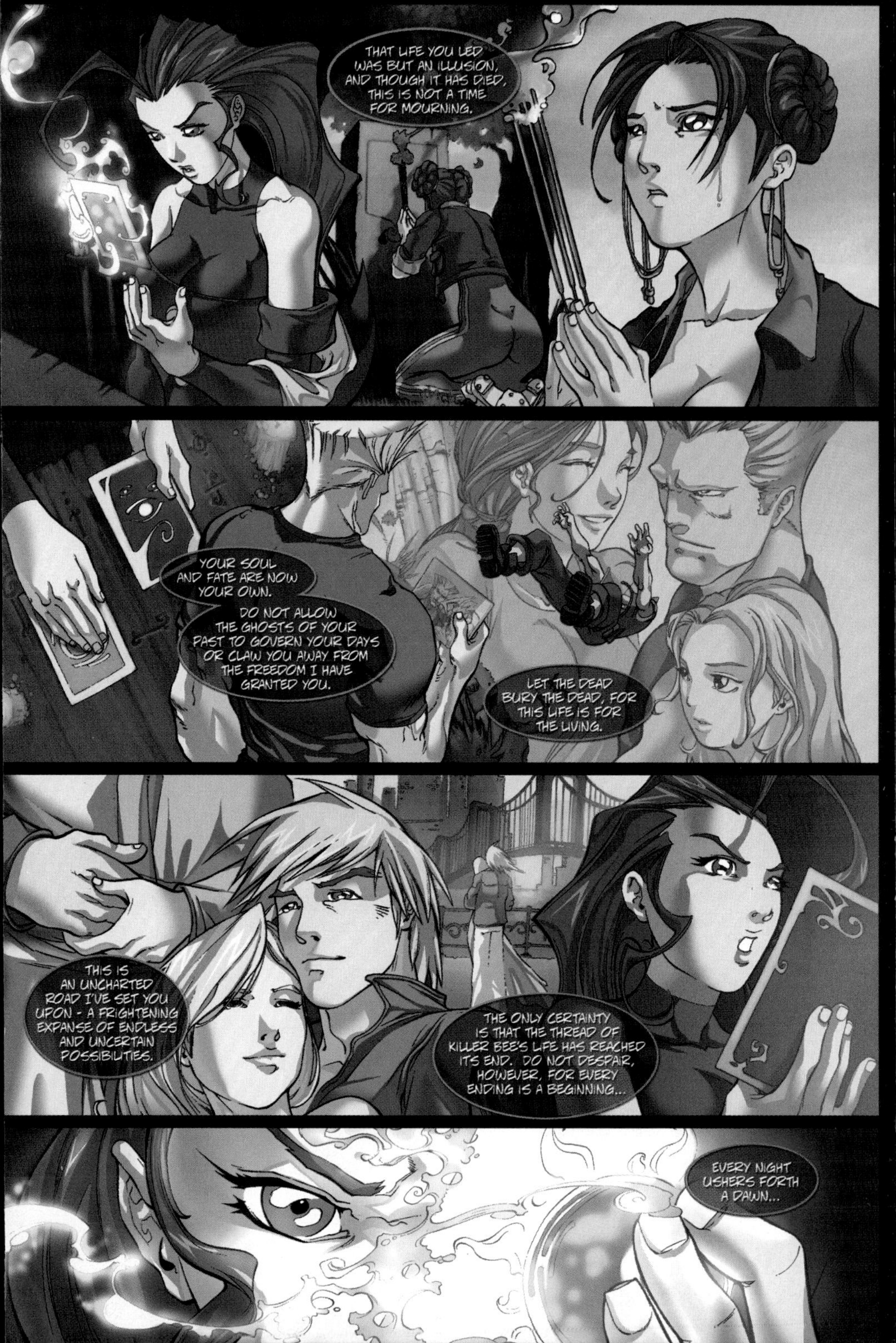
THAT LIFE YOU LED WAS BUT AN ILLUSION, AND THOUGH IT HAS DIED, THIS IS NOT A TIME FOR MOURNING.
YOUR SOUL AND FATE ARE NOW YOUR OWN.
DO NOT ALLOW THE GHOSTS OF YOUR PAST TO GOVERN YOUR DAYS OR CLAW YOU AWAY FROM THE FREEDOM I HAVE GRANTED YOU.
LET THE DEAD BURY THE DEAD, FOR THIS LIFE IS FOR THE LIVING.
THIS IS AN UNCHARTED ROAD I'VE SET YOU UPON - A FRIGHTENING EXPANSE OF ENDLESS AND UNCERTAIN POSSIBILITIES.
THE ONLY CERTAINTY IS THAT THE THREAD OF KILLER BEE'S LIFE HAS REACHED ITS END. DO NOT DESPAIR, HOWEVER, FOR EVERY ENDING IS A BEGINNING...
EVERY NIGHT USHERS FORTH A DAWN...

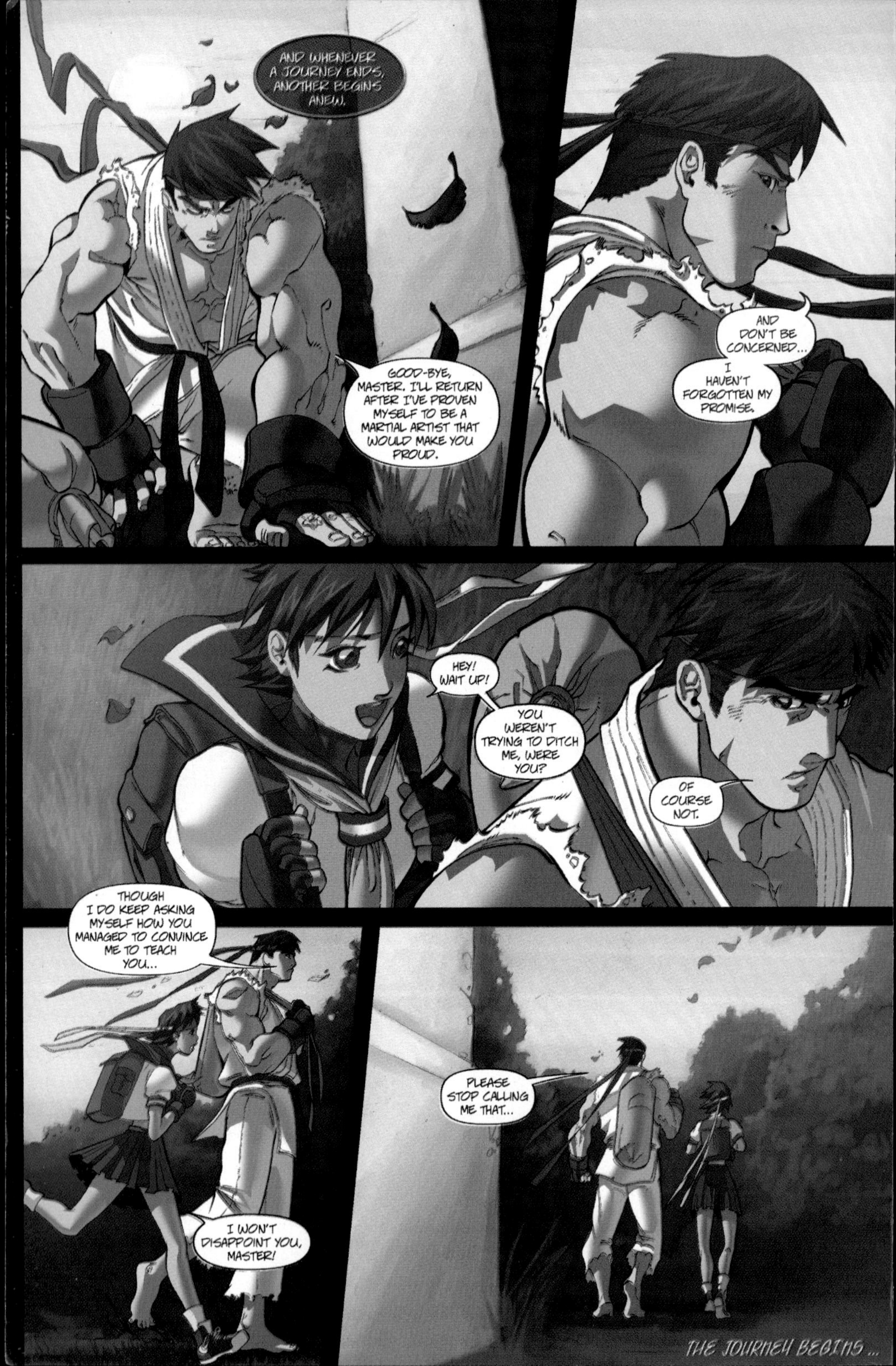
AND WHENEVER A JOURNEY ENDS, ANOTHER BEGINS ANEW.
GOOD-BYE, MASTER. I'LL RETURN AFTER I'VE PROVEN MYSELF TO BE A MARTIAL ARTIST THAT WOULD MAKE YOU PROUD.
AND DON'T BE CONCERNED...
I HAVEN'T FORGOTTEN MY PROMISE.
HEY! WAIT UP!
YOU WEREN'T TRYING TO DITCH ME, WERE YOU?
OF COURSE NOT.
THOUGH I DO KEEP ASKING MYSELF HOW YOU MANAGED TO CONVINCE ME TO TEACH YOU...
I WON'T DISAPPOINT YOU, MASTER!
PLEASE STOP CALLING ME THAT...
THE JOURNEY BEGINS ...

Cover Art by: Arnold Tsang

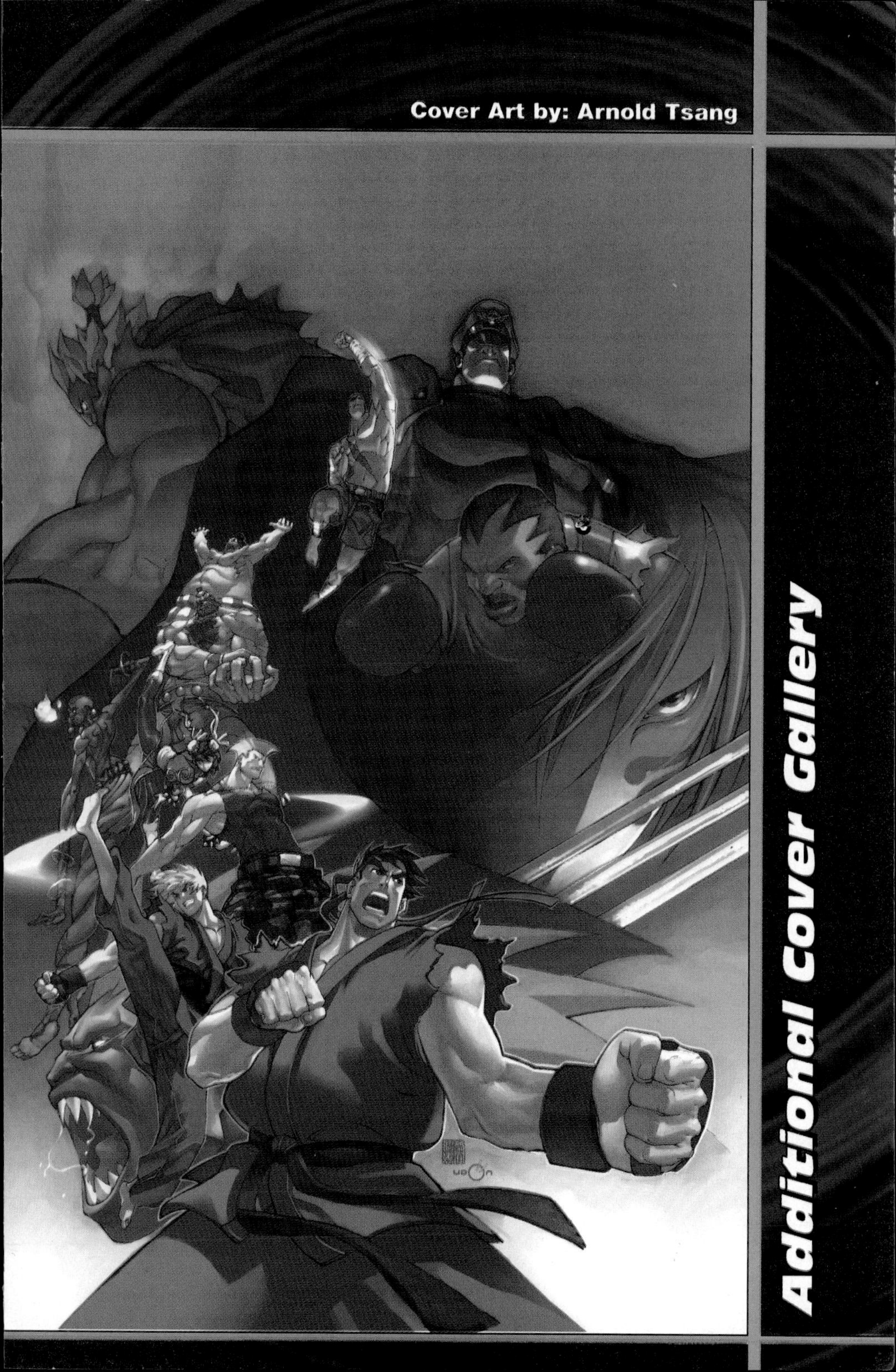

UDON

Additional Cover Gallery

Cover Art by: Long Vo and SAKA

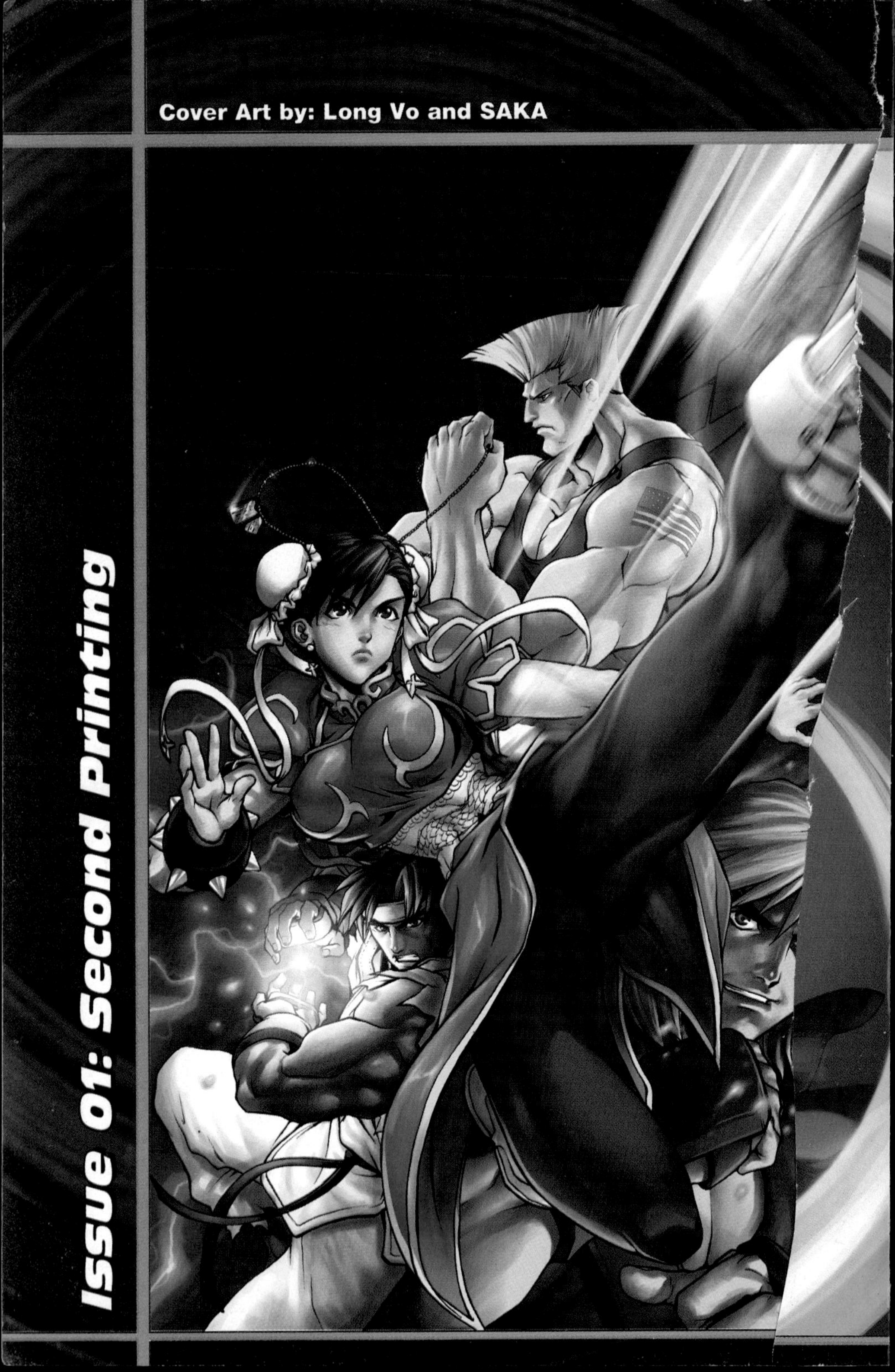

Issue 01: Second Printing

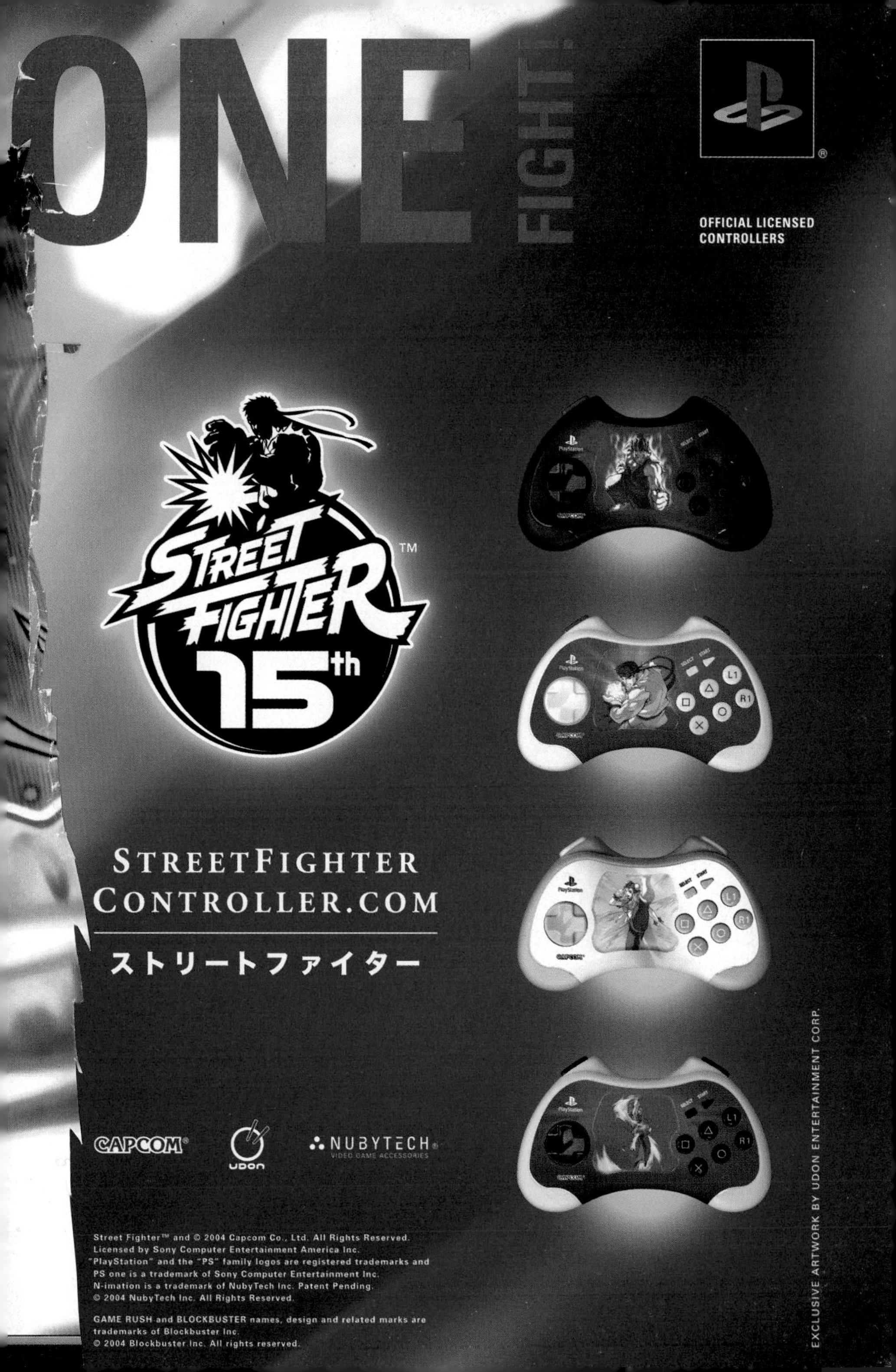

ONE FIGHT!
OFFICIAL LICENSED CONTROLLERS
STREET FIGHTER™ 15th
STREETFIGHTER CONTROLLER.COM
ストリートファイター
CAPCOM®
UDON
NUBYTECH® VIDEO GAME ACCESSORIES
Street Fighter™ and © 2004 Capcom Co., Ltd. All Rights Reserved.
Licensed by Sony Computer Entertainment America Inc.
"PlayStation" and the "PS" family logos are registered trademarks and
PS one is a trademark of Sony Computer Entertainment Inc.
N-imation is a trademark of NubyTech Inc. Patent Pending.
© 2004 NubyTech Inc. All Rights Reserved.
GAME RUSH and BLOCKBUSTER names, design and related marks are
trademarks of Blockbuster Inc.
© 2004 Blockbuster Inc. All rights reserved.
EXCLUSIVE ARTWORK BY UDON ENTERTAINMENT CORP.

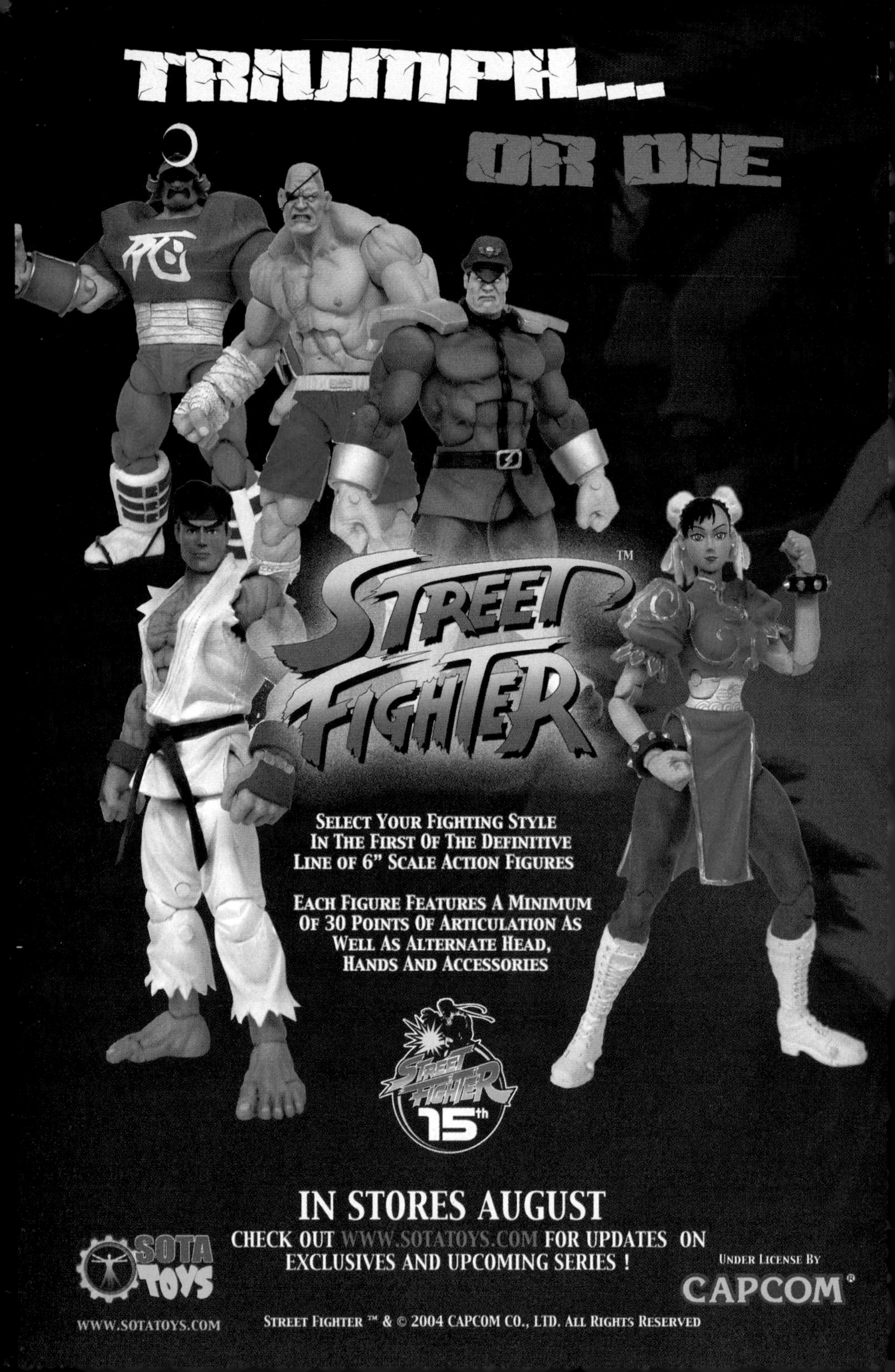
TRIUMPH...
OR DIE
STREET FIGHTER ™
SELECT YOUR FIGHTING STYLE
IN THE FIRST OF THE DEFINITIVE
LINE OF 6" SCALE ACTION FIGURES
EACH FIGURE FEATURES A MINIMUM
OF 30 POINTS OF ARTICULATION AS
WELL AS ALTERNATE HEAD,
HANDS AND ACCESSORIES
STREET FIGHTER 15th
IN STORES AUGUST
CHECK OUT WWW.SOTATOYS.COM FOR UPDATES ON
EXCLUSIVES AND UPCOMING SERIES !
SOTA TOYS
UNDER LICENSE BY
CAPCOM®
WWW.SOTATOYS.COM
STREET FIGHTER ™ & © 2004 CAPCOM CO., LTD. ALL RIGHTS RESERVED

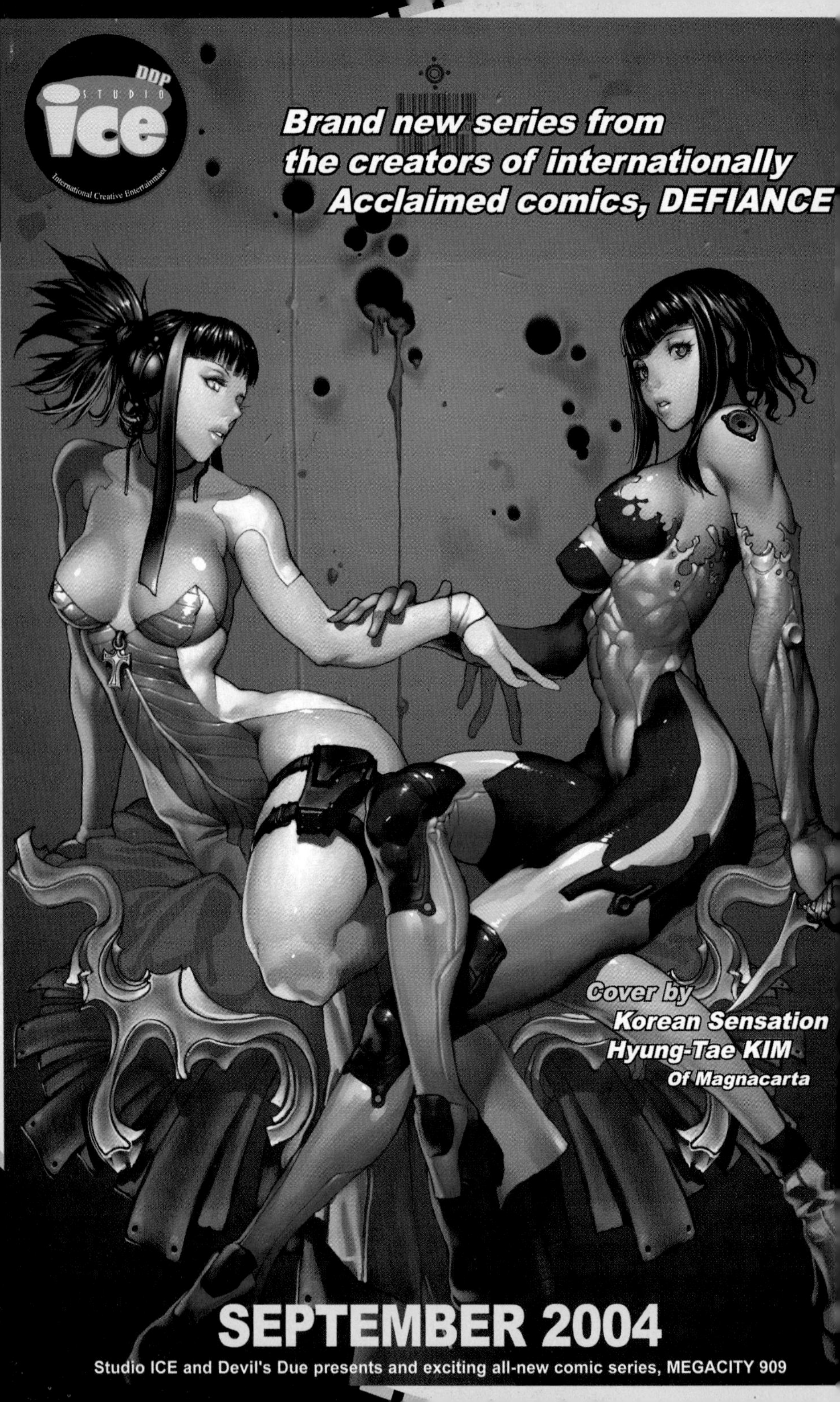
DDP STUDIO ice
International Creative Entertainmnet
Brand new series from the creators of internationally Acclaimed comics, DEFIANCE
Cover by
Korean Sensation
Hyung-Tae KIM
Of Magnacarta
SEPTEMBER 2004
Studio ICE and Devil's Due presents and exciting all-new comic series, MEGACITY 909

MEGACITY 909

Issue #1

WRITTEN BY: JACOB LEE, ANDREW DABB
ART BY: KANO KANG, ZACK SUH

In the wake of a bloody, planet-wide war, mankind stood united and completely at peace for the first time in history. Then the Pulses came.
Sentient psychic parasites that rampaged across the globe, turning those they possessed into monsters.
No one knew if they had just appeared, or if they'd been around forever, but one thing is certain; they have to be stopped. That job falls to an elite team of soldiers known as PHOBIA.

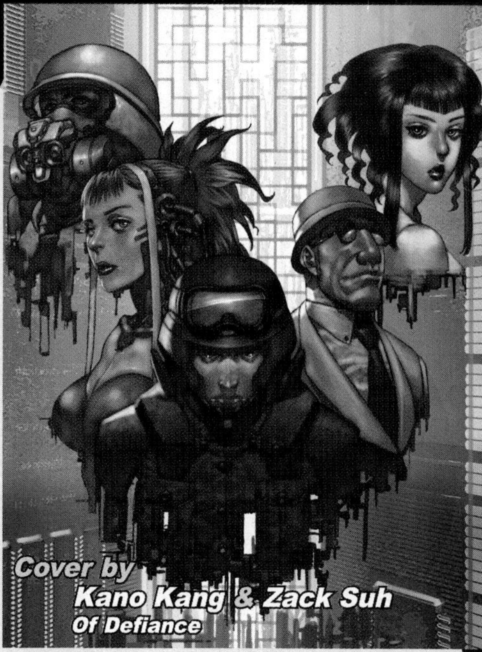

Cover by
Kano Kang & Zack Suh
Of Defiance

FULLY PAINTED INTERIOR ART!!!

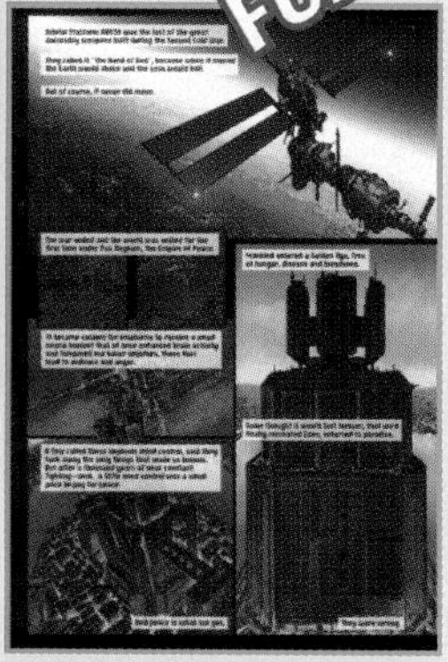

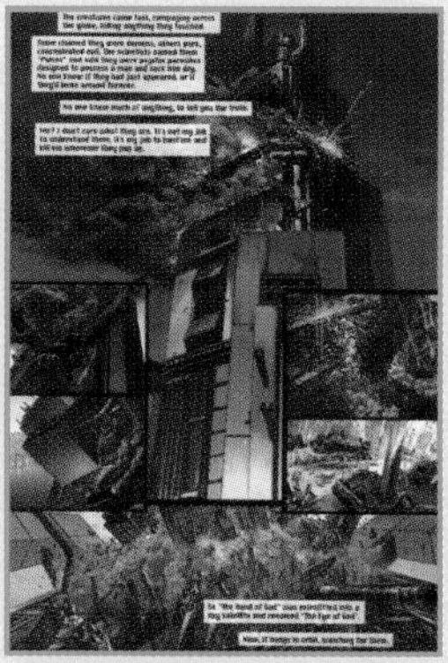

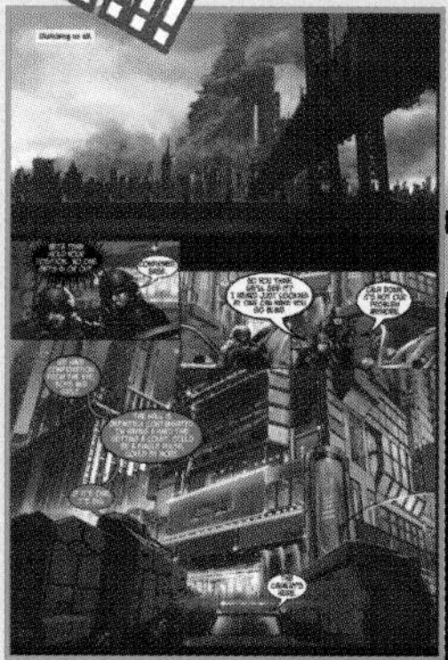

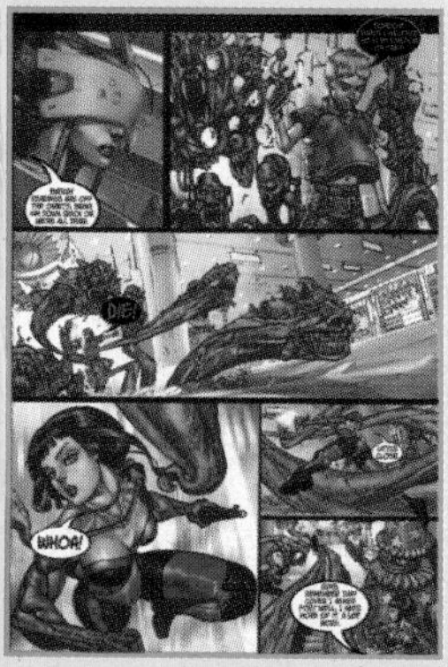
DIE!
WHOA!

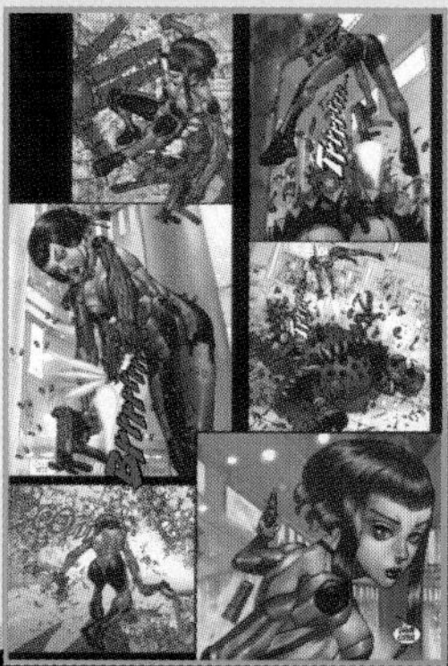

A MUST READ SCI-FI EPIC!

GET IT NOW!
Call 1-800-COMIC-BOOK
to locate a comic retailer near you

For more infomation, visit:
www.studioice.com

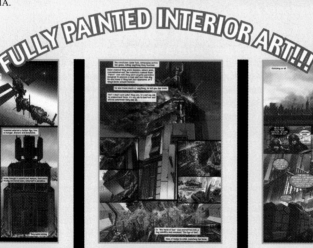

WWW.STREETFIGHTERCOMICS.COM

STREET FIGHTER®

ROUND ONE: FIGHT!
CREDITS

Cover Art by SHINKIRO of CAPCOM

Writer:
Ken Siu-Chong

Line Art:
Alvin Lee, Arnold Tsang
Long Vo, Noi Sackda
Rob Ross, Alan Tam
and Andrew Hou

COLORS:
Arnold Tsang, Andrew Hou
Joy Ang, Hanna Chen
Gary Yeung, Shane Law
Saka, Ben Huen
& Herbert Kwan

Lettering:
Simon Yeung of Cyber Graphix

Power Foil Covers by:
Jo Chen and Arnold Tsang

Assistant Script Editor: Marina Siu-Chong
UDON Chief of Operations: Erik Ko
www.streetfightercomics.com designed by: Kenneth Wu
web master: Calvin Lo

For CAPCOM Licensing:
Toshi Takumaru and Taki Enomoto of CAPCOM Co., Ltd.
Marc Mostman of Most Management

Special Thanks To:
Adam Fortier, Jim Zubkavich, Ramil Sunga, Rey, Omar Dogan, Charles Park, Joe Vriens
Eric Vedder, Mark Brooks, Scott Hepburn, Sacha Heilig, TheRealT!, Jeff Woo
Joe Madureira, J. Scott Campbell, Adam Warren, Kevin Lau,
Kaare Andrews, Kim Hyung Tae, Dustin Nguyen
Nick Barrucci, Eddie Yu, Andy Shepherd, Jim Lee, John Nee, Joe Quesada, C.B. Cebulski
Jim Valentino, Traci Hale, Brent Braun, Eric Stevenson, Jon Malin, Brett Evans, Allen Hui

For Devil's Due Publishing:
Josh Blaylock: President
Mike Norton: Art Director
Chris Crank: Web Developer
Marshall Dillon: Project Manager
Susan Bishop: Office Manager
Tim Seeley: Staff Artist

STREET FIGHTER ®: Vol.1. AUGUST 2004 Published by Devil's Due Publishing, Inc. Office of publication 4619 N. Ravenswood Ave. #204, Chicago, IL 60640. **Printed in Canada. ISBN 1-932796-08-8**

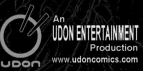

An UDON ENTERTAINMENT Production
www.udoncomics.com

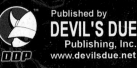

Published by
DEVIL'S DUE
Publishing, Inc.
www.devilsdue.net